■ The Massachusetts State Constitution

The Oxford Commentaries on the State Constitutions of the United States

G. Alan Tarr, Series Editor

Professor G. Alan Tarr, Director of the Center on State Constitutional Studies at Rutgers University, serves as General Editor for this important new series which in its entirety will cover each of the 50 states. Each volume of The Oxford Commentaries on the State Constitutions of the United States contains a historical overview of the state's constitutional development, plus a section-by-section analysis of the state's current constitution. Other features included in the volumes are the text of the state's constitution, a bibliographic essay, table of cases, and index. This series provides essential reference tools for those investigating state constitutional development and constitutional law.

The Massachusetts State Constitution

Lawrence Friedman

AND

Lynnea Thody

THE OXFORD COMMENTARIES ON THE STATE CONSTITUTIONS OF THE UNITED STATES

G. Alan Tarr, Series Editor

OXFORD
UNIVERSITY PRESS

OXFORD
UNIVERSITY PRESS

Oxford University Press, Inc., publishes works that further Oxford University's objective of excellence in research, scholarship, and education.

Oxford New York
Auckland Cape Town Dar es Salaam Hong Kong Karachi Kuala Lumpur Madrid Melbourne Mexico City Nairobi New Delhi Shanghai Taipei Toronto

With offices in
Argentina Austria Brazil Chile Czech Republic France Greece Guatemala Hungary Italy Japan Poland Portugal Singapore South Korea Switzerland Thailand Turkey Ukraine Vietnam

Published by Oxford University Press, Inc.
198 Madison Avenue, New York, New York 10016

Library of Congress Cataloging-in-Publication Data

Friedman, Lawrence Meir, 1930-
The Massachusetts State Constitution / Lawrence Friedman and Lynnea Thody.
p. cm. — (The Oxford commentaries on the state constitutions of the United States)
Includes bibliographical references and index.
ISBN 978-0-19-977868-3 (hardback)
1. Constitutions—Massachusetts. 2. Constitutional law—Massachusetts.
3. Constitutional history—Massachusetts.
I. Thody, Lynnea. II. Massachusetts. Constitution. III. Title.
KFM28011780.A6 F75 2010
342.744—dc22 2010049342

Note to Readers
This publication is designed to provide accurate and authoritative information in regard to the subject matter covered. It is based upon sources believed to be accurate and reliable and is intended to be current as of the time it was written. It is sold with the understanding that the publisher is not engaged in rendering legal, accounting, or other professional services. If legal advice or other expert assistance is required, the services of a competent professional person should be sought. Also, to confirm that the information has not been affected or changed by recent developments, traditional legal research techniques should be used, including checking primary sources where appropriate.

(Based on the Declaration of Principles jointly adopted by a Committee of the American Bar Association and a Committee of Publishers and Associations.)

CONTENTS

■ SERIES FOREWORD

In 1776, following the declaration of independence from England, the former colonies began to draft their own constitutions. Their handiwork attracted widespread interest, and draft constitutions circulated up and down the Atlantic seaboard, as constitution-makers sought to benefit from the insights of their counterparts in sister states. In Europe, the new constitutions found a ready audience seeking enlightenment from the American experiments in self-government. Even the delegates to the Constitutional Convention of 1787, despite their reservations about the course of political developments in the states during the decade after independence, found much that was useful in the newly-adopted constitutions. And when James Madison, fulfilling a pledge given during the ratification debates, drafted the federal Bill of Rights, he found his model in the famous Declaration of Rights of the Virginia Constitution.

By the 1900s, however, few people would have looked to state constitutions for enlightenment. Instead, a familiar litany of complaints was heard whenever state constitutions were mentioned. State constitutions were too long and too detailed, combining basic principles with policy prescriptions and prohibitions that had no place in the fundamental law of a state. By including such provisions, it was argued, state constitutions deprived state governments of the flexibility they needed to respond effectively in changing circumstances. This—among other factors—encouraged political reformers to look to the federal government, which was not plagued by such constitutional constraints, thereby shifting the locus of political initiative away from the states. Meanwhile, civil libertarians concluded that state bills of rights, at least as interpreted by state courts, did not adequately protect rights and therefore looked to the federal courts and the federal Bill of Rights for redress. As power and responsibility shifted from the states to Washington, so too did the attention of scholars, the legal community, and the general public.

During the early 1970s, however, state constitutions were "rediscovered." The immediate impetus for this rediscovery was former President Richard Nixon's appointment of Warren Burger to succeed Earl Warren as Chief Justice of the United States Supreme Court. To civil libertarians, this appointment seemed to signal a decisive shift in the Supreme Court's jurisprudence, because Burger was expected to lead the Court away from the liberal activism that had characterized the Warren Court. They therefore sought ways to safeguard the gains they had achieved for defendants, racial minorities, and the poor during Warren's tenure from erosion by the Burger Court. In particular, they began to look to state bills of rights to secure the rights of defendants and to support other civil-liberties claims that they advanced in state courts.

The "new judicial federalism," as it came to be called, quite quickly advanced beyond its initial concern to evade the mandates of the Burger Court. Indeed, less than two decades after it originated, it became a nationwide phenomenon. For when judges and scholars turned their attention to state constitutions, they discovered an unsuspected richness. They found not only provisions that paralleled the federal Bill of Rights, but also constitutional guarantees of the right to privacy and of gender equality, for example, that had no analogue in the U.S. Constitution. Careful examination of the text and history of state guarantees revealed important differences between even those provisions that most resembled federal guarantees and their federal counterparts. Looking beyond state declarations of rights, jurists and scholars discovered affirmative constitutional mandates to state governments to address such important policy concerns as education and housing. Taken altogether, these discoveries underlined the importance for the legal community of developing a better understanding of state constitutions.

Yet the renewed interest in state constitutions has not been limited to judges and lawyers. State constitutional reformers have renewed their efforts with notable success: since 1960, ten states have adopted new constitutions and several others have undertaken major constitutional revisions. These changes have usually resulted in more streamlined constitutions and more effective state governments. Also, in recent years political activists on both the left and the right have pursued their goals through state constitutional amendments, often enacted through the initiative process, under which policy proposals can be placed directly on the ballot for voters to endorse or reject. Scholars too have begun to rediscover how state constitutional history can illuminate changes in political thought and practice, providing a basis for theories about the dynamics of political change in America.

Lawrence Friedman and Lynnea Thody's excellent study of the Massachusetts Constitution is the latest contribution to the series, *The Oxford Commentaries on the State Constitutions of the United States*, which reflects the renewed interest in state constitutions and will contribute to our knowledge about them. Because the constitutional tradition of each state is distinctive, the volume begins with the history and development of constitutionalism in Massachusetts. It then provides the complete text of the state's current constitution, with each section accompanied with commentary that explains the provision and traces its origins and its interpretation by the courts and by other governmental bodies. Finally, the book concludes with a bibliography, a table of cases cited in the volume, and a topical index.

G. Alan Tarr

PREFACE

This book aims to make Massachusetts state constitutional law accessible to lawyers and judges and, we hope, general readers. The constitution's authors drafted the document in 1780 to be read and used by the people. The history of the Commonwealth supported the framers in the view that the value of written constitutions lay in the uses to which they could be put by an alert citizenry. In 1634, for example, representatives of the towns of the Massachusetts Bay Colony demanded to see the colony's original 1629 charter when they believed that Governor John Winthrop's actions violated its provisions; when review of the document proved them right, the governor changed his ways. With such incidents in mind, John Adams drafted Part II of the constitution, outlining the "Frame of Government," in clear terms, drawing on the familiar language of previous Massachusetts charters. And, in Part I, he addressed the "Declaration of Rights" to the people, reminding them of what they ought, of right, to demand from their government. The language of Article XVIII of the Declaration of Rights offers evidence of this spirit:

> A frequent recurrence to the fundamental principles of the constitution, and a constant adherence to those of piety, justice, moderation, temperance, industry, and frugality, are absolutely necessary to preserve the advantages of liberty, and to maintain a free government. The people ought, consequently, to have a particular attention to all those principles, in the choice of their officers and representatives: and they have a right to require of their lawgivers and magistrates, an exact and constant observance of them, in the formation and execution of the laws necessary for the good administration of the commonwealth.

To make the document readily available for popular use, Adams required in the last article (Chapter VI, Article XI) that the constitution be "enrolled on parchment and deposited in the secretary's office, and be a part of the laws of the land—and printed copies thereof shall be prefixed to the book containing the laws of this commonwealth, in all future editions of the said laws." And, to keep the people capable of effectively availing themselves of the constitution, he provided in Chapter V, Section II:

> Wisdom, and knowledge, as well as virtue, diffused generally among the body of the people, being necessary for the preservation of their rights and liberties; and as these depend on spreading the opportunities and advantages of education in the various parts of the country, and among the different orders of the people, it shall be the duty of legislatures and magistrates, in all future periods of this commonwealth, to cherish

> the interests of literature and the sciences, and all seminaries of them; especially the university at Cambridge, public schools and grammar schools in the towns.

As the printed Bible had by 1780 made available to the citizens of the Commonwealth of Massachusetts the founding principles of their religion, so the written constitution would make available to them the founding principles of their secular state.

In the years since 1780, the citizenry of Massachusetts has grown distant from its constitution. Over a period of many years following its ratification, the U.S. Constitution (which draws upon the model of the Massachusetts Constitution) increasingly eclipsed state constitutions as the source of fundamental political principle, just as the federal government increasingly eclipsed state governments as the center of fundamental political power. As well, the people have adopted more than one hundred amendments to the constitution of 1780 in the last two centuries, during which time the courts of Massachusetts have produced a significant body of authoritative interpretations of the various provisions of the constitution. These amendments and court decisions have made the process of reading the constitution more complicated and somewhat off-putting, such that it seems fair to say that, to fully understand the Massachusetts Constitution, one can no longer rely upon a simple reading of the document itself.

With this volume, we hope to provide an aid to the people of Massachusetts, and in particular its bench and bar, who seek to rediscover their state constitution. We begin, in Part I, with a brief treatment of the rich constitutional history of Massachusetts. Part II presents the whole of the current Massachusetts Constitution, together with annotations that provide some explanation of the meaning of the constitution's provisions. Because the current Massachusetts Constitution consists of the original 1780 constitution plus more than one hundred amendments, it challenges presentation in an accessible and concise form. To conserve space and to simplify for the reader the task of determining which portions of the constitution are currently in effect, we have edited what follows into an "integrated" constitution. All explicitly amended provisions are presented only in their amended form, and all provisions that have been explicitly annulled are removed. Removed on this ground are amendments V, IX, XXI–XXIII, XLII, LVIII, LXVI, LXX–LXXII, LXXVI, LXXX, and XCII. To further economize, we have removed any amendment that had no continuing vitality beyond its effect in explicitly annulling or amending the language of an earlier provision. Removed on this ground are amendments XI, XXVI, XXVII, XXXI, XXXII, XXXIV–XXXVI, XXXIX, XL, XLVI, LIII–LV, LVII, LXVII, LXVIII, LXXIII–LXXV, LXXVII, LXXIX, LXXXI, LXXXII, LXXXIV, LXXXV, LXXXIX, XC, XCIII–XCV, XCVII, XCVIII, C, CII–CX, CXII, CXIII, CXVI, and CXVII. We note where provisions have been implicitly amended or annulled (by later amendments which contradict their terms without explicitly acting upon them). Throughout, we have used the terms "General Court"—the name by which the Massachusetts legislature is known—and "Legislature" interchangeably.

The annotations that accompany the text provide information regarding the legislative history of each provision and discuss the major interpretive issues which have arisen under it. They do not, however, cover every issue that may have arisen or that may arise in the future, and they should not be considered as necessarily exhaustive or as remaining up to date after the publication of this book. They should not be relied upon as legal advice or as a substitute for specific legal research on an issue.

The decisions of the Commonwealth's highest court, the Supreme Judicial Court, and its intermediate appellate court, the Massachusetts Appeals Court, constitute the main source of interpretive authority in respect to the constitution. Other sources are cited for whatever light they may shed on the meaning of the constitutional text. Included in this latter category are official legal opinions of attorneys general and important discussions in the legal literature. Also included in this category are "advisory opinions" of the justices of the Supreme Judicial Court. As their citation form suggests ("Opinion of the Justices," "Opinion of the Justices to the Senate," etc.), the justices render these opinions in response to abstract legal questions put to them by the governor, the council, or a branch of the legislature. See Mass. Const. pt. 2, ch. 3, art. 2. As such, the court views these opinions as technically not binding in cases later brought before it, and the court has noted its obligation to guard against any influence flowing from an advisory opinion. See *Loring v. Young* (1921). Still, the court's frequent citation to advisory opinions as authority in later decisions and practical realities make these opinions a reasonable indication of how the court might rule in future cases.

ACKNOWLEDGMENTS

We are grateful to Charles H. Baron of Boston College Law School, who originated this project and provided us with critical guidance and support throughout its development. Barry Bachrach contributed to the development of the parts of the book addressing the frame of government. George Dargo provided us critical insights into the constitutional history of Massachusetts and gave generously of his time. A small army of research assistants provided exemplary support; they include Jordan Baumer, Damon Clark, Alexandra Deal, Eric Nelson, Rebecca Schweitzer, Jennifer Sunderland, and Cecilia Ugarte. In a work of this size and scope, errors are bound to arise, and none of these talented lawyers should be held responsible when they do.

We received support along the way from New England School of Law and its dean, John O'Brien. And we could not have completed this work without access to the libraries and skilled librarians at New England School of Law and the Boston Athenæum.

Finally, Lynnea thanks Kenneth R. Taylor Jr. and Sharon Marini, who lent their attention to preliminary drafts; and Lawrence thanks Elizabeth Sullivan, who provided support beyond measure.

PART ONE

The History of the Massachusetts Constitution

INTRODUCTION

In many respects, the constitutional history of Massachusetts is the constitutional history of the United States. Constitutional rule in America, in its earliest forms, began with the uses to which residents of Massachusetts put the Bay Colony's royal charter of 1629, and the Massachusetts Constitution of 1780 remains the oldest functioning written constitution in the world. Though not the first of the American state constitutions to be drafted in the Revolutionary period, the Massachusetts Constitution proved to be the most influential, serving as a model for the American constitutions that followed in important respects—particularly in its attention to individual rights and the structure of government, both the inspiration primarily of John Adams; and in the novel method of its enactment, ratification by popular vote. "No constitution," the sociologist George C. Homans observed, "was ever more thoroughly studied or more democratically accepted by the people who were to abide by it."[1]

[1] George C. Homans, "John Adams and the Constitution of Massachusetts," *Proceedings of the American Philosophical Society* 125 (1981): 286, 287.

THE COLONIAL CHARTER

The roots of the Massachusetts Constitution may be found in the governing document of a business corporation, an English trading company called "the Governor and companie of the Massachusetts Bay in New England." Many of the institutions, concepts, and terms that are still associated with Massachusetts government (and that differentiate the American political structure from that of England) are contained in the royal charter that established the Massachusetts Bay Company in 1628. The charter granted to the regular meeting of the corporation's stockholders and officials (called the "Greate and Generall Court"—the name by which the Massachusetts Legislature is known to this day) the power "to make, ordeine, and establishe all manner of wholesome and reasonable orders, lawes, [and] statutes" for the governance of the plantation in Massachusetts Bay. The stockholders of the corporation (called "Freemen") were to elect the officials of the corporation on a fixed date each year (as opposed to the irregular Parliamentary elections employed by the English political system). The officials included a president (called "Governor"), vice president (called "Deputy Governor"), and a board of eighteen corporate directors (called "Assistants"). The officials (the "Court of Assistants") met at least monthly for the purpose of governance between meetings of the Great and General Court.

The Massachusetts Bay Company was not the first English trading company to employ such a structure; the charters of the East India Company and the Virginia Company of London had established similar institutions. But the Massachusetts company was the first to move its corporate headquarters from London to the colony which it governed. In the spring of 1630, Puritan stockholders, who had decided to make the Massachusetts plantation a utopian religious colony, immigrated to New England together with the corporation's charter and officials. "By the single act of transfer," wrote the historian Samuel Eliot Morison, "capitalists became colonists, and the charter of a business corporation became the constitution of a semi-independent Commonwealth."[2]

Once on American soil, the corporation's institutions developed new forms. The terms of the charter did not permit the first Governor, John Winthrop, to legislate with his Assistants alone. Under the charter's provisions, all laws were to be passed at the Great and General Court where the Freemen could be in attendance and vote. To exercise this power in a fashion most convenient to them, the Freemen began to select Deputies from the towns to represent them at the General Court. Shortly thereafter, steps were taken toward establishing America's first bicameral legislature. In 1636, in an effort to regain some of their former power, Winthrop and the Assistants secured passage of a measure that required a majority vote of the Assistants (as well as of the Deputies) for the

---

[2] Samuel Eliot Morison, *A History of the Constitution of Massachusetts* (Boston: Wright & Potter, 1917), 6.

enactment of any law. In 1644, this separation of legislative power was formalized when the General Court was officially divided into a House of Deputies and a House of Assistants, with each having a veto over legislation passed by the other.

The Bay Colony charter contained assurances from Charles I that the colonists would "have and enjoy all liberties and immunities of free and naturall subjects . . . as if they and every of them were borne within the realme of England." But early on, the colonists began formulating guarantees of individual freedom that would be more concrete and closer to home. In 1635, the Freemen requested that a detailed written code of fundamental rights and laws be drafted. The most influential response to this request—"The Body of Liberties"—was published in 1641. An amalgam of new principles drawn from a dozen years of self-government in America and old principles stemming from sources going back to Magna Carta, it contained provisions guaranteeing freedom of speech and assembly, just compensation for property taken, freedom to emigrate, the right to bail, the right to counsel, the right to trial by jury in civil cases, the right to challenge jurors, and the right to speedy trial. It also provided special protections from double jeopardy, cruel or unusual punishments, and imprisonment for debt, as well as protections for the rights of women, children, servants, aliens, and animals.

In 1648, the General Court enacted almost all of The Body of Liberties as part of a general code of laws called "The Book of the General Lawes and Libertyes Concerning the Inhabitants of Massachusetts." As the first printed collection of laws in North America and perhaps "the first modern code of the Western World,"[3] its framers intended the "General Lawes and Libertyes" to make the law understandable to every citizen in the colony.[4]

The royal charter had granted the Massachusetts Bay Company power to make only laws that were not "repugnant to the lawes and statutes of our realme of England." Despite this, the colony's codes made little effort toward legitimacy on the basis of English authority. In many ways, the colony was a theocracy in which God's will supplied the ultimate legal authority: The Holy Bible served as both the model for the colony's laws and their basic source. This necessarily

---

[3] George Lee Haskins, *Law and Authority in Early Massachusetts: A Study in Tradition and Design* (New York: Macmillan, 1960), 120.

[4] As one commentator put it:

> The alphabetical arrangement of [the book] made the law accessible to the most primitively literate. * * * A person unhappy with the price of bread had need of no other recourse than this code to resolve a dispute with a baker. [The book] provided the colonists with a bible of civil government. It made possible the same access to the laws as the Bible did to the Word of God [and] had the same potential to popularize the discussion and development of the law that the publication of a vernacular bible had for the popularization of theology.

Daniel R. Coquillette, "Radical Lawmakers in Colonial Massachusetts: The 'Countenance of Authoritie' and the *Lawes and Libertyes*," *The New England Quarterly* 67 (June 1994): 179, 200–01.

resulted in some restrictions upon individual liberties. Only members of the Congregational Church were permitted to vote as Freemen, and the government did not function as a modern democracy. Nonetheless, the colony managed to operate relatively free from interference by the King and Parliament. As a result, during this period, "the Massachusetts Bay colonists enjoyed a greater measure of self-government than any people in the world outside New England."[5]

This independence came to a temporary end in 1684 when James II revoked the charter and began merging Massachusetts (along with the colonies of Plymouth, Maine, New Hampshire, Rhode Island, Connecticut, New Jersey, and Pennsylvania) into a new entity called the "Dominion of New England." James abolished all elections and representative bodies (except town meetings), and decreed that government be conducted by a Governor and Council directly appointed by the King. The reign of James ended in 1688, however, and, when news of the "Glorious Revolution" reached Boston in the spring of 1689, the Dominion was dissolved, the Governor was imprisoned on Castle Island, and the most recently elected Assistants, together with a convention of Deputies newly elected from the towns, declared government under the 1629 charter to be provisionally re-established.

THE PROVINCE CHARTER OF 1691

On October 7, 1691, the new English monarchs, William and Mary, issued a charter for an entity called "The Province of Massachusetts Bay." The charter expanded the borders of Massachusetts to include Plymouth, Martha's Vineyard, Nantucket, Maine, and Nova Scotia. It also restructured the government of Massachusetts to tie it more closely to that of England. The charter called for the appointment by the King of a royal Governor who would function as a powerful chief executive and held an absolute veto over legislation. The Deputy Governor (now called "Lieutenant Governor") and a new official called the "Secretary" were also royal appointees. All legislation passed by the General Court (now comprising a "Council" of 28 Assistants or "Councilors" elected by the General Court and a "House of Representatives" elected by the Freemen) could be vetoed not only by the royal Governor but also (at any time within three years of enactment) by the Privy Council in London. Most decisions of the colony's newly created judicial body—the "Superior Court of Judicature" (predecessor to the current Supreme Judicial Court)—were likewise subject to review and reversal by the Privy Council if the losing party appealed.

The 1691 charter did not radically diminish the independence of the colonists: an ocean lay between London and Boston, and the colonists maintained a strong commitment to self-government. Further, some of the charter's innovations

[5] Morison, *A History of the Constitution of Massachusetts*, 8.

were, in fact, liberalizing reforms. The charter guaranteed for the first time some degree of religious liberty (for various types of Protestants, but not for Catholics), and opened the franchise to anyone who owned a qualifying amount of property, rather than restricting the vote to members of the Congregational Church.

More critically, innovations that had been instituted to increase London's control proved largely ineffective. The General Court often passed laws of only two or three years' duration so that they would expire before review in the Privy Council, and the Legislature exploited its exclusive power to tax and to make appropriations of money to maximum advantage—no appointed government official could take action which required the outlay of money without securing the cooperation of the popularly elected General Court. Further, any government officer who frustrated the will of the Legislature risked personal financial ruin since the General Court also set and appropriated salaries. As a result, "[b]y about 1745 the royal Governor became little more than a figurehead, dependent on his personal influence for what little power he was able to exert. This compromise was, needless to say, reasonably satisfactory to the people of Massachusetts; and the attempt of the ministers of George III to restore the balance in favor of imperialism caused the American Revolution."[6]

When revolution arrived, such was the commitment of Massachusetts to "the rule of law" that even opposition operated within the framework of constitutional law. In 1761, when James Otis opposed the issuance of "writs of assistance," which subjected the colonists to unreasonable searches and seizures, he appealed to English constitutional case law in demanding that the practice be declared void. Appeals to traditional English constitutional principles gradually became mixed with arguments reflecting the colonists' experience with government under their written charters. "The charter of the province invests [us] with the power of making laws for its internal government and taxation," proclaimed the General Court in its protest against the Stamp Act.[7] The colonists conceded to Parliament power to regulate only the external affairs of the colonies, and that only within bounds permitted by the English Constitution. The Massachusetts charter of 1691, like the 1628 charter before it, had guaranteed the colonists all the "Libertyes and Immunities" of free English subjects, including the principle that Englishmen had no obligation to pay any taxes or indeed obey laws unless those laws were passed by their elected Representatives.[8] From this

[6] Ibid., 10.

[7] Resolution of Oct. 23, 1765, in Alden Bradford, ed., *Speeches of the Governors of Massachusetts, from 1765 to 1775* (Boston, 1818), 45.

[8] Willi Paul Adams, *The First American Constitutions: Republican Ideology and the Making of the State Constitutions in the Revolutionary Era* (Chapel Hill: University of North Carolina Press, 1980), 13.

principle of constitutional law, the colonists came to decry taxation without representation.[9]

Until the very eve of war, the colonists looked to the English Constitution as a fundamental source of their liberties. The Glorious Revolution of 1688 and the selection of William and Mary as monarchs had established an English government based, at least in theory, upon the consent of the people. Parliament's enactment of the Bill of Rights of 1689, a document which had been accepted by William and Mary as part of the terms for their ascension to the throne, had begun a process of codification of the fundamental rights of the English people. Perhaps most important, under the English Constitution a system of "mixed government" had developed, in which each branch of government—the King, the House of Lords, and the House of Commons—functioned as a check against potential abuses of power by the others. In 1766 (at the height of the Stamp Act Crisis), a youthful John Adams could credibly describe the English Constitution as unique in having liberty as "its end, its use, its designation, drift, and scope, as much as grinding corn is the use of a mill, the transportation of burdens the end of a ship."[10] And, as late as 1775, with hostilities already erupting in Massachusetts, Adams would still be arguing (in a series of articles in the *Massachusetts Gazette* written under the pseudonym "Novanglus") that the English Constitution, properly interpreted, justified the independent status within the English realm that America demanded[11]—and that resistance to efforts to subordinate the colonies was "an affirmation of the legal order."[12]

The colonists remained committed to constitutional principle throughout the revolution. In 1774, in the wake of the Boston Tea Party, Parliament passed the "Intolerable Acts," which, among other things, gave the King power to appoint and remove members of the Council at his pleasure. When General Thomas Gage, the new military Governor of Massachusetts, dissolved the last regularly elected General Court in June of 1774, the colonists declared Parliament's new regime unconstitutional and proceeded to establish their own, one which claimed legitimacy from the consent of the people and the terms of the 1691 charter. Three provincial congresses, elected from the towns, governed from the fall of 1774 to the summer of 1775. In May of 1775, after the battles at Lexington and Concord, the Third Provincial Congress declared Gage's rule ended and arranged the election of a new General Court, which took power in July. Faced with a vacant Governor's office that could not be filled by constitutional means (because the 1691 charter gave power of appointment to the King),

---

[9] Ibid.

[10] "The Earl of Clarendon to William Pym, No. III," *Boston Gazette*, Jan. 27, 1766, in Charles Francis Adams, ed., *The Works of John Adams* (Boston: 1850–1856), III, 479.

[11] Novanglus VII, in Adams, ed., *Works of John Adams*, IV, 99–100.

[12] Daniel R. Coquillette, "Justinian in Braintree: John Adams, Civilian Learning, and Legal Elitism, 1758–1775," *Law in Colonial Massachusetts* 62 (1984): 359, 411.

the General Court placed executive power in the hands of the Council, giving as its justification the fact that "the late Governor, Lieutenant Governor or Deputy Governor of the Province have absented themselves, and have refused to govern the Province according to the charter."

■ THE CONSTITUTION OF 1780

By the spring of 1776, a break with England appeared inevitable. On May 29, 1776, the people of Pittsfield addressed a petition to the General Court requesting it to frame a new "fundamental constitution as the basis and frame-work of legislation" and refer it to the people for approval. On September 17, the House of Representatives responded by requesting the towns vote on whether the General Court should draft a new constitution and whether the draft should be made public for general comment before the General Court acted to ratify it. Most of the towns that made returns favored drafting a new constitution so long as the people would have the opportunity to comment upon and ratify the draft. In June of 1777, the General Court resolved itself into a constitutional convention and appointed a committee to draft the constitution. By February 28, 1778, a proposed constitution had been agreed upon by the convention and submitted to universal manhood suffrage for ratification by two-thirds majority vote.

The proposed constitution met with resounding defeat at the polls. Besides being inelegantly framed, the draft lacked a bill of rights, retained outmoded practices from the provincial charter, and showed inadequate attention to detail. Some of the towns filed returns criticizing the proposed constitution in detail and at length. "The Essex Result"—a pamphlet produced by a convention of delegates from the towns of Essex County but essentially the work of a young lawyer named Theophilus Parsons (later to become Chief Justice of the Supreme Judicial Court)—not only criticized the 1778 draft, but helped lay the foundation for the Constitution of 1780. Like others, Parsons condemned the proposed constitution's lack of substantive provisions delineating and protecting the people's natural rights, but he also focused upon the draft's failure to frame a governmental structure that would both check tyrannical abuse and enable effective action.

Parsons's views largely echoed advice John Adams had given two years earlier when sister colonies had sought his help in drafting their new state constitutions. In a letter, subsequently published under the title "Thoughts on Government," Adams had made many of the same suggestions as Parsons for many of the same reasons. As a constitutional consultant, Adams had brought great enthusiasm as well as expertise to his work. Adams's advice went largely unheeded in the first wave of new state constitutions, which, if they used any model other than predecessor royal charters, tended to follow a simple, radically democratic outline traceable to Thomas Paine's "Common Sense." But Paine's model, epitomized by the Pennsylvania Constitution of 1776—with its unicameral legislature and very weak executive and judicial branches—quickly came under criticism for its lack of protections against "democratic excesses." A second wave of drafting, adopting some of the checks and balances proposed by Adams and others, began with the New York Constitution of 1777, reaching a high point with Adams's 1780 constitution for Massachusetts—"the most important [constitution] to be written between 1776 and 1789."[13]

The second attempt at drafting a constitution for Massachusetts began in 1779, this time by a convention of delegates elected by all resident Freemen twenty-one years of age or older. The convention held its first meeting in Cambridge on September 1, and its members immediately elected a committee of thirty persons to prepare a draft. Shortly thereafter, the drafting committee met in Boston and delegated its work to a subcommittee consisting of James Bowdoin (the President of the Convention), Samuel Adams, and John Adams. The subcommittee, in turn, delegated its work to a committee of one: John Adams. By October 28, 1779, when the convention opened its second session, Adams's draft, with some additions by the whole committee, was ready to be reported out to the floor. There followed a period of discussion and refinement prolonged by travel problems due to an unusually cold and snowy winter.

On March 2, 1780, the convention submitted the result of its deliberations to a two-thirds majority vote of the adult Freemen. The convention requested the towns to record votes, comments, and suggestions on each article separately. Thus, when the convention met again on June 5, the delegates faced a complicated task in accurately tabulating the results. Though, as Samuel Eliot Morison concluded, the convention actively "juggled the returns," almost all the articles seemed to be supported by the requisite two-thirds majority, and all were supported by at least a simple majority.[14] The mood of the people demanded decisive action, and, on June 15, 1780, the convention voted that the people had adopted the new constitution.

Though the constitution as approved bore Adams's imprint in almost every important respect, there were some notable exceptions; as Robert Taylor aptly observed, "the convention debated freely, patiently, and at length to bend his draft to its wishes."[15] And so, the convention inserted Article III of the Declaration of Rights (which essentially established the Congregational Church as a state-supported institution) and Article I of Chapter VI of the Frame of Government (which required elected officials to take a "test oath" excluding non-Protestants from office) over Adams's objections. Moreover, the convention had pared down

[13] Donald Lutz, *Popular Consent and Popular Control: Whig Political Theory in the Early State Constitutions* (Baton Rouge: Louisiana State Univ. Press, 1980), 129.

[14] Samuel Eliot Morison, "The Struggle over the Adoption of the Constitution of Massachusetts, 1780," *Proceedings of the Massachusetts Historical Society* 50 (1917): 356, 400.

[15] Robert J. Taylor, "Construction of the Massachusetts Constitution," *Proceedings of the American Antiquarian Society* 90 (1980): 317, 344.

Article XVI of the Declaration of Rights to protect only freedom of the press (leaving out Adams's provision protecting freedom of speech) and had diluted Adams's absolute veto for the Governor by empowering the General Court to override it by a two-thirds vote.

On the whole, however, the document reflected Adams's ideas. The Great and General Court was bicameral, with a House of Representatives and a Senate. The constitution restricted the Senate to forty members distributed among the senatorial districts in proportion to the amount of tax paid from each district. The people would directly elect the Governor (whom the constitution guaranteed a fixed and "honorable" salary), who wielded such power that his would become (as of that time) the strongest executive office in America. In addition to his veto over legislation, the constitution granted him power to appoint numerous important officers (including all judges) with the advice and consent of a nine-member Governor's Council. The Council, elected by and from the membership of the Senate, was intended to serve as a check against any gubernatorial tendencies toward abuse of power. And, as a check against abuse of power from any source, the constitution provided for an independent judiciary—a Supreme Judicial Court whose members would "hold their offices during good behavior" so that they could be counted upon to provide "an impartial interpretation of the laws, and administration of justice" and thus preserve "the rights of every individual."[16]

Individual rights would be protected as well by placing a list of the most prominent at the beginning of the constitution. The thirty articles of the Declaration of Rights featured provisions as old as the Magna Carta and others traceable to documents such as the "Lawes and Libertyes" of 1648 and the Bill of Rights of 1688, along with still others of more recent vintage. Adams's version of a bill of rights went beyond those that had been drafted for such states as Pennsylvania and Virginia, employing mandatory language in at least some of its provisions. Article XII, for example, states in no uncertain terms: "No subject shall be held to answer for any Crimes or offence, until the same is fully and plainly, substantially and formally, described to him; or be Compelled to accuse, or furnish evidence against himself."

Still, many of the provisions of the Declaration of Rights as adopted retained a merely admonitory tone and seemed aimed primarily at ensuring that the people, as well as government officials, would keep the first principles of republican government in mind. Article V, for example, served to remind the reader that all power resides "originally in the people, and being derived from them, the several magistrates and officers of government, vested with authority, whether legislative, executive, or judicial, are their substitutes and agents, and are at all times accountable to them." Similarly, Article VII states: "Government is

---

[16] Mass. Const., Frame of Government, Chapter III, Art. I.

instituted for the Common good; for the protection, safety, prosperity and happiness of the people; and not for the profit, honor, or private interest of any one man, family or Class of men: Therefore the people alone have an incontestible, unalienable, and indefeasible right to institute government; and to reform, alter, or totally change the same, when their protection, safety, prosperity and happiness require it."

Though Adams hoped Article XXX of the Declaration of Rights would help to guarantee "a government of laws and not of men" by prohibiting each branch of government from attempting to exercise the power of another, the new constitution would require an active and enlightened electorate to secure the preservation of freedom. No wonder, then, that Adams counted as his favorite provision Chapter V, Section II of the Frame of Government,[17] which committed the government of Massachusetts to the education of its people as a first principle of democracy:

> Wisdom, and knowledge, as well as virtue, diffused generally among the body of the people, being necessary for the preservation of their rights and liberties; and as these depend on spreading the opportunities and advantages of education in the various parts of the country, and among the different orders of the people, it shall be the duty of the Legislatures and Magistrates, in all future periods of this Commonwealth, to cherish the interests of literature and the sciences, and all seminaries of them; especially the university at Cambridge, public schools and grammar schools in the towns.

■ JUDICIAL ENFORCEMENT OF THE CONSTITUTION

The new constitution provided the judiciary—"distinct from both the legislative and the executive, and independent upon both"—a base from which it might act to keep the other branches of government in check.[18] The members of the Supreme Judicial Court did not have to rely upon the largesse of the Legislature for their salaries or the good graces of the executive for their continued tenure: the new constitution provided that the justices, unlike their predecessors on the late Superior Court of Judicature, whose pay the Legislature varied from time to time, should enjoy "honorable salaries ascertained and established by standing laws" and retain tenure in office "as long as they behave themselves well." From its inception, the court's membership could turn to an elite and learned bar for assistance in interpreting and enforcing the constitution; it could rely upon the

[17] David McCullough, *John Adams and the Good Life of the Mind* (Boston: Boston Athenæum, 2004), 6–7. On Adams's own devotion to liberal education and the influence of his learning on his legal and political thinking, see generally Coquillette, "Justinian in Braintree: John Adams, Civilian Learning, and Legal Elitism, 1758–1775."

[18] John Adams, "Thoughts on Government," in Adams, ed., *Works of John Adams*, IV, 198.

bar as well to supply eminent candidates for service on the bench. Early Chief Justices, such as William Cushing (1777–1789), Theophilus Parsons (1806–1813), Isaac Parker (1814–1830), and Lemuel Shaw (1830–1860), established the court's authority vis-à-vis the other branches of government.

Following the adoption of the constitution in 1780, such confidence as the Supreme Judicial Court possessed in its authority revealed itself in few constitutional matters; in cases raising constitutional questions, the court typically showed great deference to principles of popular rule. Still, in 1783, Chief Justice Cushing notably questioned the compatibility of slavery with Article I's declaration that "[a]ll men are born free and equal" when charging the jury in *Commonwealth v. Jennison.*[19] In 1799, the court engaged in an early instance of the exercise of judicial review—the power to strike down governmental acts that violate the constitution—when it ruled an act of the legislature of a sister state—Georgia—to be unconstitutional as a "flagrant, outrageous violation of the first and fundamental principles of social compacts" as well as Article I, §10 of the U.S. Constitution.[20] In an 1805 case, *Mountfort v. Hall,* defense counsel challenged the lack of appeal from a judgment of a justice of the peace and in so doing assumed the court had the power to declare a legislative act unconstitutional; the justices duly considered the argument, though it did not prove dispositive.[21] Less than a decade later, in 1814, the court, again without elaboration, viewed a resolve of the General Court purporting to suspend a statute of limitations as it applied to a named individual creditor as contrary to "the first principles of civil liberty and natural justice, and . . . the spirit of our constitution and laws."[22]

The court would not hold a state statute unconstitutional until 1854, during the watch of Chief Justice Lemuel Shaw, later called "America's greatest magistrate" for his role in reshaping the common law to respond to the economic and technological challenges of the mid–nineteenth century.[23] Shaw set the tone in the period before the Civil War; when presented with a challenge to the constitutionality of a statute, he believed that the court should generally "approach the question with great caution, examine it in every possible aspect, and ponder

---

[19] "Commonwealth v. Jennison," *Proceedings of the Massachusetts Historical Society (1873–1875)* 13 (1875): 292. See also John D. Cushing, "The Cushing Court and the Abolition of Slavery in Massachusetts: More Notes on the 'Quock Walker Case,'" *American Journal of Legal History* 5 (1961): 118, and Robert Cover, *Justice Accused: Anti-Slavery and the Judicial Process* (New Haven: Yale University Press, 1975), 44–50.

[20] Reported as *Derby v. Blake* in a supplement to the *Massachusetts Reports,* 226 Mass. 619 (1917), the case anticipated the decision of the U.S. Supreme Court in *Fletcher v. Peck,* 10 U.S. (6 Cranch) 87 (1810).

[21] Mountfort v. Hall, 1 Mass. 443 (1805).

[22] Holden v. James, 11 Mass. 396, 405 (1814).

[23] Leonard W. Levy, "America's Greatest Magistrate," in *Ranters Run Amok, and Other Adventures in the History of the Law* (Chicago: Ivan R. Dee, 2000), 217.

upon it as long as deliberation and patient attention can throw any new light on the subject, and never declare a statute void, unless the nullity and invalidity of the act are placed, in their judgment, beyond reasonable doubt."[24] Shaw notably made some exceptions to this general rule when laws encroached upon certain civil liberties, at least in the area of criminal procedure, and in 1854 led the court to hold a state statute unconstitutional, in *Fisher v. McGirr*, a case involving the validity of a law regarding the manufacture and distribution of alcohol, and in particular the law's allocation of discretion to local authorities. Shaw justified the decision on the ground that laws endangering private rights "[must] be so clear and well-defined, that they may serve as a safe guide to all . . . officers and magistrates in their respective duties; and in these respects, the statute itself must, on its face, be conformable to the constitution."[25]

Shaw did not extend this stricter constitutional scrutiny much beyond criminal procedure. When, in the 1830s, a jury convicted Abner Kneeland of blasphemy for having published atheistic statements in his *Investigator*, Shaw's court refused to consider the relevant statute invalid under either Article II (providing that "no subject shall be hurt . . . for his religious profession or sentiments") or Article XVI (providing that "[t]he liberty of the press [ought not] to be restrained in this Commonwealth").[26] As to the former, Shaw concluded that the constitution protected the formation of opinions and the profession of religious sentiments, but not those having a tendency to disturb the peace;[27] and as to the latter, Shaw concluded that the constitution left "every citizen responsible for any offence capable of being committed by the use of language."[28] When in the 1840s a neighborhood primary school denied Sarah Roberts admission because she was an African-American, the Shaw court created the doctrine of "separate but equal" in refusing to invalidate Boston's segregated school system under Article I.[29]

After the Civil War, the Supreme Judicial Court, like the high courts of many other states and the Supreme Court of the United States, took a less deferential view when litigants sought to have the judiciary enforce principles of constitutional law. Whereas from 1780 to 1860 the Massachusetts court had struck down only ten statutes, forty-one were invalidated between 1860 and 1916—thirty-one of these from 1860 to 1893 alone. The vast majority of these decisions voided legislation deemed to infringe economic rights—in some cases, because

[24] Wellington et al. Petitioners, 16 Pick. 87, 95–97 (1834).

[25] Fisher v. McGirr, 1 Gray 1, 40 (1854).

[26] Commonwealth v. Kneeland, 20 Pick. 206 (1838).

[27] Ibid., 221.

[28] Ibid., 219.

[29] Roberts v. City of Boston, 59 Mass. (5 Cush.) 198 (1850). The U.S. Supreme Court later relied upon *Roberts* to uphold state laws mandating racially segregated railroad facilities under the Fourteenth Amendment to the U.S. Constitution. See Plessy v. Ferguson, 163 U.S. 537, 544 (1896).

the Legislature appropriated taxes to assist only one class of individuals, rather than promoting the "common good,"[30] in others, because the Legislature unduly limited liberty of contract in its effort to protect workers,[31] or because the Legislature took property for a nonpublic purpose or had done so without "due process of law."[32]

Like the U.S. Supreme Court's "economic due process" opinions during this era, those of the Supreme Judicial Court were often formalistic and the court offered little in the way of useful clues as to why it decided one case one way and another a different way.[33] In one day in 1909, for instance, the Supreme Judicial Court struck down a regulation which required all undertakers to be licensed embalmers, concluding that the plaintiff's constitutional right to engage in a calling of his choosing outweighed the speculative benefits the Legislature thought might flow from the embalmers' training in the post mortem signs of contagious diseases, and then went on, without any real effort to distinguish the two cases, to uphold a statute that regulated assignment of wages by an employee, because the justices would not second guess the Legislature's determination that the regulation would advantage to the community as a whole.[34]

It appeared from the pattern and the reasoning of these "economic due process" decisions that, under cover of constitutional theory, the justices were practicing economic conservatism. Oliver Wendell Holmes, Jr., who served on the court for twenty years (1882–1902), the last three of those as Chief Justice, suggested as much in dissent in at least one Massachusetts case.[35] Holmes carried this view with him to the U.S. Supreme Court,[36] which in the 1930s abandoned economic due process. The Supreme Judicial Court subsequently began to view economic legislation with greater deference. Unlike its federal counterpart, however, the Massachusetts high court never completely abandoned the application of more intense judicial review to certain economic regulations that lacked a demonstrable rational basis. In 1965, for example, the Supreme Judicial Court struck down legislation that attempted to protect the Massachusetts dairy

---

[30] See, for example, Lowell v. Boston, 111 Mass. 454 (1873); Mead v. Acton, 139 Mass. 341, 1 N.E. 413 (1885); and Brown v. Russell, 166 Mass. 14, 43 N.E. 1005 (1896).

[31] Commonwealth v. Boston & Maine Railroad, 222 Mass 206, 110 N.E. 264 (1915).

[32] Commonwealth v. Perry, 155 Mass. 117, 28 N.E. 1126 (1891).

[33] Lawrence Friedman, "Ordinary and Enhanced Rational Basis Review in the Massachusetts Supreme Judicial Court: A Preliminary Investigation," *Albany Law Review* 69 (2006): 415.

[34] Compare Wyeth v. Board of Health of the City of Cambridge, 200 Mass. 474, 86 N.E. 925 (1909) and Mutual Loan Co. v. Martell, 200 Mass. 482, 86 N.E. 916 (1909).

[35] Commonwealth v. Perry, 155 Mass. 117, 124, 28 N.E. 1126 (1891).

[36] See, for example, Holmes's famous dissent in *Lochner v. New York*, 198 U.S. 45 (1905): "This case is decided upon an economic theory which a large part of the country does not entertain. If it were a question whether I agreed with that theory, I should desire to study it further and long before making up my mind. But I do not conceive that to be my duty, because I strongly believe that my agreement or disagreement has nothing to do with the right of a majority to embody their opinions in law."

industry (at the expense of consumers) by prohibiting the sale of nondairy coffee creamers. The court found the pretextual consumer-protection reasons given for the legislation to be "more fanciful than real" and stated: "What is permissible under the Federal Constitution in matters of State economic regulation is not necessarily permissible under State law . . . . The Constitution of a State may guard more jealously against the exercise of the State's police power."[37]

Beginning in the mid-1970s, the Supreme Judicial Court demonstrated a willingness to "guard more jealously against the exercise of the State's police power." Under Chief Justices Edward F. Hennessey, Paul Liacos, and Herbert P. Wilkins, the court interpreted the Massachusetts Constitution to extend greater protection than the U.S. Constitution to the right to free expression,[38] the right to religious freedom,[39] the "right to die,"[40] the right to choose abortion,[41] the right to engage in political action,[42] the right to education,[43] the right to be free from unreasonable searches and seizures,[44] the right to confront witnesses,[45] the right to be free from cruel and unusual punishment,[46] and the right to a jury chosen on a nondiscriminatory basis.[47]

In seeking to give independent meaning to its state constitution, the Supreme Judicial Court did not toil alone. To be sure, the U.S. Supreme Court took center stage in developing a jurisprudence of individual rights from the 1930s to the 1970s, meaningfully enforcing the Bill of Rights against the federal government and applying it to the states by way of the Due Process Clause of the Fourteenth Amendment. But when the U.S. Supreme Court began to dilute the extent of federal protection for individual rights under the U.S. Constitution in the 1970s, lawyers appearing before state courts drew the attention of judges to the long-neglected rights provisions of their state constitutions. Since that time, state

---

[37] Coffee-Rich, Inc. v. Commissioner of Public Health, 348 Mass. 414, 204 N.E.2d 281 (1965).

[38] Commonwealth v. Sees, 374 Mass. 532, 373 N.E.2d 1151 (1978).

[39] Society of Jesus of New England v. Boston Landmarks Commission, 409 Mass. 38, 564 N.E.2d 571 (1990).

[40] Superintendent of Belchertown State School v. Saikewicz, 373 Mass. 728, 370 N.E.2d 417 (1977).

[41] Moe v. Secretary of Administration and Finance, 382 Mass. 629, 417 N.E.2d 387 (1981).

[42] Batchelder v. Allied Stores International, 388 Mass. 83, 445 N.E.2d 590 (1983).

[43] McDuffy v. Secretary of the Executive Office of Education, 415 Mass. 545, 615 N.E.2d 516 (1993).

[44] Commonwealth v. Blood, 400 Mass. 61, 507 N.E.2d 1029 (1987); Commonwealth v. Panetti, 406 Mass. 230, 547 N.E.2d 46 (1989); Horsemen's Benevolent and Protective Association v. State Racing Commission, 403 Mass. 692, 532 N.E.2d 644 (1989); Guiney v. Police Commissioner of Boston, 411 Mass. 328, 582 N.E.2d 523 (1991).

[45] Commonwealth v. Amirault, 424 Mass. 618, 677 N.E.2d 652 (1997).

[46] District Attorney v. Watson, 381 Mass. 648, 411 N.E.2d 1274 (1980) and Commonwealth v. Colon-Cruz, 393 Mass. 150, 470 N.E.2d 116 (1984).

[47] Commonwealth v. Soares, 377 Mass. 461, 387 N.E.2d 499 (1979).

supreme courts increasingly have availed themselves of these provisions, part of a movement dubbed the "New Judicial Federalism." The effort has received the praise of many observers who predict that we "can expect state judges to play an increasingly prominent role in state constitutional development."[48]

THE CONSTITUTIONAL CONVENTION OF 1820

The major engine of popular constitutional change to the present has been the amendment process, though this was not the case at first. The 1780 Massachusetts Constitution, like many state constitutions of the era, did not provide an ongoing procedure for amendment. Article X of Chapter VI of the Frame of Government provided for a vote to be taken in 1795 to determine whether the electorate desired to call a new constitutional convention. When such a vote was taken, only a majority, not the necessary two-thirds, favored holding such a convention. Problems that a majority saw in their constitution went uncorrected, and the constitution contained no explicit provision for correcting them thereafter.

Relief came in 1820 when, as part of the Missouri Compromise, Maine detached itself from Massachusetts. The Maine counties had been included in Massachusetts since the 1691 charter and they were integral to the representation scheme of the 1780 constitution. Though the Legislature thought secession could be handled without constitutional change, the people of the Commonwealth manifested a belief that it should be taken as an opportunity for consideration of amendments. Accordingly, drawing upon the precedent of the 1779 convention and the language of Article VII that declared the right of the people to reform government "when their protection, safety, prosperity and happiness require it," the Legislature called for a constitutional convention if a majority of the voters approved; that approval came on August 21, 1820, by a count of nearly two to one.

On November 15, a body of 485 delegates (the largest group ever to attend a Massachusetts constitutional convention) met in the old Representatives Chamber in the State House. The extraordinarily distinguished group included such luminaries from the bench and bar as Justice Joseph Story of the U.S. Supreme Court, Chief Justice Isaac Parker of the Supreme Judicial Court, future Massachusetts Chief Justice Lemuel Shaw, Daniel Webster, and Josiah Quincy. John Adams himself attended, declining the invitation to preside over the convention on grounds of advanced age; the position went to Chief Justice Parker.

---

[48] Alan G. Tarr, *Understanding State Constitutions* (Princeton; Princeton University Press, 1998), 169; see also Charles H. Baron, "The Supreme Judicial Court in its Fourth Century: Meeting the Challenge of the 'New Constitutional Revolution,'" *Mass. L. Rev.* 77 (1992): 35.

Most of the major issues raised by the delegates struck themes that would characterize the amendment process for the next century and a half. Of the fourteen amendments that the convention proposed to the people for ratification, four attempted to increase religious tolerance. Proposition 1 was an amendment to Article III of the Declaration of Rights which would have deleted the second paragraph empowering the Legislature to require church attendance. It was one of five of the convention's proposed amendments which the people declined to ratify. Adams and others had suggested more radical revisions, some of which found their way into the constitution in 1833 in Amendment XI. Proposition 10, which would have amended Chapter V of the Frame of Government to open the Board of Harvard to Christian ministers outside the Congregational Church, was also defeated. But the people ratified propositions 11 and 12, amending Chapter VI of the Frame of Government to, among other things, eliminate from the oaths of office a declaration of belief in the Christian religion; they became Amendments VI and VII.

A second important theme in the proposed amendments was reform of the election process. Proposition 6 eliminated property qualifications for voting in state elections by extending the franchise to all taxpaying male citizens of the age of majority who were not paupers or under guardianship. Proposition 8, which dealt with voting for officers in the militia, extended the vote to all militia members without regard to age or taxpayer status. Large majorities ratified both provisions and they became Amendments III and V, respectively. Proposition 2 provided for all state elections to be held on the second Monday in November and for the political year to begin on the first Wednesday in January. Seemingly inconsequential, this change met stiff opposition for undermining the "election week" festivities to which citizens looked forward each spring. It failed when proposed by the convention, but resurfaced a decade later and was ratified by the people as Amendment X in 1831. Proposition 5 would have revised the system of representation in the General Court to reflect changes in the size and distribution of the state's population. In light of the fact that the secession of Maine had provided the pretext for calling the convention, it is ironic that this proposition was among those the delegates failed to ratify. Amendment XII in 1836 and Amendment XIII in 1840 would achieve more radical revisions in respect to representation.

Several proposed amendments concerned constitutional checks and balances. Rather than attempting to reduce checks on legislative power, the convention delegates sought to increase them. Proposition 3, ratified as Amendment I, buttressed the Governor's veto power by providing for its effective exercise even after the General Court has adjourned. Proposition 7, ratified as Amendment IV, broadened the Governor's appointment power to include notaries public and interim selections for Secretary and Treasurer. Proposition 13, ratified as Amendment VIII, added new prohibitions against joint office holding to the old ones contained in Article II of Chapter VI.

The people ratified the remaining two proposals. Proposition 4, which empowered the Legislature to establish city governments upon request of a majority of the voting inhabitants of any area with population of 12,000 or more, became Amendment II. There had been strong opposition to this encroachment on the tradition of government by town meeting, but an overwhelming vote out of Boston carried the day. Proposition 14, the last and most fundamentally important of the proposals, established a procedure for amending the constitution outside the calling of a constitutional convention. By its terms, amendments could be added by majority vote in two consecutive sessions of the Senate, of two-thirds majorities in two consecutive sessions of the House of Representatives, and of a majority of the electorate voting at a statewide election. It became Amendment IX.

THE CONSTITUTIONAL CONVENTION OF 1853

The new amendment procedure initially seemed sufficient for the Commonwealth's needs. Amendment X, ratified in 1831, adopted the 1820 convention's proposed changes in the calendar for elections and the political year. Amendment XI, ratified in 1833, brought an end to the Congregational Church's reign as the established church of Massachusetts; it eliminated the General Court's power to support churches with public funds, to require attendance at services, and to discriminate by law in favor of one religious group over another. But mounting evidence suggested that the Amendment IX process would not solve at least one problem: Section II of Chapter I of the Frame of Government gave one Representative in the House of Representatives to every town with 150 voters and added another Representative for each additional 225 voters, and growth in the state's population had driven membership of the House to unwieldy numbers. Moreover, under the apportionment system the smallest towns enjoyed more political power per voter than the large towns and cities.

In 1833, the House of Representatives asked the justices of the Supreme Judicial Court for an advisory opinion as to whether specific amendments could be made to the constitution by some process other than that of Amendment IX, or whether the Legislature could limit a constitutional convention to the consideration of amendments on only certain subjects. Chief Justice Shaw, writing for the court, stated that, in the absence of a "great emergency," the constitution provided for no method of amendment other than that contained in Amendment IX; further, should the people decide to call a convention "to consider the expediency of altering the constitution in some particular part," they could not then "propose amendments in other parts of the constitution not so specified."[49]

[49] Opinion of the Justices of the Supreme Judicial Court, 60 Mass. 573 (1833).

A constitutional convention would not be called until 1853. In the meantime, the people ratified Amendment XII in 1836 as a response to the representation problem. It quickly proved inadequate. Though it reduced somewhat the extent of malapportionment, the number of legislators still exceeded five hundred. In 1840, Amendment XIII provided more radical changes in the representation system, effecting important reforms in the Senate and the Governor's Council. Senate seats would be apportioned thereafter on the basis of population, not on the amount of taxes paid in a given county. Council members would be elected thereafter from the people at large rather than from the membership of the Senate. The provision removed property qualifications for candidates who stood for election to the Council and the General Court. The Amendment also revised the system for apportioning the House, but this revision proved no more satisfactory than earlier efforts.

In 1850, the citizens of small towns led the call for a constitutional convention; by this time, they were losing legislative power to the more populous parts of the state. The old Representatives Chamber in the State House again served as the site of the convention, but the 1853 convention bore little similarity to its 1820 predecessor. From the outset, party divisions plagued the proceedings, with voting largely determined by politics rather than reason.

Though the convention ultimately suggested more than thirty changes in the constitution on a broad range of topics, the question of apportionment of the House mattered most, with the conservative, rural small towns pressing for constitutional reform, and the progressive, manufacturing and mercantile cities and counties resisting it. Eight propositions emerged from the convention to be submitted to the people for ratification. Proposition 1 offered a revised constitution that incorporated some twenty-eight changes. Propositions 2 through 8 specified several reforms that could be adopted regardless whether the people ratified the new constitution as a whole.

Most of the changes contained in Proposition 1 related to the election process, and included: changes to voter eligibility; the institution of secret balloting; holding state and national elections on the same day; eliminating property qualifications for Governor and Lieutenant Governor, as they had been for all other offices; instituting popular election of the Council; and making many appointive offices elective. Much of this represented compromise. As to representation in the House, the new constitution would have granted one Representative to each town of 1,000 inhabitants and additional representation for each additional 4,000 inhabitants. Towns with fewer than 1,000 inhabitants would also be permitted representation; they could either combine with other towns to achieve a total population that would entitle them to representation every year or they could choose to be represented once in every five years (and in the tax valuation year as well). The original proposal would have granted full representation to towns under 1,000 inhabitants and put a cap of 30 on the number of Representatives from the largest cities. It would have enabled two hundred small towns comprising one-fourth the population of the state to elect one-half of the House of Representatives. The counterproposal would have instituted the system we have today—representative districts of equal population. As part of the compromise, the majority agreed to a provision requiring the 1856 session of the General Court to submit to the people an amendment adopting such a pure district system.

The seven additional propositions that emerged from the convention covered a variety of topics. Four of them involved aspects of court process. Proposition 2 would have bolstered the writ of habeas corpus, Proposition 3 would have granted juries the right to try issues of law as well as fact in criminal cases, Proposition 4 would have eliminated the doctrine of sovereign immunity, and Proposition 5 would have constitutionally prohibited imprisonment for debt. Proposition 6 would have forbidden the General Court to spend public money in support of sectarian education; the terms of this proposition, the most popular of the propositions put before the voters, were substantially those of Amendment XVIII which would be ratified in 1855. Proposition 7 would have regulated the power of the General Court with respect to incorporation of businesses, and Proposition 8 would have further regulated these powers in the special instance of banking corporations.

Though several of the reforms these proposed amendments contained would be added later to the constitution as individual amendments, the electorate rejected all of the proposed amendments in the fall of 1853; they were dragged down by the weight of Proposition 1. As Morison concluded in his comprehensive study of the 1853 convention, "It was the country against the city, the old order against the new, and the new won by preserving the old Constitution."[50]

■ CONSTITUTIONAL CHANGE FROM 1853 TO 1917

The people approved more than a dozen constitutional amendments in the next fifty years. The changes those amendments made concerned such matters as the conditions for voting and holding public office and adjustment of the Governor's power to remove justices of the peace. Other changes included: providing a means for filling vacancies in the Senate and the Council; eliminating the property requirement for running for Governor; and permitting voting machines to replace paper ballots, so long as the ballots remain secret. As well, beginning in 1911, amendments intended to enhance the power of the Legislature appeared. In that year the people adopted Amendment XXXIX, granting to the General Court the power to condemn land for road building that exceeded the need for the road, and to resell it, so long as the taking was limited to suitable building lots on both sides of the road.

---

[50] Morison, *A History of the Constitution of Massachusetts*, 63.

In 1912, Amendment XLI granted the General Court the power to prescribe for wild or forest lands methods of taxation that would develop and conserve the forests and resources of the Commonwealth. In 1913, Amendment XLII gave the General Court discretion to allow matters to go before the voters in a referendum. And in 1915, Amendment XLIII expanded the police power of the General Court in respect to urban renewal, authorizing the Legislature to buy and sell and improve land for the purpose of relieving congestion and providing homes for citizens, provided that the same could not be resold for less than the cost to the commonwealth. Also in 1915, Amendment XLIV authorized the General Court to tax different kinds of income at different rates, though uniformly as to the types of property from which the income flowed.

THE CONSTITUTIONAL CONVENTION OF 1917–1918

In 1912, the Progressive Party in Massachusetts had placed in its election platform a call for a convention. In 1914, Governor David Walsh in his inaugural address urged a convention because the consideration of individual amendments was taking up too much of the Legislature's time. Walsh repeated his suggestion in 1915. Though the General Court defeated the proposal, pressure started to mount, particularly from the proponents of initiative and referendum procedures. In 1915, a "Union for a Progressive Constitution" was formed, and the major issue was whether the Commonwealth should embrace some form of direct democracy through the adoption of the initiative and referendum. The new Governor, Samuel McCall, raised the idea of a convention in his 1916 inaugural address. Finally, on April 3, 1916, the Legislature passed a law sending the question to the people. The size of the convention was for the first time limited, to 320, by a new apportionment. As well, the law required for the first time that every Representative live in the district he represented. The people in November 1916 voted to hold the convention.

World War I had an immediate impact on the convention, with many delegates called to Europe. And it was a long convention: debates extended for 116 days over two years. Further, the convention seemed to raise fewer fundamental issues than had been raised at the start of the 1853 convention. The main issue the convention faced was the Progressive concern with the initiative and referendum. By this time, some nineteen states had adopted some form of one or the other, or both. These procedures gave the people a way around the Legislature, to prevent laws they did not favor from being executed (referendum), or to have laws enacted that the Legislature would not enact (initiative). The provisions adopted in state constitutions varied widely. Some did not provide for constitutional amendment by initiative, while others allowed for direct initiative (obviating the need for the Legislature to act as an intermediary in the process), and some allowed only for indirect (requiring the Legislature to act in before the law or the amendment would become effective).

Quickly it became clear that some form of initiative and referendum would be adopted at the convention. Advocates argued that the procedures would serve, in one delegate's words, "to make legislation as far as possible in the general public interest."[51] Still, other delegates expressed concern about turning the constitution into something more like a statute, which could be changed at the will of a temporary majority of the voters. Ultimately, the convention elected to exclude certain kinds of constitutional amendments from the process, including amendments related to the judiciary, religious institutions, and many of the rights contained in the Declaration of Rights. This compromise led to Amendment XLVIII replacing the Amendment IX procedure and the optional referendum procedure of Amendment XLII. In this way, as Morris Goldings remarked, the convention created one of "the most complicated [amending processes] in any state constitution."[52]

A second major cause at the convention was the anti-aid amendment. Amendment XVIII's prohibition against allocating public moneys exclusively for public schools did not extend beyond grade schools to apply to colleges and seminaries of learning and hospitals that might be under sectarian control. The convention extended the prohibition to apply to these other institutions in what because Amendment XLVI, superseding Amendment XVIII.

The convention also addressed issues regarding the structure of government, establishing two-year terms for state officers, Councillors, Senators, and Representatives; changing the order of succession to eliminate Councillors; and prohibiting members of the General Court from taking advantage of any office created or compensation by the Legislature during the period of their election. Further, though the movement to adopt the initiative and referendum succeeded, at the same time the convention adopted a variety of amendments that continued the process of augmenting the Legislature's authority—to exercise the power of eminent domain when the public purpose doctrine might not have been satisfied, to address issues regarding the environment and ancient landmarks, and to restrict advertising on public ways.

■ CONSTITUTIONAL CHANGE FROM 1918 TO THE PRESENT

In the next four decades, fifteen more amendments would be made to the constitution concerning such sundry matters as exempting emergency measures from the referendum process delay, granting women the rights to vote and to run for office, and adding to Article XVI of the Declaration of Rights a prohibition against abridging "[t]he right to freedom of speech." Between 1950 and 1964,

---

[51] John. J. Dinan, *The American State Constitutional Tradition* (Lawrence: University of Kansas, 2006), 88 (quoting *Debates in the Massachusetts Constitutional Convention*, 1917–1918, II: 282).

[52] Morris M. Goldings, "Massachusetts Amends: A Decade of State Constitutional Revision," *Harvard Journal on Legislation* 5 (1968): 373, 380.

the people adopted no new amendments, and in 1962, the General Court authorized the establishment of a "Commission Relative to the Need for Amendment, Revision, or Simplification of the Constitution of the Commonwealth," to investigate the need for amendment, revision, or simplification of the constitution.

The Commission submitted an Initial Report in 1963 and a Final Report in March of 1967. In its Initial Report, the Commission concluded that no pressing need existed for amendment of the Declaration of Rights. The Commission voiced the belief that changes that could appropriately be effected through legislation ought not be the subject of constitutional amendment, which should be restricted to those provisions "deemed so basic—and so potentially tempting in moments of political stress—that they should be difficult to change."[53] The Commission nonetheless concluded some changes should be suggested regarding the structure of government.

The Commission focused its attention on proposals for amendments beginning in 1945. Advocates had pressed for changes in the structure of government, including the terms of the Governor and other constitutional officers, abolishing the Council, reapportionment of the House of Representatives, and further enhancements to the powers of the Legislature. As well, the Commission reviewed proposals related to election matters and the procedure by which constitutional amendments could be made. In respect to these proposals, the Commission noted the conservative nature of Massachusetts constitutional history—the fact that the citizens of the Commonwealth had been governed by a document in its essence unchanged since its initial adoption. Notwithstanding historical periods of relatively liberal amendment, the Commission determined that neither the Declaration of Rights nor the Frame of Government required a substantial overhaul.

By the time the Commission had issued its final report, eight additional amendments had been adopted. The 1964 amendments concerned such matters as extension of the terms of the Governor and other executive officers; authorizing the General Court to provide for prompt and temporary succession of power in the event of disaster caused by enemy attack; and extending the jurisdiction of the Supreme Judicial Court to authorize—and, indeed, require—it to give advisory opinions to the Governor or Council upon request. The 1966 amendments concerned such matters as executive department reorganization, with the cooperation of the Legislature; authorizing the Legislature to address issues related to industrial development at the municipal level; and home rule—Amendment LXXXIX gave to cities and towns the power to revise their charters

[53] Massachusetts Special Commission on Revision of the Constitution, *Initial Report* (1963), 13–14.

to provide for the exercise of many powers previously exclusive to the Legislature.

In view of this amending activity and given other proposals discussed at the time, the Commission elected to devote its energy to improvements to the amendment procedure itself, trusting to that process all the substantive matters that might be raised. The most significant proposal to emerge was an amendment that would explicitly authorize and regulate the process of future constitutional conventions. It would have required the Legislature to ask the people every ten years, beginning in 1974 (the next gubernatorial election year), whether they would like to hold a constitutional convention. The origins of this recommendation may be traced to proposals debated and defeated at both the 1853 and 1917 conventions—defeated largely because a majority of delegates viewed such a measure as unnecessary in light of the precedents of 1820, 1853, and 1917. The recommendation also recalls one made by the town of Beverly in 1778, arguing in Jeffersonian fashion that a constitutional convention should be held every twenty years.[54]

The Commission also proposed that the time for adopting provisions in the General Court be shortened. Following the adoption of Amendment XLVIII, it could take as long as three years, ten months, for an amendment to pass; under Amendment IX, the maximum time had been one year, ten months. In addition, the Commission recommended changes in the kinds of legislative votes that should be required, as well as how many signatures ought to be required on amendment petitions.

Whether the Commission's work influenced the period of constitutional amendment that followed is a matter of debate. In the nearly forty-year period from 1968 to 2007, the people adopted thirty amendments to the constitution. These amendments liberalized voting rights by eliminating durational residency requirements, lowering the voting age, extending absentee balloting rights to those individuals with physical disabilities and those who could vote on a particular election day because of religious beliefs, and allowing "paupers" to vote. Other amendments extended equal protection rights, recognizing sex as a protected class and prohibiting discrimination on the basis of sex, race, color, creed, or national origin, and on the basis of a disability.

In addition, this period saw amendments recognizing environmental rights on the part of the people, authorizing the Legislature to protect agricultural land and extending its power to preserve forest lands, and providing for the use of gasoline taxes to support mass transit. As well, the people added a new anti-aid amendment which broadened the General Court's power to spend money on

---

[54] As Thomas Jefferson explained in 1816, we should rid ourselves of the belief entertained by some that constitutions should be viewed with "sanctimonious reverence . . . like the ark of the covenant, too sacred to be touched." "Letter to Samuel Kercheval of July 12, 1816," in Paul L. Ford, *Works of Thomas Jefferson* (New York and London: G.P. Putnam's Sons, 1904–1905), XII, 3.

private institutions by empowering it to make grants in aid to private higher educational institutions or to students or their tuition paying parents; modified Amendment XLVIII to provide information to voters about proposed constitutional amendments; augmented, again, the General Court's taxing power; and addressed the problem of legislators voting large raises for themselves or fearing retaliation for voting even reasonable raises by tying compensation to the median income level of the commonwealth.

Amendment CXVI, adopted in 1982, warrants particular mention. By this amendment, the people essentially overruled the Supreme Judicial Court's decision in *District Attorney v. Watson*, in which the court held the death penalty invalid under the Massachusetts Constitution as a violation of the prohibition on cruel and unusual punishment.[55] The amendment states that "No provision of the Constitution . . . shall be construed as prohibiting the imposition of the punishment of death." The court nonetheless determined in a later case, *Commonwealth v. Colon-Cruz*, that "nothing in the new language" prevents a Massachusetts court "from invalidating a particular death penalty statute under the Massachusetts Constitution on a ground other than that the imposition of the punishment of death is forbidden."[56]

The court's treatment of Amendment CXVI reflects the tension between proposals to amend the constitution to represent the will of a contemporary majority and the court's obligation to enforce the essential protections of the Declaration of Rights. The court's effort to reconcile Amendment CXVI with the existing provisions of the Declaration of Rights, moreover, may indicate its approach in future cases involving the reach of constitutional amendments that seek to constrict rather than enlarge rights contained in the Massachusetts Constitution. At least one such amendment has been adopted: Amendment CXX, adopted in 2002, prohibits persons incarcerated as a result of felony convictions from voting. And in 2007, the Legislature addressed the popular pressure to adopt a constitutional amendment overruling the Supreme Judicial Court's decision in *Goodridge v. Department of Public Health*, in which the court held invalid the denial of marriage licenses to same-sex couples.[57] The proposed amendment ultimately failed to receive sufficient votes in the Legislature to be placed on the ballot.

■ CONCLUSION

Whether the amendments at the end of the twentieth century and the like efforts at the beginning of the twenty-first foretell a new wave of state constitutional revision in Massachusetts is at this writing unclear. What does seem likely,

---

[55] District Attorney for the Suffolk District v. Watson, 381 Mass. 648, 411 N.E.2d 1274 (1980).

[56] Commonwealth v. Colon-Cruz, 393 Mass. 150, 159, 470 N.E.2d 116, 121 (1984).

[57] Goodridge v. Department of Public Health, 440 Mass. 309, 798 N.E.2d 941 (2003).

looking at more than two hundred years of Massachusetts constitutional history, is that pressure for change will build whenever the citizens of Massachusetts and their Representatives confront societal developments the framers of the constitution and its amendments could not have imagined, much less planned for. In other words, as James Bowdoin observed when presiding over the 1780 convention, constitutional change in Massachusetts will come "as Experience, that best instructor, shall . . . point out to be expedient or necessary."[58]

[58] *Journal of the Convention for Framing a Constitution of Government for the State of Massachusetts Bay* (Boston: Dutton and Wentworth, 1832), 217.

PART TWO

The Massachusetts Constitution and Commentary

Preamble and the Decalaration of Rights

"[A constitution] is the body of elements, to which you can refer, and quote article by article; and which contains . . . everything that relates to the complete organization of a civil government, and the principles on which it shall act, and by which it shall be bound."

THOMAS PAINE, "Rights of Man" (1791)

PREAMBLE

The end of the institution, maintenance, and administration of government, is to secure the existence of the body politic, to protect it, and to furnish the individuals who compose it with the power of enjoying in safety and tranquility their natural rights, and the blessings of life: and whenever these great objects are not obtained, the people have a right to alter the government, and to take measures necessary for their safety, prosperity and happiness.

The body-politic is formed by a voluntary association of individuals: it is a social compact, by which the whole people covenants with each citizen, and each citizen with the whole people, that all shall be governed by certain laws for the common good. It is the duty of the people, therefore, in framing a constitution of government, to provide for an equitable mode of making laws, as well as for an impartial interpretation, and a faithful execution of them; that every man may, at all times, find his security in them.

We, therefore, the people of Massachusetts, acknowledging, with grateful hearts, the goodness of the great Legislator of the universe, in affording us, in the course of His providence, an opportunity, deliberately and peaceably, without fraud, violence or surprise, of entering into an original, explicit, and solemn compact with each other; and of forming a new constitution of civil government, for ourselves and posterity; and devoutly imploring His direction in so interesting a design, do agree upon, ordain and establish the following

Declaration of Rights, and Frame of Government, as the CONSTITUTION OF THE COMMONWEALTH OF MASSACHUSETTS.

The Preamble to the Massachusetts Constitution stands as it was penned in 1780. The question whether the Preamble itself operates to make any grant of governmental power or to place any limit upon the exercise of governmental power has been left open. See *Opinion of the Justices* (1939). Among the methods employed by the Supreme Judicial Court to interpret a provision of the state constitution is that of seeking the "natural and obvious sense" of the terms of the provision, "according to common and approved usage at the time of [the provision's] adoption." *McDuffy v. Sec'y of Executive Office of Educ.* (1993) (quotation omitted). The court has stated that the constitution "is to be interpreted in the light of the conditions under which it and its several parts were framed, the ends which it was designed to accomplish, the benefits which it was expected to confer, and the evils which it was hoped to remedy." *Id.* In light of these interpretive precepts, it would seem that at least the spirit of the Preamble should play a role as an aid to interpreting the constitution.

PART THE FIRST: THE DECLARATION OF RIGHTS

ARTICLE I. Equality and Natural Rights of All People

All people are born free and equal and have certain natural, essential and unalienable rights; among which may be reckoned the right of enjoying and defending their lives and liberties; that of acquiring, possessing and protecting property; in fine, that of seeking and obtaining their safety and happiness. Equality under the law shall not be denied or abridged because of sex, race, color, creed or national origin.

Amended in 1976, this Article originally spoke of "men" rather than "people" and it lacked its last sentence. The language is strongly reminiscent of predecessor provisions in the Virginia and Pennsylvania constitutions. Those constitutions, however, held men to be "by nature equally free and independent" rather than "born free and equal." Adams's draft had used the more stinting terminology of the state constitutions, but the Massachusetts convention chose to replace it with the more radical language of the Declaration of Independence, suggesting a more general political and legal equality. Article I equality protections were made more explicit when the "Massachusetts Equal Rights Amendment" added the last sentence in 1976. The declaration of the existence of "natural, essential and unalienable" human rights suggests that the explicitly stated rights are merely "among" those that are not given up as the price for enjoying the benefits of civil society and government; the existence of others is clearly envisaged.

Three years after ratification of the Massachusetts Constitution, the Supreme Judicial Court suggested the equality provisions of Article I prohibit slavery in the Commonwealth. See *Jackson v. Phillips* (1867) (discussing Supreme Judicial

Court's 1783 decision in *Commonwealth v. Jennison*). In 1850, however, the court in *Roberts v. City of Boston* (1850) rejected a claim that Boston's racially segregated public schools violated the state constitution. See *id.* Five years later, the Massachusetts Legislature outlawed racial discrimination in "any place of public accommodation, resort or amusement" in the Commonwealth. Mass. St. 1865, c. 277 (codified at Mass. G.L. c. 272, § 98). But the U.S. Supreme Court, in 1896, drew upon the "separate but equal" language and reasoning of *Roberts* to uphold state laws mandating racially segregated railroad facilities under the Equal Protection Clause of the Fourteenth Amendment to the U.S. Constitution. See *Plessy v. Ferguson* (1896).

The U.S. Supreme Court overruled *Plessy* in a series of decisions, beginning with *Brown v. Board of Education* (1954), that prohibited state-sanctioned racial discrimination as part of the court's general tightening of standards for state laws under the Equal Protection and Due Process clauses of the Fourteenth Amendment. The Supreme Judicial Court, like most of its sister state supreme courts, participated in this "rights revolution" by not only following those decisions when the court applied federal provisions to the cases that came before it but also by employing them as "persuasive authority" when it interpreted analogous provisions of the Massachusetts Constitution. Accordingly, although there is no explicit equal protection clause in the state constitution, Massachusetts courts have developed what they have called "equal protection" doctrine under the language of Articles I, VI, VII, X, and (occasionally) XII of the Declaration of Rights and have largely tracked the decisions of the U.S. Supreme Court in doing so. See *Brest v. Comm'r of Ins.* (1930) (observing that "[t]he Declaration of Rights of the Constitution of this Commonwealth in arts. 1, 6, 7, [and] 10 . . . contain [s]ample guarantees for equal protection."). A similar phenomenon has taken place in respect to the development of "due process" jurisprudence under the state constitution, and Article I has been cited, in conjunction with Articles X and XII and Part II, C. 1, § 1, Art. IV, as guaranteeing individuals due process of law. See, e.g., *Eastern Cas. Ins. Co., Inc. v. Roberts* (2001) (describing the right to due process of law as contained in Articles I, X, and XII of the Massachusetts Constitution).

Under the Fourteenth Amendment, the general run of state legislation enjoys a presumption of constitutionality that can be defeated only upon a showing that the law is "arbitrary" or lacking in "minimum rationality." Laws that discriminate on the basis of race or some other "suspect classification," or that impinge upon a "fundamental right," however, are denied that presumption and will be held unconstitutional unless they can be shown to serve a "legitimate and compelling state interest" that could not be achieved by some "less restrictive state means." The U.S. Supreme Court supplemented these two levels of scrutiny—designed to steer a middle course between too little and too much judicial review of legislation—in the 1970s with an "intermediate scrutiny" standard applicable to laws employing semi-suspect classifications, such as gender. The constitutionality of those laws requires a showing that the use of such a classification serves an "important state interest" and is "substantially related" to the achieving of that interest. Notably, some U.S. Supreme Court opinions have suggested the application of a nuanced, sliding scale of review based upon the degree to which a class is suspect or a right is fundamental, rather than a rigid system of three levels of scrutiny. See, e.g., *City of Cleburne v. Cleburne Living Center* (1985) (invalidating zoning restrictions on housing for the mentally retarded under purported minimum rationality equal protection review).

As a starting point, the Supreme Judicial Court has adopted the general approach to equal protection of the U.S. Supreme Court. See *Tobin's Case* (1997). The constitutional commitment to equal protection does not "protect against burdens and disabilities as such but against their unequal imposition." *Opinion of the Justices* (1996). Equal protection requires that "all persons in the same category and the same circumstances be treated alike." *Opinion of the Justices* (1955). Accordingly, when faced with an equal protection challenge to the constitutionality of governmental action, state courts will seek to determine whether that action classifies individuals or groups of persons in a particular way, and whether the classification is unfair. In determining whether the government has violated equal protection guarantees under the Massachusetts Constitution, the courts follow the federal approach in applying "strict scrutiny" to governmental action that discriminates between or among individuals or groups on the basis of a "suspect classification," or that infringes upon a "fundamental right," and they require a showing of "compelling state interest" and use of means that are "necessary" for the advancement of that interest. See *Tobin's Case, supra.*

As with the Fourteenth Amendment, suspect classifications subject to strict scrutiny under the Massachusetts Constitution include those employing race, alienage, or national origin. See *Commonwealth v. King* (1977). Because the 1976 Equal Rights Amendment to Article I explicitly prohibits discrimination based upon sex, gender discrimination is also subject to strict scrutiny. See *Lowell v. Kowalski* (1980). Amendment CXIV of the Massachusetts Constitution, ratified in 1980, presumably establishes disabled individuals as a suspect class as well. This proposition is untested because disabled individuals have preferred to raise their claims of discrimination under the Massachusetts civil rights acts rather than under the constitution. Massachusetts' fairly comprehensive scheme of civil rights legislation often affords relief when discrimination is based upon classifications not deemed to be "suspect" under the Massachusetts Constitution. See, e.g., *Rock v. Massachusetts Comm'n Against Discrimination* (1981) (age discrimination).

A difference from federal constitutional doctrine is the relative lack in Massachusetts of a body of case law that develops in detail the "fundamental rights" branch of equal protection strict scrutiny review. While the Supreme Judicial Court has held, for example, that the right to move freely within the Commonwealth, see *Commonwealth v. Weston W.* (2009), the right to vote, see *Dane v. Board of Registrars of Voters* (1978), the protection of property, see *Campbell v. Boston* (1935), and the right or private employees to strike, see *Pickett v. Walsh* (1906), are fundamental rights, most Massachusetts case law tends to demarcate the rights that should not be considered "fundamental" for equal protection purposes. See, e.g., *Tobin's Case* (no fundamental right to receive workers' compensation benefits); *Williams v. Secretary of EOHS* (1993) (no fundamental right to receive mental health services); *Commonwealth v. Conceicao* (1983) (right to appeal not fundamental); *Commonwealth v. Henry's Drywall Co.* (1974) (right to pursue one's work or one's business not fundamental); *Commonwealth v. Leis* (1969) (right to smoke marijuana not fundamental). Often, the Supreme Judicial Court has elected to protect fundamental rights under the due process provisions of the Massachusetts Constitution, rather than under the equal protection framework. See, e.g., *Moe v. Secretary of Administration & Finance* (1981) (discussing fundamental privacy rights under Massachusetts Constitution); *Superintendent of Belchertown State School v. Saikewicz* (1977) (discussing right to bodily integrity under rubric of substantive due process).

Governmental action that does not infringe upon a fundamental right or implicate a suspect classification will survive equal protection review if it can be shown to advance any legitimate state interest through means that are not wholly irrational or arbitrary. See *Rushworth v. Registrar of Motor Vehicles* (1992). The court has stated that "[t]he Legislature has wide discretion to create statutory classifications that do not burden a fundamental interest or discriminate against a suspect class. As long as the classification rationally furthers some legitimate, articulated state purpose, it will not be overturned." *Murphy v. Department of Correction* (1999) (quotation omitted) ("Department of Correction"). If, however, the plaintiff can prove that the classifications are arbitrary, capricious, or irrational, then the court will strike down the law. See *Goodridge v. Department of Public Health* (2003); *Murphy v. Comm'r of the Dept. of Indus. Accidents* (1993) ("Industrial Accidents"). As a general matter, an arbitrary statutory classification is one that fails to rest on some ground of difference having "fair and substantial relation to the object of the legislation." *Russell v. Treasurer and Receiver Gen.* (1954).

The courts show great deference to legislative solutions and line drawing under rational basis review, even if distinctions may appear to be imprecise or unwise. See *Department of Correction*; see also *Shell Oil Co. v. City of Revere* (1981) ("it is not the province of the court to sit and weigh conflicting evidence supporting or opposing a legislative enactment"). In pressing a violation of equal protection under the Massachusetts Constitution, a plaintiff bears the burden of proving that the legislative classification is invalid. See *Zeller v. Cantu* (1985). Classifications need not be perfect to survive an equal protection challenge. *Commonwealth v. Petralia* (1977). A legislative difference in treatment reasonably related to a legitimate public purpose is permissible. *Henry's Drywall Co.* "[R]ough accommodations that to some extent result in dissimilarity of treatment" will not be overturned, *id.*, and the government is not constitutionally required to choose between attacking every aspect of a problem and not attacking it at all. See *Mobil Oil Corp. v. Attorney General* (1972).

Notwithstanding the deference accorded legislative judgments under rational basis review, such review is not wholly without force. In cases involving noneconomic legislation, for example, the court has long held that the state constitution "may guard more jealously against the exercise of the State's police power." *Coffee-Rich, Inc. v. Commissioner of Pub. Health* (1965). Even under rational basis review, "equal protection analysis requires the court to look carefully at the purpose to be served by the statute in question and at the degree of harm to the affected class." *English v. New England Medical Center, Inc.* (1989). The *English* court reasoned that "characterizing the test to be applied to determine the constitutional validity of legislation as 'reasonable relation' and 'strict scrutiny'" is simply a "shorthand for referring to the opposite ends of a continuum of constitutional vulnerability determined at every point by the competing values involved." *Id.* (quotations omitted). Thus the court has recognized the need, in appropriate cases, to apply nonstrict scrutiny equal protection review pragmatically and flexibly.

Those appropriate cases typically involve personal interests that are significant but do not rise to the level of recognized fundamental rights. Consider, in this regard, *Industrial Accidents, supra,* in which the court, applying rational basis scrutiny, held unconstitutional the requirement of a fee for workers' compensation claims filed with the assistance of counsel. Acknowledging the Legislature's legitimate interests in reducing the costs of an administrative proceeding, deterring frivolous appeals and lowering the cost of litigation for "financially disadvantaged litigants," the court nonetheless rejected the filing fee requirement because the relationship between the fee and those legitimate goals was "so attenuated as to render the distinction arbitrary or irrational." *Id.* (quotation omitted). In the court's view, the filing fee requirement served only to penalize "claimants who [chose] to engage counsel." *Id.* The court's relatively close review of the fee in question may be explained by the importance under the Massachusetts Constitution of a citizen's right of access to the courts. The court has held that, pursuant to Article XI of the Declaration of Rights, citizens shall enjoy such access "without discrimination." *Id.* (quotation omitted). While the right of access to the courts apparently is not fundamental for the purpose of equal protection review, see *Paro v. Longwood Hospital* (1977) (applying identical rational basis review under Articles I and XI), still the Supreme Judicial Court has stated that, when governmental action implicates access to the courts, "[n]o obstacles can be thrown in the way of some which are not interposed in the path of others." *Industrial Accidents* (quotation omitted).

In *Goodridge v. Department of Public Health*, the court undertook a particularly thorough rational basis review of the Commonwealth's proffered justifications for limiting civil marriage to opposite-sex couples. In *Goodridge*, the plaintiffs, all same-sex couples, appealed the Commonwealth's decision to deny them marriage licenses. The court overturned the denial. The court concluded that neither the state's interest in promoting a favorable setting for procreation or child-rearing, nor its interest in preserving scarce financial resources, presented a rational basis for excluding same-sex couples from marriage. The court viewed these justifications as unreasonable because they were "starkly at odds with the comprehensive network of vigorous, gender-neutral laws promoting stable families and the best interests of children." *Id.* Though the court's inquiry in *Goodridge* was sharp, it was still rational basis review: to justify the exclusion of same-sex couples from civil marriage, the Commonwealth did not have to present a compelling justification for the statutory classification, but it did have to present a justification that harmonized that classification with the many other laws pertaining to the benefits and protections afforded all Massachusetts families and children. The Commonwealth having failed to do so, the court deemed irrational—and likely motivated by historical prejudice—a law limiting whom one might choose to marry.

ARTICLE II. The Right and Duty of Public Religious Worship
It is the right as well as the duty of all men in society, publicly, and at stated seasons to worship the Supreme Being, the great Creator and Preserver of the universe. And no subject shall be hurt, molested, or restrained, in his person, liberty, or estate, for worshipping God in the manner and season most agreeable to the dictates of his own conscience; or for his religious profession or sentiments; provided he doth not disturb the public peace or obstruct others in their religious worship.

Though this Article has never been amended, in 1855 voters ratified Article of Amendment XVIII, prohibiting money raised by taxation from being appropriated to any religious sect for the maintenance of its own school. Article of Amendment XLVI, ratified in 1917, superseded Amendment XVIII; it states that "No law shall be passed prohibiting the free exercise of religion."

Article II guarantees "absolute freedom as to religious belief and liberty unrestrained as to religious practices, subject only to the conditions that the public peace must not be disturbed nor others obstructed in their religious worship or the general obligations of good citizenship violated." *Nicholls v. Mayor and School Committee of Lynn* (1937) (quotation omitted). Until 1990, the standard established by the U.S. Supreme Court for evaluating free exercise of religion claims under the First Amendment had been adopted by the Supreme Judicial Court in interpreting Article II of the Massachusetts Constitution. See *Opinion of the Justices* (1982). Shortly after the U.S. Supreme Court's 1990 decision in *Employment Division v. Smith* (1990), in which the court ruled that a statute violates freedom of religious expression under the First Amendment only when it specifically targets religion, the Massachusetts Supreme Judicial Court chose to rely on Article II of the state constitution to provide broader protection to religiously inspired conduct. See *Society of Jesus of New England v. Boston Landmarks Commission* (1990). The Supreme Judicial Court, in *Society of Jesus,* adopted a two-tiered balancing test, which offers more rigorous protection of individual religious rights than the U.S. Supreme Court's test.

Article II "guarantees freedom of religious belief and religious practice subject only to the conditions that the public peace not be disturbed and the religious worship of others not be obstructed." *Id.* In applying Article II, the first question is whether a law burdens the free exercise of religion. See *Attorney Gen. v. Desilets* (1994). If there is a burden, the next step is to inquire whether the religiously inspired conduct falls within the ambit of the provisos—that is, whether it disturbs the public peace or obstructs others in their religious worship, in which case the religiously inspired conduct is exempt from absolute protection. When religiously motivated conduct falls within an exemption, the permissibility of applying a statute burdensome to that conduct is determined by balancing the Commonwealth's interests in enforcing the law against the individual's interests in worshiping as he or she chooses. The Commonwealth has the burden of proving that its interest in maintaining public peace outweighs the individual's interest in practicing religion in whichever manner he or she chooses.

In *Society of Jesus,* for example, the Supreme Judicial Court held that Article II protected the right of the plaintiffs to design interior spaces meant for religious worship in any manner worshipers saw fit, provided questions of public safety did not arise, thereby barring the government from regulating interior changes through a landmark preservation program. The court ruled that the religious conduct burdened by the landmark preservation (including, among other things, removal of an altar) was not exempt from Article II protection. Since the religiously inspired conduct of the Society of Jesus—the desire to maintain the placement of an altar—did not harm the public or the religious practices of others, the conduct received absolute protection under Article II. The court went on to explain that even if the Society of Jesus' desire to maintain an altar had triggered an exemption listed in the proviso, when weighing the two interests against each other, the right to worship in whichever manner a religious organization saw fit within their place of worship far outweighed the landmark preservation's interest in restoring the church.

The Supreme Judicial Court also applied this standard in *Attorney General v. Desilets,* in which landlords refused to rent to an unmarried, cohabitating couple because of a sincerely held religious belief. The couple commenced the action under General Laws c. 151B, § 4(6), which provides in part that it shall be an unlawful practice for the owner of a multiple dwelling to refuse to rent or lease to persons because, among other things, of marital status. The Supreme Judicial Court concluded that there was a direct conflict between the law and the landlords' sincerely held religious belief that allowing an unmarried couple to live together would have been facilitating sinful conduct. The court then considered whether the landlords' refusal to rent to unmarried couples would constitute a breach of the public peace. The majority concluded that the Commonwealth had not offered enough evidence upon which to base a ruling.

In a concurring opinion, Justice Liacos criticized the majority for not taking the opportunity to develop further the court's analysis of state constitutional jurisprudence. Through a close reading of the language of Article II, Liacos argued that citizens are unambiguously "free to decide for [themselves] the method by which [they] will worship." *Id.* He stated:

> I cannot agree that particular conduct will not be recognized as worship by this court merely because that conduct is not within the conception of worship espoused by a majority of the Justices of this court, past or present. Nor can I agree that conduct must be "commonly regarded as religious conduct" for it to fall within the scope and protection of art. 2. These propositions suggest that only those forms of worship that are acceptable in the opinion of the majority of society will receive consideration under art. 2. In my view, these propositions are contrary to the essence of art. 2, as shown in both the plain language of that provision and in our case law interpreting it.
>
> *Id.*

As noted above, Article II does not provide absolute religious protection. In *Commonwealth v. Nissenbaum* (1989), for example, a majority of the Supreme Judicial Court concluded that Article II permitted the state to criminalize the religiously inspired use of marijuana and hashish. After balancing the state's interests against the individual's, the court concluded that the state's interest in preventing use of a "dangerous" substance outweighed the religious conflict. *Id.* The majority reached its conclusion by reasoning that, "in a broad sense," all offenses are breaches of the public peace, and by relying on precedent established by federal and other state courts. *Id.* In a dissent, Justice Liacos reasoned that the framers intended Article II to protect practitioners of minority religions and that whether the use of marijuana was intended for a sincerely held religious belief was a question of fact for a jury to decide. He argued that, assuming the family's possession and use of marijuana resulted in no harm to the public and in no victim, the religiously inspired conduct should have received absolute protection by Article II since it did not trigger an exemption from the proviso.

For further provisions as to religious freedom, see Part I, Art. III; Amendment XVIII, replaced by Amendment XLVI (Anti-Aid Amendment); and Amendment XLVIII ("religion, religious practices or religious institutions" not subject to initiative or referendum).

ARTICLE III. Religious Societies

As the public worship of God and instructions in piety, religion and morality, promote the happiness and prosperity of a people and the security of a

> **republican government;—therefore, the several religious societies of this commonwealth, whether corporate or unincorporate, at any meeting legally warned and holden for that purpose, shall ever have the right to elect their pastors or religious teachers, to contract with them for their support, to raise money for erecting and repairing houses for public worship, for the maintenance of religious instruction, and for the payment of necessary expenses: and all persons belonging to any religious society shall be taken and held to be members, until they shall file with the clerk of such society, a written notice, declaring the dissolution of their membership, and thenceforth shall not be liable for any grant or contract which may be thereafter made, or entered into by such society: — and all religious sects and denominations, demeaning themselves peaceably, and as good citizens of the commonwealth, shall be equally under the protection of the law; and no subordination of any one sect or denomination to another shall ever be established by law.**

The current text of Article III was ratified by Amendment XI in 1833. The earlier version of Article III was adopted as a part of the original Massachusetts Constitution in 1780. Before its amendment, Article III essentially established the Congregational Church as the favored church of Massachusetts.

In interpreting Article III, the Supreme Judicial Court has time and again relied upon standards developed by the U.S. Supreme Court under the Establishment Clause of the First Amendment. See *Colo v. Treasurer and Receiver General* (1979). In *Colo*, the court applied the federal standard and held that a statute or governmental practice does not violate the establishment clause so long as (1) there is a secular legislative purpose, (2) the primary effect of the challenged practice neither advances nor inhibits religion, (3) there is an avoidance of excessive governmental entanglement with religion, and (4) the challenged practice has no divisive political potential. The court noted that this standard is not a rigid test, but rather a "guideline" for establishment clause analysis.

In applying this "guideline," the Supreme Judicial Court has held that expending public monies to finance the salaries of legislative chaplains who daily open legislative sessions with brief prayers is not unconstitutional. In *Colo*, the opening prayers were voluntary and directed toward adults, whose religious beliefs or nonbeliefs were most likely already formed and were therefore not impressionable. The court stated that "[t]he hermetic separation of church and State is an impossibility which the [U.S.] Constitution has never required." *Id.* Massachusetts courts have also followed federal standards in *Wheeler v. Roman Catholic Archdiocese of Boston* (1979) (allowing hierarchical religious organization to manage its own property dispute); *Commonwealth v. Anderson* (1930) (holding that religious nature of books sold did not negate need for a license); and *Commonwealth v. Plaisted* (1889) (holding that musician performing in streets for religious reasons not exempt from needing a license).

ARTICLE IV. Right of Self-Government; Reservation of Powers

The people of this commonwealth have the sole and exclusive right of governing themselves, as a free, sovereign, and independent state; and do, and forever hereafter shall, exercise and enjoy every power, jurisdiction, and right, which is not, or may not hereafter, be by them [expressly] delegated to the United States of America in Congress assembled.

This provision reflects the text of Article II of the Articles of Confederation, which was in force in 1780. That Article provided: "Each State retains its sovereignty, freedom and independence, and every power, jurisdiction and right, which is not by this confederation expressly delegated to the United States, in Congress assembled." Congress enacted Article II of the Articles of Confederation on November 15, 1777; the Massachusetts Constitution was ratified in 1780. Article IV has never been amended or explicitly superseded. The word "expressly" has been placed in brackets to reflect the differing language of the Tenth Amendment to the U.S. Constitution, ratified in 1791, which states: "The powers not delegated to the United States by the Constitution, nor prohibited by it to the States, are reserved to the States respectively, or to the people."

Massachusetts courts have not had occasion to interpret Article IV. Presumably, the provision establishes, to the extent that doubt might exist, that the people of Massachusetts declare themselves to be citizens of a state government and not subject to the authority of any other governmental power, save the government of the United States of America, except as they shall expressly allow it. In connection with this provision, see also Amendment II of the Massachusetts Constitution, ratified in 1821 (as supplemented or amended by Amendments XLVII (1910), LXX (1926), and LXXXIX (1966), each of which concerns the power of self-government in towns and cities).

ARTICLE V. Magistrates and Officers as Agents of and Accountable to the People

All powers residing originally in the people, and being derived from them, the several magistrates and officers of government, vested with authority, whether legislative, executive, or judicial, are their substitutes and agents, and are at all times accountable to them.

This Article has not been amended.

This Article is another announcement of the constitutional commitment to the social compact theory of government in Massachusetts: by its terms, Article V provides that government has only those powers delegated to it by the people, in whom all powers originally resided. Accordingly, the people's representatives are just that—representatives who act for the people in their stead, or as their agents. And those representatives are properly limited in exercising their powers to doing those things that the people themselves would do. Representatives will learn of the people's wishes, presumably, through public debate, elections, and such "instructions" as they are given via "questions of instruction" from the voting public. See Mass. G.L. c. 53, sec. 19 (concerning questions of instruction by ballot).

Importantly, the declaration that the "magistrates and officers of government" are "at all times accountable" to the people does not mean that individuals have the right to compel their representatives, or other governmental officials, to take particular action. In other words, whether governmental officials have transcended their political (as opposed to legal) mandate is, under Article V, an essentially nonjusticiable question, to be remedied, if at all, at the polls. In *Manning v. Municipal Court* (1977), for example, the court ruled that Article V confers no individual right to compel a criminal prosecution, or to direct the conduct of a public prosecutor.

In connection with this provision, see also Part I, Art. XXIX.

ARTICLE VI. Title to Obtain Advantages or Privileges

No man, nor corporation, or association of men, have any other title to obtain advantages, or particular and exclusive privileges, distinct from those of the community, than what arises from the consideration of services rendered to the public; and this title being in nature neither hereditary, nor transmissible to children, or descendants, or relations by blood, the idea of a man born a magistrate, lawgiver, or judge, is absurd and unnatural.

This Article has not been amended.

Article VI concerns the use of state power for private interests; the provision "recognizes that advantages distinct from those of the community may be conferred upon the consideration of services rendered to the public." *Opinion of the Justices* (1900). So long as the conferral of a benefit, privilege, or right is only an incidental effect of a statute primarily concerned with the public welfare, the statute will withstand constitutional challenge. See, e.g., *Boston & A.R.R. v. Reardon* (1917) (because the real estate of railroads "is in a sense impressed with a public use," the Legislature may protect such property from claims of adverse possession).

Article VI has been used to challenge veterans' preference legislation. These challenges have been largely unsuccessful. Legislation requiring that preference be given to veterans in hiring for civil service positions has been overturned only when the statute in question requires that veterans be given an absolute preference, without regard to qualifications. See *Brown v. Russell* (1896) (overturning absolute statutory preference for veterans be appointed before nonveterans, even if veterans in question had not taken civil service examination). The *Brown* court reasoned that "it is inconsistent with the nature of our government, and particularly with articles VI and VII of our Declaration of Rights, that the appointing power should be compelled by legislation to appoint to public offices persons of a certain class in preference to all others, without the exercise on its part of any discretion." *Id.* The court has upheld preferential legislation that leaves room for the discretion of the appointing party to take the applicant's qualifications into account. See, e.g., *White v. City of Boston* (1998) (preference for disabled police employees not unconstitutional because employees must be otherwise qualified).

In upholding veterans' preference legislation, the Supreme Judicial Court has followed a rationale that allows special treatment for certain groups if the public interest is thereby served. The court has stated that most veterans' preference legislation does not violate the Massachusetts Constitution because the public interest would be served in two ways through a veterans' preference for civil service positions. First, veterans are likely to possess certain qualities that would make them good civil servants; second, patriotism would be stimulated by supporting veterans. *Opinion of the Justices* (1896).

This reasoning reflects a different understanding of the rationale justifying statutory preferences than the text of Article VI appears to endorse; under the language of Article 6, it would seem logical that veterans could be granted preference simply for "consideration of services rendered to the public"—in other words, in recognition of their military service. The court, however, has not chosen to proceed according to this logic, and, as it stands, all preferential treatment must be couched in terms of serving the society as a whole to survive constitutional scrutiny. See *Leigh v. Bd. of Registration in Nursing* (1987) (Article VI "does not impose a constitutional prohibition on the conferral of benefits to individuals where the public is served"). While this rationale dovetails with the traditional equal protection scrutiny of economic legislation under Part I, article I of the Massachusetts Constitution, it does allow for the possibility of more searching judicial review of a statutory preference if that preference is absolute. In a 1939 advisory opinion, for example, the court concluded that a proposed bill to exclude married women whose husbands were capable of supporting them from public employment (ostensibly in order to provide more jobs for single women with no other support) violated Article VI because the exclusion was not related to obtaining a higher quality of public employee and would therefore not serve the public interest. *Opinion of the Justices* (1939). Like the veterans' preference legislation rejected in *Brown v. Russell*, moreover, the exclusion would have established an absolute preference for single women in hiring decisions.

The creation of absolute preferences by statute is rare. The majority of legislative classifications challenged under Article VI have been upheld as long as they rest on rational bases related to the public interest. See, e.g., *Jewel Companies v. Town of Burlington* (1974) (legislation requiring supermarkets, but not restaurants, to close between certain hours held constitutionally valid because maintaining quiet in residential neighborhood is legitimate end).

ARTICLE VII. Government Instituted for the Common Good

Government is instituted for the common good; for the protection, safety, prosperity and happiness of the people; and not for the profit, honor, or private interest of any one man, family, or class of men: Therefore the people alone have an incontestable, unalienable, and indefeasible right to institute government; and to reform, alter, or totally change the same, when their protection, safety, prosperity and happiness require it.

This Article has not been amended.

In an 1896 case involving a constitutional challenge to a statutory veterans' preference in civil service positions, the Supreme Judicial Court explained that, under Article VII, "public offices, which are the instrumentalities of government," ought to be created or filled "only for the protection, safety, prosperity, and happiness of the people, and for the common good." *Brown v. Russell* (1896). Since that time, Article VII has been interpreted by the Massachusetts courts, in conjunction with Articles I, VI, and X of the Declaration of Rights, to provide individuals some protection from arbitrary discrimination through governmental action. See *Connor v. Metro. Dist. Water Supply* (1943). In *Corning Glass Works v. Ann & Hope, Inc.* (1973), for example, the Supreme Judicial Court did not differentiate among Articles I, VI, VII, and X in stating that the Commonwealth may exercise the police power only when legislation "bears a real and substantial relation to the public health, safety, morals, or some other phase of the general welfare."

Still, Article VII has not been held to provide specific equal protection guarantees to individuals or groups. The court has observed that, while "equal protection . . . considerations may arise" under Article VII, *Opinion of the Justices* (1990), it has "never held that art. 7 creates an equal protection right." *Town of Brookline v. Sec'y of the Commonwealth* (1994). In the court's view, Article VII "speaks essentially to a right of the people to institute and change government and not to challenge statutory classifications." *Id.* The court has not elaborated what this right entails, or how it might be enforced. The majority of cases citing to Article VII involve its use with Article I and Article VI in the context of equal protection.

In contrast to the Supreme Judicial Court, courts interpreting other state constitutions have reached different conclusions as to the meaning of provisions similar to Article VII. The Vermont Supreme Court, for example, has interpreted chapter 1, article 7 of the Vermont Constitution—the "common benefits clause"—as a specific equality guarantee, pursuant to which a reviewing court must determine whether "the omission of a part of the community from the benefit, protection, and security of [a] challenged law bears a reasonable and just relation to [the law's] purpose." *Baker v. State* (1999). And the West Virginia Supreme Court has held that the common benefits clause in the West Virginia Constitution may provide greater individual rights protection than the Equal

Protection Clause of the U.S. Constitution. See *United Mine Workers of America, Int'l Union v. Parsons* (1983).

ARTICLE VIII. Regular Elections and Appointments
In order to prevent those, who are vested with authority, from becoming oppressors, the people have a right, at such periods and in such manner as they shall establish by their frame of government, to cause their public officers to return to private life; and to fill up vacant places by certain and regular elections and appointments.

This Article has not been amended.

The Massachusetts Constitution, through Articles VIII and IX, as well as Amendments LXIV and LXXXII, mandates regular elections for public office in the Commonwealth. See *Bates v. Director of the Office of Campaign and Political Finance* (2002). The Supreme Judicial Court has, in the few cases in which it has considered Article VIII, interpreted the provision to mean what it says. In *Lamson v. Secretary* (1960) of the Commonwealth, for example, the court considered an Article VIII challenge to a statute reapportioning senatorial and councillor districts in the Commonwealth. The court held that the time between redistricting and the next election was "sufficient," such that there was "no violation of the requirement [in Article VIII] of certain and regular elections." *Id.* And, when faced with the question whether the Legislature could constitutionally authorize absentee ballots for primaries and preliminary elections, the court confirmed that Article VIII concerns itself only with "elections," and not primaries or nominations. *Opinion of the Justices* (1971).

ARTICLE IX. Free Elections; Equality of Right to Elect and Be Elected
All elections ought to be free; and all the inhabitants of this commonwealth, having such qualifications as they shall establish by their frame of government, have an equal right to elect officers, and to be elected, for public employments.

This Article has never been amended.

The Supreme Judicial Court has held that the primary purpose of Article IX is "to guarantee equality among all . . . [qualified] voters." *Opinion of the Justices* (1975) (quotation omitted). Notwithstanding this constitutional commitment, the Legislature has the authority to "reasonably regulate elections and access to a place on the ballot." *Id.* The court has concluded, for example, that "[t]he preservation of the integrity of various routes to the ballot is a proper state objective" and affirmed the validity of a law barring independent candidates from the ballot if they were members of a political party within twenty-eight days of the last days for filing nomination papers. The court has made clear, however, that the Legislature's authority "must be exercised consistently with the protections of art. 9." *Opinion of the Justices* (1978).

Elaboration upon the meaning and importance of Article IX's free elections guarantee, and the limitations it places on the regulation of elections, has come in cases involving both the right of citizens to elect officers, and the right of individuals to stand for election.

The Right to Elect

The Supreme Judicial Court has held that "[t]he right to vote is a precious personal prerogative to be sedulously guarded." *Swift v. Registrars of Voters of Quincy* (1932). The "rightful exercise of the franchise" is paramount, and election laws must secure that right, not obstruct it. *Id.* Because voting rights are fundamental, "derogations from those rights are subject to strict, not rational basis scrutiny." *McSweeney v. City of Cambridge* (1996). With this principle in mind, the *McSweeney* court suggested that, while a preferential municipal voting scheme designed to provide for the representation of minority groups or for the possibility of greater representation would not necessarily fail to survive strict scrutiny review under Article IX, "perhaps a showing [could] be made that in the actual operation of the scheme some equalities come in, that they are substantial enough to raise constitutional doubts, and that the scheme [could] be more narrowly tailored to represent accurately the wishes of all the voters." *Id.*

Strict scrutiny does not apply in every instance in which voting procedures are challenged; a more relaxed standard applies "in reviewing mechanisms for filling vacancies." *Id.* "Insofar as the issue relates to each voter's right to an equal voice in the electoral process, a scheme for filling vacancies need only meet rational basis review." *Id.* In *McSweeney*, for instance, the plaintiff challenged a means of filling vacancies on a city council that involved recounting the ballots credited to the candidate whose vacancy was being filled and, if no candidate received a majority, the ballots of the candidate lowest in the poll would be transferred accordingly according the voters' next indicated preference, and so on until a candidate received a majority. The court concluded that this means of filling vacancies was rationally related "to the legitimate goal of allowing those who voted for the councilor whose [seat] was vacated to choose the successor." *Id.*

In construing laws aimed at regulating electoral procedures generally, the intent of voters should be honored and the laws construed to "secure the rights of duly qualified voters, ... not to defeat them." Swift. The law challenged in Swift dealt with voting machines and ballot counting; due to the malfunction of one machine, a number of ballots were not canceled as required by law, and thus not counted in the election. The court concluded that the law should be read to contain an implied exception for errors resulting not from voter misconduct or mistakes made by election officials, but rather from mechanical malfunctions beyond human control. The court reached this conclusion after consideration of the paramount importance of free elections and the promotion of the intent of the voters, as long as the voters' actions comported with the relevant laws. By construing the statute in this way, the court avoided "grave doubts as to [the statute's] constitutionality" and demonstrated the importance of the right to vote under Article IX.

The state constitution qualifies the right to vote. In order to exercise the franchise, an individual must be an inhabitant of the Commonwealth. See *In re Opinion of the Justices* (1922). The court has understood "inhabitant" to be synonymous with "citizen." *Id.* Thus, so long as a person is a citizen of the Commonwealth, he or she is eligible to elect public officials therein. Following the ratification and adoption of the Nineteenth Amendment to the U.S. Constitution, which granted suffrage to women, the Massachusetts Constitution could not be read to contain any "limitation of sex upon the right to vote." *Id.* In *Sears v. Secretary of the Commonwealth* (1975), the court noted that the Constitution would not tolerate "[d]evices designed to circumvent the rights of voters on account of race." Other qualifications that must be met in order to exercise the franchise include an age requirement (Amendments III and XCIV) and a limited literacy requirement (Amendment XX).

Significantly, the court has ruled that there is no "state action" requirement under Article IX. See *Batchelder v. Allied Stores International, Inc.* (1983). This means that individuals can maintain a cause of action for abridgement of election rights, as against both the government and private actors. For example, the *Batchelder* court, recognizing the fundamental importance of ballot access in the election process, held that a shopping mall could not prevent a candidate from seeking signatures and distributing materials in support of his nomination to public office. It remains, however, that when a grant of relief would disrupt the election process, relief may be denied. See *Tsongas v. Secretary of the Commonwealth* (1972).

The Right to Stand for Election

The state constitution qualifies the right to seek election: a person seeking office must be an inhabitant of the Commonwealth. The court has stated the inhabitancy requirement as a condition of standing for election. Following the passage of the Nineteenth Amendment, the Supreme Judicial Court assumed that women would thereafter be eligible to hold office on equal grounds as men. As to other constitutional limitations, "All persons possessing the requisite qualifications have a right to invite the votes of their fellows and to be elected to office." *Wood v. Board of Election Commissioners of Cambridge* (1929) (citation omitted).

The right to stand for election is subject to regulation reasonably necessary to achieve legitimate public objectives. While the Legislature may not add or change qualifications explicit in the Massachusetts Constitution, if the constitution does not name qualifications for a certain public office, the Legislature may establish reasonable qualifications, so long as it remains open for any person to secure those qualifications. *In re Opinion of the Justices* (1922). Accordingly, the Legislature may, for example, require that candidates for district attorney be members of the Massachusetts Bar.

As a general matter, the dictates of Article IX apply only to elected officials and not to appointed positions. See *Sheridan v. Gardner* (1964). Further, the right to vote does not include the right to select candidates at primaries or elect delegates to a national party convention. Among the cities and towns of the Commonwealth, different modes of electing public officers are permissible. See *Graham v. Roberts* (1908). Thus, a municipal government may devise an election plan for its city and town officers that is not in accordance with other election plans in the state. It does not matter if the newly devised plan is more limiting than other plans already in effect in other municipalities, as duly qualified voters in each city are still afforded an equal right to elect officers when a plan applies with equal force to every voter in a city.

For further provisions as to voter and public employment qualifications, see Mass. Const. Pt. 2, c. 1, § 2, Art. II (inhabitancy requirements); Amendment III (as amended by Amendment XCIII, XCIV and C) (age and residence requirements); Amendment XX (limited literacy requirement); Amendment XXVIII (as amended by Amendment XXXI) (voting rights of veterans); Amendment XXX (change of residence); and Amendment XXXII.

ARTICLE X. Enjoyment of Life, Liberty, and Property

Each individual of the society has a right to be protected by it in the enjoyment of his life, liberty and property, according to standing laws. He is obliged, consequently, to contribute his share of the expense to this protection; to give his personal service, or an equivalent, when necessary: but no part of the property of any individual can, with justice, be taken from him, or applied to public uses, without his own consent, or that of the representative body of the people. In fine, the people of this Commonwealth are not controllable by any other laws than those to which their constitutional representative body have given their consent. And whenever the public exigencies require that the property of any individual should be appropriated to public uses, he shall receive a reasonable compensation therefor.

The legislature may by special acts for the purpose of laying out, widening or relocating highways or streets, authorize the taking in fee by the commonwealth, or by a county, city or town, of more land and property than are needed for the actual construction of such highway or street: provided, however, that the land and property authorized to be taken are specified in the act and are no more in extent than would be sufficient for suitable building lots on both sides of such highway or street, and after so much of the land or property has been

appropriated for such highway or street as is needed therefor, may authorize the sale of the remainder for value with or without suitable restrictions.

This Article was amended by Amendment XXXIX, ratified in 1911, which added the second paragraph. Related amendments designed to extend the power of the General Court to authorize the use of eminent domain are Amendments XLIII, ratified in 1915; XLVII, ratified in 1917; XLIX, ratified in 1918 (as amended by Amendment XCVII, ratified in 1972); and LI, ratified in 1918.

The language of the first two sentences of Article X seems to suggest that the framers intended that they be read together to mean that, because the society protects each citizen according to the standing laws, each citizen owes a duty to contribute taxes or personal service to the society. In fact, the common law interpretation of the article has isolated the first sentence as a freestanding prohibition against specialized lawmaking for the benefit or detriment of a particular individual or group. In this sense, Article X represents another equal protection provision. In addition, the provision could also be read as placing an affirmative obligation upon government to protect people in the enjoyment of life, liberty, and property according to standing laws. The second sentence, read alone, provides a constitutional basis for the collection of taxes and requiring of military service. Article X has been interpreted by the Massachusetts courts to establish constitutional requirements governing special legislation, due process, taxation and eminent domain, and land use regulation.

Special Legislation

The Supreme Judicial Court has interpreted the first sentence of Article X, or the "standing laws" provision, to prohibit "special legislation." The court has defined special legislation as legislation "addressed to a particular situation, that does not establish a rule of future conduct with any substantial degree of generality, and may provide ad hoc benefits of some kind for an individual or a number of them." *Commissioner of Public Health v. The Bessie M. Burke Memorial Hospital* (1975). A party—under the constitution, only individual persons or groups of persons, as well as private corporations independent of the Commonwealth of Massachusetts, see *Comm'rs of Hampden County v. Town of Agawam* (1998)—bears a heavy burden in arguing that a law amounts to special legislation; a reviewing court will grant all rational presumptions in favor of the constitutionality of a legislative enactment. See *Kienzler v. Dalkon Shield Claimants Trust* (1997). The challenging party must prove, beyond reasonable doubt, that no conceivable grounds exist upon which the enactment could be found rational. The court will uphold laws that benefit single individuals, but do "no specific injury to any other person or entity." *Id.* In addition, the court will uphold an enactment that benefits one person or group at the expense of another so long as the legislation promotes some legitimate public purpose.

Thus, in *Holden v. James* (1814), and *Paddock v. Brookline* (1964), the court struck down laws that allowed a single named individual to maintain a suit that would have been barred by a general statute, for the reason that "they served no discernible purpose and operated only to aggrandize the personal interests of a single party." *Kienzler*. In *Kienzler*, by contrast, the court upheld a statute that specifically enlarged the limitations period in which individuals could sue in connection with injuries caused by use of the Dalkon Shield intrauterine device. The court concluded that the Legislature could have reasoned that the traditional limitations period on lawsuits was unfair to women injured by the Dalkon Shield, which constituted a legitimate justification for the law under Article X.

Due Process

Article X has been a primary source of due process jurisprudence in Massachusetts. We refer here principally to substantive due process and procedural due process. The Supreme Judicial Court has endorsed the distinction between substantive and procedural due process embraced by the U.S. Supreme Court. Substantive due process implicates governmental actions that either "shock the conscience" or interfere with rights considered to be fundamental to the concept of ordered liberty. *Aime v. Commonwealth* (1993). As is the case with a claim arising under Article I, when the challenged governmental action involves a right deemed to be fundamental, the court typically will uphold only those laws "that are narrowly tailored to further a legitimate and compelling governmental interest." *Id.* If the governmental action does not implicate a fundamental right, the law need only bear "a reasonable relation to a permissible legislative objective." *Id.*

As discussed above in respect to Part I, Article I, the Supreme Judicial Court has classified certain rights as "fundamental" for purposes of substantive due process, and expressed a willingness to hold the Massachusetts Constitution more protective in this area than its federal counterpart. For example, the court has interpreted the right to choose to obtain an abortion more broadly under the state constitution than the right has been framed under the federal constitution. See *Moe v. Secretary of Administration & Finance* (1981). Other fundamental rights include the right to freedom from bodily restraint, see *Kenniston v. Dep't. of Youth Services* (2009), as well as the right of an individual to marry, establish a home, and bring up children, see *Tarin v. Comm'r of Div. of Medical Assistance* (1997), and associated parental interests, see *Adoption of Olivia* (2002).

Procedural due process refers to the constitutional requirement that governmental action be implemented in a fair manner. In matters of procedural due process, the Supreme Judicial Court has applied the same standards under the state constitution as the U.S. Supreme Court has applied under the federal constitution. See *Liability Investigative Fund Effort, Inc. v. Massachusetts Medical Prof. Ins. Assoc.* (1994).

In reviewing a procedural due process challenge, courts undertake a two-part inquiry. See *Lotto v. Commonwealth* (1976). First, the court will seek to define the interest involved; procedural due process applies only to the deprivation of an interest in liberty or property. "Liberty" has been understood to include such interests as the freedom to engage in lawful private occupations, such as employment or business activity. A "property" interest must be one to which the plaintiff had an entitlement. For example, attachment of a lien to an individual's residence affects a constitutionally protected property interest. See *Leger v. Comm'r of Revenue* (1995). An individual may have a property interest in a benefit, provided that the relevant law "establishes certain eligibility criteria which, if met, entitle [the] individual to the benefit." *Doyle v. Dep't of Industrial Accidents* (2000). Such claim of entitlement will be negated, however, if the relevant law provides that a governmental entity has discretion to determine whether an individual should receive the benefit.

Second, the court must balance the individual interest at stake against the nature of the governmental interest and the risk of erroneous deprivation of liberty or property under the procedures that the state seeks to use, to determine whether due process has been satisfied. See *Gray v. Comm'r of Revenue* (1996). As the Supreme Judicial Court has put it, "How much and what process is due is a function of the gravity of the consequences that government decision making may visit on those subject to it." *In re Hill* (1996). The minimum due process required will vary with the context. See *Spence v. Gormley* (1982). In respect to a deprivation of property, for example, due process generally will require than an individual receive notice and an opportunity to be heard prior to the deprivation. Postdeprivation procedures will typically satisfy due process when the deprivation concerns the assessment and collection of taxes.

In addition to substantive and procedural due process, Article X has been a source of authority in cases involving retrospective legislation. Retroactive application of a statute raises constitutional issues if the law deprives an individual of a vested right. See *Connolly's Case* (1994). If an individual has no vested right, he or she has no claim under the state constitution. Vested rights include such interests as contractual property rights, see *Frank Kumin Co. v. Marean* (1933), and rights in a final judgment, see *Casieri's Case* (1934). In *St. Germaine v. Pendergast* (1993), for example, the court concluded that a statute retroactively exposing the defendant to liability for personal injuries suffered in connection with certain construction work was unconstitutional. The court reasoned that, because the statute would subject the defendant's prior conduct to a standard that differed from the law at the time in question, it would have a substantial effect on his rights.

Due process also operates to ensure that laws do not suffer from insufficient clarity. Due process requires that laws be clear so as to give a person of ordinary intelligence a reasonable opportunity to know what the law proscribes, that he or she might act accordingly. See *Commonwealth v. Butler* (1996). In addition, the law must be clear enough that a putative enforcer "would be able to apply it without discrimination." *Id.* In *Butler,* for instance, the court concluded the words "no contact," as used in a restraining order, were not unconstitutionally vague; by anonymously sending the complainant flowers, the defendant had acted indirectly to achieve communication with her that amounted to prohibited contact.

In addition to Article X, the courts have found due process protections in Pt. I, Article I; Pt. I, Article XII; and Pt. II, c. 1, §1, Article IV. See *In re McKnight* (1990).

Taxation

Article X has been held to be specifically applicable in the taxation context. The Supreme Judicial Court has recognized the importance of taxation "in order that governmental functions may be discharged." *Napir v. City of Springfield* (1939). The classification of property for taxation purposes does not violate the constitution so long as legislative distinctions have a fair and rational relationship to the object the Legislature seeks to accomplish. *Seiler Corp. v. Comm'r of Revenue* (1981). Further, courts will presume that legislation related to taxation is based on "adequate facts justifying its adoption in the public interest." *Thompson v. Chelsea* (1970).

Article X imposes particular restrictions on taxation legislation. The court has interpreted the words "his share" in the second sentence of Article X as a prohibition against disparate taxation; the provision prohibits "the imposition upon one taxpayer of a burden relatively greater or relatively less than that imposed upon other taxpayers." *Opinion of the Justices* (1955). Applying this principle, the court has concluded that a proposed act that would allow corporations to defer tax payments for as long as forty-five years, while requiring individual taxpayers to pay taxes annually, would produce disproportion and be unconstitutional. Article X also obligates assessors to assess real property at full and fair cash value. See *Coomey v. Bd. of Assessors of Sandwich* (1975). To the extent assessors fail to so value property, the constitution nonetheless requires that each taxpayer bear only his proportionate share of the tax burden. Article X provides that any taxpayer whose property was disproportionately assessed is entitled to an adequate remedy for any injury suffered as a result. *Axelrod v. Bd. of Assessors of Boxborough* (1984).

Amendment XLIV, ratified in 1915, effectively amended Article X to grant the Legislature the authority to tax income derived from different classes of property at different rates, providing that taxation within a class is at a uniform rate. In addition, the amendment allows the Legislature to grant reasonable exemptions and abatements of tax burdens. The Legislature can grant exemptions reasonably related to the public interest. See *City of Springfield v. Bd. of Assessors of Granville* (1979). The Legislature can exempt real property in whole or in part, so long as exemptions do not create a disparate impact within a class. See *Opinion of the Justices* (1957). For example, an urban redevelopment corporation formed in order to revitalize a "blighted open area" may constitutionally be given a tax advantage not available to an ordinary corporation. *Opinion of the Justices* (1956). In contrast, a development commission planning to redevelop an open area mainly for private resale could not be granted an exemption although the incidental effects of the plan would provide a public benefit.

Eminent Domain and Land Use Regulation

Article X establishes that, at a minimum, permanent physical occupations that amount to a transfer of a traditional estate in land are takings of property for which the Commonwealth is obligated to pay just compensation. See *Goulding v. Cook* (1996). Under Article X, the Commonwealth can take property only for a public purpose, which the court has defined as "one the enjoyment and advantage of which are open to the public on equal terms." *Machado v. Bd. of Public Works of Arlington* (1947) (quotation omitted). The laying out of sewers, for example, is a public purpose that would justify the taking of private property by eminent domain. Article X nonetheless forbids the seizure of private property for an ostensibly public use and its later diversion to a private use. See *Sellors v. Town of Concord* (1952) (quotation omitted). Further, if the plaintiff has no property right in the property seized, no taking has occurred. See *German v. Commonwealth* (1991).

Like its federal counterparts in the Fifth and Fourteenth Amendments to the U.S. Constitution, Article X requires the Commonwealth to provide compensation for any property seized through eminent domain; accordingly, the Legislature must provide for the means by which a property owner will be compensated, such that he or she will suffer neither risk nor unreasonable delay. See *Bromfield v. Treasurer and Receiver-General* (1983). The protections of Article X in this regard are no greater than those afforded under the federal constitution. As a general matter, the Legislature has the constitutional authority to delegate the power of eminent domain to cities and towns. See *Burnham v. Mayor and Aldermen of Beverly* (1941).

Governmental regulation of property does not necessarily effect a taking for which just compensation must be provided. Property may be subject to reasonable restraints and regulations in the public interest. See *Lovequist v. Conservation Comm'n of Town of Dennis* (1979). Forbidden governmental action under the state constitution is only that which strips private property of all practical value. Restrictions need only be reasonably related to the implementation of a policy "expected to produce a widespread public benefit and applicable to all similarly situated property." See *Moskow v. Comm'r of Dep't of Environ. Management* (1981). Controlling and restricting the filling of wetlands, for example, falls within the scope of the Commonwealth's police power.

For purposes of determining whether governmental regulation effects a taking, the court will not view a single parcel in discrete segments and determine whether rights in a particular segment have been abridged. See *Daddario v. Cape Cod Comm'n* (1997). The court instead will focus on the "character of the action and the nature of the interference with the rights in the property as a whole." *Id.* Absent a permanent, physical occupation of the property, the analysis is fact dependent, and restrictions on a landowner's use of property will not necessarily result in a regulatory taking if the property as a whole retains substantial value.

The amendments to Article X all define certain governmental functions to have public purposes, thereby allowing governmental regulation or takings of private property to serve one of several specified purposes. Amendment XXXIX (1911) allows the General Court to take land by eminent domain for the purpose of widening or relocating streets. Amendment XLIII (1915) allows the taking of land for the purpose of relieving congestion and providing homes for citizens. Amendment XLVII (1917) allows the taking of property during wartime or public emergency for the purpose of providing food and shelter at reasonable rates. Amendment XLIX (1918) allows for takings to conserve and develop natural resources. Amendment XCVII (1972) replaces Amendment XLIX and expands it to include environmental protection as a proper public purpose. Amendment L (1918) brings public advertising into the realm of activities state government may properly regulate. Finally, Amendment LI (1918) allows the taking of historical or antiquarian property for the purpose of preserving such property. These purposes all constitute the "public exigencies" of the original article for which property may be taken upon payment of reasonable compensation.

ARTICLE XI. Right to a Remedy and Access to the Courts; Speedy Trial
Every subject of the commonwealth ought to find a certain remedy, by having recourse to the laws, for all injuries or wrongs which he may receive in his person, property, or character. He ought to obtain right and justice freely, and without being obliged to purchase it; completely, and without any denial; promptly, and without delay; conformably to the laws.

Article XI has not been amended.

Article XI has been interpreted by the Massachusetts courts as providing, in the context of civil cases, rights to a remedy and access to the courts; and, in criminal cases, the right to a speedy trial.

Right to a Remedy

Article XI guarantees individuals "a certain remedy, by having recourse to the laws, for all injuries or wrongs which [one] may receive." The Supreme Judicial Court has construed this language as expressing a concern for the preservation of procedural and not substantive rights. See *Pinnick v. Cleary* (1971). Thus the court has concluded, for example, that Article XI does not create a fundamental right to recover unlimited damages. See *Hallett v. Town of Windham* (1986). And the court has held that Article XI does not grant to any person "a vested interest in any rule of law" that would entitle him "to insist that it shall remain unchanged for his benefit." *Decker v. Black and Decker Manuf. Co.* (1983) (quotation omitted). The court has reasoned that to construe Article XI as granting such an interest would be to prevent the common law from being altered by the Legislature or the courts in future cases, thereby undermining checks and balances between and among the branches of government and "the flexibility required for the healthy growth of the law." *Id.* (quotation omitted).

The Legislature accordingly may enact a statute that effectively abolishes a common law cause of action without providing a substitute remedy so long as the statute "is rationally related to a permissible legislative objective." *Klein v. Catalano* (1982). In *Soares v. Gotham Ink of New England* (1992), for example, the plaintiff brought an Article XI challenge to a statutory enactment abolishing the common law rights of spouses and children of an injured employee unless the employee preserved his or her common law rights. The plaintiff argued that Article XI prohibits the Legislature from eliminating common law rights without providing a substitute remedy. The Massachusetts Appeals Court rejected this argument, concluding that the plaintiffs had no fundamental right to sue in tort and the Legislature could reasonably determine that, in the interest of the general public welfare, certain wrongs should not be compensable or should be compensable only on a limited basis. "Rules of the common law," the court observed, "are not above all change except by constitutional amendment." *Id.* (quotation omitted).

Access to the Courts

Article XI's promise of justice freely obtained has been interpreted by the Supreme Judicial Court as a promise of equal justice, such that "all litigants similarly situated may appeal to the courts both for relief and for defense under like conditions and with like protection and without discrimination." *Old Colony R.R. v. Assessors of Boston* (1941) (quotations omitted). Article XI forbids the Legislature from raising obstacles to the ability of some individuals to pursue their rights in court, but not others similarly situated. See *Murphy v. Commissioner of Dep't of Industrial Accidents* (1993). And it prohibits a court from refusing litigants access to a judicial forum to resolve justiciable disputes. See *Graizzaro v. Graizzaro* (1994). The court has held that the right of equal access under Article XI is coextensive with the equal protection clause of the Fourteenth Amendment to the U.S. Constitution. See *Paro v. Longwood Hospital* (1977).

In *Paro v. Longwood Hospital*, for example, the plaintiffs challenged the requirements of a law establishing a tribunal to screen medical malpractice cases. The plaintiffs argued that the requirement of a $2,000 bond as a condition for a continuance violated their rights under Article XI. The court concluded that, because the Legislature rationally could have determined that the imposition of screening procedures and bond requirements would discourage frivolous medical malpractice claims, the law satisfied federal equal protection requirements. Accordingly, the malpractice law did not violate Article XI. In *Murphy v. Commissioner of Dep't of Industrial Accidents*, by contrast, the court held unconstitutional under Article XI a law providing that an employee who seeks to challenge an administrative judge's denial of worker's compensation benefits must pay a fee if the case involved a medical issue and the employee desired to proceed with the assistance of counsel. The court concluded that, under equal protection principles, there existed no rational basis to impose a premium upon those litigants who chose to proceed with counsel. The law having failed to survive rational basis scrutiny, the court ruled that it also violated Article XI.

Relatedly, Article XI has also been viewed by the Massachusetts courts, along with Part I, Articles XXIX and XXX, as a source of the concept of "inherent judicial powers"—those powers "whose exercise is essential to the function of the judicial department, to the maintenance of its authority, [and] to its capacity to decide cases." *First Justice of the Bristol Div. of the Juvenile Court Dept. v. Clerk-Magistrate of the Bristol Div. of the Juvenile Court Dept.* (2003) (quotation omitted). We discuss inherent judicial powers more thoroughly in respect to Articles XXIX and XXX.

Speedy Trial

The Supreme Judicial Court has concluded that, in the criminal context, Article XI's second sentence provides a speedy trial guarantee. That guarantee serves to protect an accused from prolonged preliminary incarceration; to relieve an accused of the anxiety and public suspicion that may attend an untried accusation; and to ensure the accused that the means by which innocence might be proved will not be minimized due to unavailability of witnesses or faded memories. See *Commonwealth v. Hanley* (1958). The court has also emphasized the public interest in having criminal cases tried expeditiously, noting that the trial court "is as much responsible for protecting" that interest as he or she is "for protecting the right of the individual defendant to a speedy trial." *Commonwealth v. Dabrieo* (1976).

The court has indicated that, in cases involving a claim that a defendant was denied the right to a speedy trial under Article XI, it will apply the criteria developed by the U.S. Supreme Court to analyze federal speedy trial claims. See *Commonwealth v. Green* (1968) (stating that Article XI and the Sixth Amendment to the U.S. Constitution are "analogous mandates"). The four factors the court weighs in evaluating a speedy trial claim are: (1) the length of the delay; (2) the reasons for the delay; (3) the extent, if any, to which the defendant asserted the right to a speedy trial; and (4) the prejudice, if any, resulting from the delay. See *Commonwealth v. Beckett* (1977). Such claims under Article XI apply only to trials; the guarantee does not apply to the appellate process. See *Commonwealth v. Latimore* (1996).

Speedy trial determinations under Article XI are fact-specific. See *Commonwealth v. Lutoff* (1982). In evaluating the reason for the delay, court congestion will not be considered the responsibility of the defendant, and must be weighed against the Commonwealth, but not so heavily as a deliberate effort by the prosecution to create delay. Similarly, a delay caused by the Commonwealth's negligence will be weighed less heavily than "one calculated to frustrate the defense of an accused." *Commonwealth v. Look* (1980). Further, if the record reveals a defendant's indifference to the date of trial, the defendant will not be able to support a claim that Article XI was violated. In *Commonwealth v. Beckett*, the court concluded that a delay of fifty-five months was not unconstitutional when the defendant failed to assert the right to a speedy trial for more than four years after indictment, and when she could not demonstrate prejudice.

The defendant has the burden of demonstrating prejudice, by showing, for example, that due to the delay witnesses had become unavailable, or that memories had suffered. When a defendant has diligently pressed the right to a speedy trial and the delay is substantial, prejudice will be presumed and the burden shifted to the Commonwealth to demonstrate that no prejudice resulted. See *Lutoff*. In *Commonwealth v. Green*, for instance, the court presumed prejudice in a delay of some fifteen years. See *Green, supra.*

The current standard for determining when and how to approach speedy trial issues is found in Massachusetts Rule of Criminal Procedure 36. Most modern speedy trial cases have been analyzed under the rule and not Article XI per se. See, e.g., *Commonwealth v. Amidon* (1998) (discussing speedy trial issues raised under Rule 36).

ARTICLE XII. Prosecutions, Criminal Procedure, and Jury Trials

No subject shall be held to answer to any crimes or offence, until the same is fully and plainly, substantially and formally, described to him; or be compelled to accuse, or furnish evidence against himself. And every subject shall have a right to produce all proofs, that may be favorable to him; to meet the witnesses against him face to face, and to be fully heard in his defence by himself, or his counsel, at his election. And no subject shall be arrested, imprisoned, despoiled, or deprived of his property, immunities, or privileges, put out of the protection of the law, exiled, or deprived of his life, liberty, or estate, but by the judgment of his peers, or the law of the land. And the legislature shall not make any law,

that shall subject any person to a capital or infamous punishment, excepting for the government of the army and navy, without trial by jury.

Part of the original Massachusetts Constitution in 1780, this Article has not been amended. This Article is frequently cited as a source of constitutional due process protection. See *Commonwealth v. Acen* (1986). As the Supreme Judicial Court has observed, Article XII protects individuals

> against being deprived of property, immunities or privileges, life, liberty or estate except by judgment of peers or the law of the land. This is one of the great landmarks of human freedom. It cannot be cut down or invaded by an act of legislation. It is an additional shield to protect rights declared in article 10.

Attorney General v. Brissenden (1930). In addition to being a source of due process protection, this Article provides the basis for many of the key constitutional protections in connection with criminal prosecutions. In applying the dictates of this Article to issues arising in the context of criminal prosecutions, the Massachusetts courts have, in certain circumstances, been inclined to interpret its protection of individual liberties more broadly than the comparable provisions of the U.S. Constitution.

The breadth of substantive and procedural due process protections is discussed above, in connection with Article X. Here we discuss some of Article XII's criminal procedure protections, including the right to a description of the offense charged, the right against self-incrimination, the right to counsel, the right of confrontation, the right to a jury trial, the right to exculpatory evidence, and certain unenumerated rights that are considered to be part of "the law of the land" under the constitution. Note that this chapter touches upon only some of the criminal procedure protections that Massachusetts jurists and commentators have identified as within Article XII's purview.

The Right to a Description of the Offense Charged

Article XII provides criminal defendants the right to a sufficient description of the crime or offense with which they are charged. This provision is analogous to the Sixth Amendment's guarantee that all criminal defendants "be informed of the nature and cause of the accusation." It has been interpreted by the Supreme Judicial Court to afford a defendant "only such particularity of allegation as may be of service to a person charged with a crime in enabling him to understand the charge and prepare his defense." *Commonwealth v. Farmer* (1914).

Importantly, Article XII does not require that the Commonwealth lay out every element of the crime charged, so long as the complaint or indictment is of "sufficient clarity to show a violation of law and to permit the defendant to know the nature of the accusation against him." *Commonwealth v. Green* (1987). With the adoption of the Massachusetts Rules of Criminal Procedure, the right to a description of the offense charged has been codified as a requirement that a complaint or indictment contain a "plain, concise description of the act which constitutes the crime or an appropriate legal term descriptive thereof." Mass. R. Crim. P. 4(a).

The Right Against Self-Incrimination

Article XII secures the fundamental right of an individual to be free from coerced self-incrimination. Analogous to the Fifth Amendment to the U.S. Constitution, which provides that no person shall "be compelled in any criminal case to be a witness against himself," this Article forms the basis of a criminal defendant's right to remain silent and to insist that no presumption be drawn against him or her as a result of a decision to remain silent. See *Commonwealth v. Paradiso* (1975); *Commonwealth v. Harlow* (1872). The Article also applies to civil proceedings; a witness may, pursuant to Article XII, "refuse to testify unless it is perfectly clear that his testimony cannot incriminate him." *In the Matter of the Enforcement of a Subpoena* (2001). The Supreme Judicial Court confirmed in 1938 that the right against self-incrimination is of constitutional dimension in an advisory opinion. See *Opinion of the Justices* (1938).

The court has held that the right against self-incrimination must be liberally construed in favor of the person claiming it. See *Commonwealth v. Koonce* (1994). Massachusetts courts have often applied federal standards to determine whether an Article XII claim will be upheld. See *Commonwealth v. Martin* (1996) (noting that Massachusetts standards under Article XII are "consistent with Federal standards"). In certain circumstances, however, the court has interpreted Article XII to afford individuals greater protection than the Fifth Amendment. In *Commonwealth v. Lydon* (1992), for example, the court held that Article XII precludes admission of evidence that a defendant on trial for first degree murder refused to have his hands swabbed. The court reasoned that, if, as the Commonwealth argued, the defendant's refusal shows consciousness of guilt, "such refusal rises to the level of a self-accusation." *Id.* At bottom, Article XII bars the government from compelling a criminal defendant to choose between potentially inculpatory alternatives: testifying or having his refusal introduced against him at trial. See *Commonwealth v. Conkey* (1999).

One important way in which the court has interpreted Article XII differently from the Fifth Amendment concerns the degree of immunity that must be provided a witness to avoid his Article XII rights. The federal standard, first spelled out in *Kastigar v. United States* (1972), demands only that the government provide "use and derivative-use immunity"; that is, a proscription of the use in a criminal case of compelled testimony and any evidence directly or indirectly derived from that compelled testimony. The Supreme Judicial Court, by contrast, has held that the Massachusetts Constitution requires no less than a grant of absolute immunity from prosecution for offenses to which the compelled testimony relates. See *Attorney General v. Colleton* (1982). Relying on its 1872 decision in *Emery's Case* (1871), the *Colleton* court confirmed that the language "or furnish evidence against himself" must be presumed to add something to the preceding "compelled to accuse" language.

In general, however, the Massachusetts courts have recognized the same limits on the reach of a defendant's right against self-incrimination as their federal counterparts. In *Commonwealth v. Brennan* (1982), the Supreme Judicial Court held that breathalyzer and field sobriety tests administered to determine whether a driver was under the influence of alcohol did not violate Article XII (or the Fifth and Fourteenth Amendments). The defendant had been charged with driving under the influence and was given a choice of submitting to the tests or having his license automatically suspended for ninety days. He asserted that the words "furnish evidence" encompassed real or physical evidence as well as testimonial or purely communicative evidence, requiring a more expansive interpretation than that given the Fifth Amendment, which contains only the "compelled to accuse" language. The court reasoned that this sort of liberal construction of Article XII would also apply to fingerprints, photographs, line-ups, blood samples, voice, and handwriting exemplars, and even the defendant's appearance at trial for identification purposes, none of which the framers of Article XII had intended to prohibit. The court accordingly held that Article XII protection extends only to tests of a testimonial or communicative nature.

A final note in respect to the right against self-incrimination: as is true under the Fifth Amendment, Massachusetts courts have held that criminal suspects must be informed of their rights against self-incrimination and to counsel, and that any waiver must be knowing, intelligent, and voluntary. See *Commonwealth v. Vao Sok* (2002). As it relates to self-incrimination, though, Article XII, has been held to have a broader reach than the Fifth Amendment in at least one important respect: the Supreme Judicial Court has held that Article XII requires police officers to inform a suspect that an attorney seeks to provide him or her with legal advice. See *Commonwealth v. Mavredakis* (2000). "When an attorney identifies himself or herself to the police as counsel acting on a suspect's behalf, the police have a duty to stop questioning and to inform the suspect of the attorney's request immediately." *Id.* Further, the Commonwealth bears the burden of proving that a suspect declined an offer of legal advice. Applying this standard in *Mavredakis*, the court held unconstitutional a municipal police department's policy forbidding officers from informing suspects under interrogation that their attorneys had sought to contact them.

The Right to Counsel

Article XII provides individuals with the right to counsel in all criminal proceedings. Though there is no language in Article XII analogous to the language of the Sixth Amendment to the U.S. Constitution that "the accused shall . . . have the Assistance of Counsel for his defence," in 1958, the Supreme Judicial Court, in an exercise of its rulemaking authority, adopted a rule requiring the appointment of counsel in all noncapital felony cases. See Sup. Jud. Ct. Rule 10

(1958). The court thus anticipated the U.S. Supreme Court's seminal decision in *Gideon v. Wainwright* (1963). In 1964, the Supreme Judicial Court expanded the right to counsel to indigent defendants charged with crimes for which imprisonment might be imposed. The court has stated that "the right to counsel under art. 12 provides a defendant with at least the same safeguards as the Sixth Amendment." *Lavallee v. Justices in the Hampden Superior Court* (2004).

The Supreme Judicial Court has held that the right to counsel attaches "at or after the initiation of adversary judicial criminal proceedings—whether by way of formal charge, preliminary hearing, indictment, information, or arraignment." *Commonwealth v. Simmonds* (1982). On this point the Supreme Judicial Court is in agreement with the U.S. Supreme Court. The *Simmonds* court concluded that Article XII does not provide a right to counsel at a preindictment identification. In that case, a defendant challenged the denial of counsel in connection with his participation in a police line-up for purposes of identification, before his indictment and before prosecutors formally charged him with an offense. The court has also held that the issuance of a complaint and arrest warrant are not necessarily coincident with the commencement of adversary proceedings sufficient to trigger the protections of Article XII. See *Commonwealth v. Jones* (1988). Once it attaches, the right to counsel extends to every critical stage of the criminal process. *Lavalee.*

This Article also guarantees a criminal defendant the effective assistance of counsel, which includes assistance in making decisions about specific defenses and trial strategies. In respect to this right, the Supreme Judicial Court has declined to adhere strictly to the U.S. Supreme Court's interpretations of the Sixth Amendment. Though there are many bases upon which a defendant could challenge the effectiveness of counsel, in respect to conflict of interest claims the defendant's burden under Article XII is lighter than that which he or she would be expected to carry under the federal constitution. "A defendant is entitled to the untrammeled and unimpaired assistance of counsel free of any conflict of interest and unrestrained by commitments to others." *Commonwealth v. Davis* (1978). Because effective counsel is fundamental, a defendant need not prove that a genuine conflict of interest resulted in an adverse effect on counsel's performance, or even that prejudice resulted. See *Commonwealth v. Hurley* (1984). Rather, proof of a conflict of interest alone is sufficient to establish a denial of the effective assistance of counsel to which defendants are constitutionally entitled. See *Commonwealth v. Hodge* (1982). In *Commonwealth v. Hodge,* for instance, the court agreed that a conflict of interest existed when the defendant's counsel's law partner concurrently represented a prosecution witness in an unrelated civil matter; in such circumstances, the defendant was denied his right to conflict-free counsel.

The Right to Confront Witnesses

Article XII also secures to a criminal defendant the right to "meet the witnesses against him face to face." As the Supreme Judicial Court observed in

Commonwealth v. Bergstrom (1982), "constitutional language more definitively guaranteeing the right to a direct confrontation between witness and accused is difficult to imagine." The purpose of Article XII "was to put beyond the possibility of alteration except by the people themselves the principle already established as a part of the common law that the witness should confront the accused face to face." *Commonwealth v. Richards* (1836). Face to face confrontation allows a jury to observe the demeanor of a testifying witness, an aid to assessing his or her credibility. See *Commonwealth v. Johnson* (1994). In determining whether this standard has been satisfied, the court has turned to federal case law interpreting the confrontation clause of the Sixth Amendment to the U.S. Constitution. See, e.g., *Bergstrom* (relying upon federal cases in interpreting Article XII).

The right to confront witnesses under Article XII encompasses two primary protections: that a probative statement by a witness at trial be made under oath or its functional equivalent; and that witnesses be subject to cross-examination. See *Opinion of the Justices* (1989). In addition, Article XII has been held to provide defendants a right "to be present personally throughout [the] trial." *Bergstrom*. The confrontation right is subject to limited exceptions. For example, hearsay will be constitutionally admissible if the witness is shown to be unavailable and the statement satisfies a hearsay exception that is premised upon a particularized guarantee of trustworthiness. Further, the right must yield in certain circumstances, such as prison disciplinary proceedings involving an informant whose safety could be jeopardized by face-to-face confrontation. See *Murphy v. Superintendent* (1986). Notably, such exceptions are not crime-specific: Article XII, the court has stated, "does not discriminate against classes of defendants," or "distinguish among categories of crimes." *Bergstrom*.

Applying the dictates of Article XII, the court in *Bergstrom* struck down a complex statutory scheme to provide for the testimony of minors in sexual abuse and other sensitive cases by electronic means, outside the physical presence of the defendant and the jury. In that case, the Commonwealth charged a father with rape and indecent assault and battery on his two minor daughters; they testified against him by use of closed-circuit television. The court concluded that this arrangement denied the defendant his right to a confrontation with the witnesses against him. Article XII simply does not permit the introduction of available witness's testimony outside of the defendant's presence. "For constitutional purposes, no principled distinction can be drawn between a child witness and any other class whom the Legislature might in the future deem in need of special treatment." *Id.*

Nonetheless, special procedures may be taken to decrease stress and trauma a trial witness may suffer by testifying, but the trial judge must take care to make a finding of compelling need for protection of witness before such procedures are used. The age of a witness alone, however, does not qualify as a compelling need. Accordingly, the court in *Commonwealth v. Johnson* reversed a rape conviction on the ground that a special seating arrangement at trial, whereby the child-victims sat near the court reporter's table, facing the jury box with the questioning attorney between the child witness and the jury, violated defendant's right to confront witnesses "face to face."

The Right to a Trial by Jury

This Article also provides a right to trial by jury. The substance of the right to trial by jury is the protection from arbitrary judgment secured through a fact-finding process conducted by a fairly numerous and impartial body of representatives of the community. See *Commonwealth v. Bellio* (1947). In the interest of preserving that substantive protection, the Supreme Judicial Court has understood the right to embrace a "living principle capable of reasonable adaptation to a constantly changing society." *Id.* Thus the court has long adhered to the view that the framers did not intend to preserve in Article XII the minor details and unessential formalities of the trial by jury as it existed at the time of the American Revolution. See *Bothwell v. Boston Elev. Ry.* (1913). For instance, though prior to the Revolution a jury was typically composed of twelve men, the Article does not expressly state the number of persons to serve on the jury, and a jury of fewer than twelve in cases involving certain lesser crimes has been held to be constitutional. See *Opinion of the Justices* (1971). The framers likely contemplated a jury composed of twelve men. See *Commonwealth v. Gallo* (1961). The Legislature made women eligible for jury duty by statute in 1949. See Mass. G.L. c. 234, § 1.

The right to a trial has been the subject of a variety of constitutional challenges. In *Commonwealth v. Soares* (1979), for example, the defendants contested the composition of the jury that heard their case; they alleged that the prosecutors used peremptory challenges to exclude persons from the jury on the basis of race. The defendants were African-American, while the victims were white. Prosecutors peremptorily challenged twelve of thirteen eligible black jurors. The defendants argued that such exclusion of black jurors effectively deprived them of their right to be tried by an impartial jury under the Massachusetts Constitution. The court noted that the constitutional mandate that a jury be drawn fairly from a representative cross-section of the community is "critical." Though the court concluded that Article XII does not require absolute proportionality, it could not condone the exercise of peremptory challenges so as to exclude prospective jurors "solely by virtue of their membership in, or affiliation with, particular, defined groupings in the community." *Id.*

The *Soares* court held that the discrete groups recognized under Article XII include those identified by sex, race, color, creed, or national origin. The court also established a framework for effectuating its holding: the analysis begins with the presumption that peremptory challenges are properly exercised; either party can seek to rebut that presumption by showing a pattern or exclusion and that there is a likelihood that individuals were excluded by reason of their group membership. In *Soares,* the court found both a pattern and the requisite connection, at which point the issue became whether to draw the inference that the prosecution had used peremptory challenges to exclude individuals on the basis of their group affiliation. If the trial court so concluded, the prosecution would have an opportunity to demonstrate that its exercise of peremptory challenges did not hinge on group affiliation.

At the time the court decided *Soares,* its interpretation of the Massachusetts Constitution differed from the U.S. Supreme Court's interpretation of the federal constitution in respect to the scope of the right to a fair jury trial vis-à-vis the use of peremptory challenges. The U.S. Supreme Court has since held that the protections under the federal constitution are similar to those under the Massachusetts Constitution and other state constitutions. See, e.g., *Batson v. Kentucky* (1986) (prohibiting use of prosecutorial use of peremptory challenges based upon race).

An individual's right to a trial by jury can be burdened indirectly by legislation as much by the decisions of prosecutors. In *Commonwealth v. Colon-Cruz* (1984), the defendants challenged the constitutionality of a Massachusetts death penalty statute under Article XII. Under the statutory scheme at issue, if a defendant were to plead guilty to murder in the first degree, he could not be sentenced to death. The court concluded that the scheme effectively chilled a defendant's rights under Article XII to free of self-incrimination, and to have a trial by jury of the charges brought against him.

Individuals have also sought to raise Article XII as a bar to the statutory qualifications of jurors in the Commonwealth. In *Commonwealth v. Acen,* the defendants argued that Article XII guarantees them a trial by jury *de medietate linguae,* and that statutory requirements that jurors speak English and be U.S. citizens are unconstitutional. A trial by jury *de medietate linguae* means literally "of the half tongue." *Id.* The practice in England in the Middle Ages was to allow a *de medietate linguae* jury, which would be composed of six of an alien's own countrymen and six English citizens. On a historical analysis of old English law, the Supreme Judicial Court rejected the defendants' argument: though the origins of Article XII's protections may be traced to the Magna Charta, the court concluded that, "[w]hatever else may be said of a jury de medietate linguae, its relative obscurity alone demonstrates it is not among th[e] great fundamental principles" that the Magna Charta was designed to secure. *Id.* The *Acen* defendants also argued that the statutory requirements for jurors of citizenship and command of English were unconstitutional because non-English speakers and noncitizens formed discrete groups within the community who could not be excluded form the jury under *Soares.* The court rejected this argument as well, holding that those groups were not protected classes under the Massachusetts Constitution.

The Right to Exculpatory Evidence

Due process under Article XII includes a defendant's right to have the Commonwealth disclose potentially exculpatory evidence. The obligation upon prosecutors to disclose such evidence derives from a constitutional concern for the fair administration of justice. Under the Fifth and Fourteenth Amendments to the U.S. Constitution, the government must disclose to a criminal defendant favorable evidence in its possession that could aid in his or her defense. See *Brady v. Maryland* (1963). To prevail on a motion for a new trial when the government did not disclose potentially exculpatory evidence, the federal constitutional standard requires that the defendant show that, had the evidence been disclosed by the prosecution in response to either a specific or a general request for evidence, the result at trial would have been different. See *United States v. Bagley* (1985).

The Supreme Judicial Court, by contrast, has held that, under the Massachusetts Constitution, when a prosecutor's failure to disclose exculpatory evidence in his or her possession following a defendant's specific request for such evidence, "a standard of prejudice more favorable to the defendant is justified in order to motivate prosecutors to be alert to defendants' rights to disclosure." *Commonwealth v. Tucceri* (1992). Further, rather than press a defendant to demonstrate beyond a reasonable doubt that the result at trial would have been different, as required under federal law, in Massachusetts a defendant need only demonstrate that, on a "full and reasonable assessment of the trial record, the absent evidence would have played an important role in the jury's deliberations and conclusions." *Id.*

Applying this analysis to the circumstances presented in *Commonwealth v. Tucceri*, the court concluded that the photographic evidence prosecutors failed to produce required the ordering of a new trial. In *Tucceri*, the court reasoned that the defendant's motion for exculpatory evidence should have been understood by prosecutors to include a request for the production of photographs integral to the identification of the victim's assailant. Because the photographs could have cast doubt on the identification of the defendant as the offender, it could have played an important role in the jury's consideration of the charges against him, and its absence warranted a new trial for the defendant.

The "Law of the Land" and Massachusetts Criminal Procedure

The Massachusetts Constitution does not expressly provide for some of the criminal procedure protections featured in the federal constitution or other state constitutions. For example, there is no Massachusetts constitutional analog to the guarantee of the Fifth Amendment (and many other state constitutions) that no one shall be "subject for the same offense to be twice put in jeopardy of life and limb." Nonetheless, the Supreme Judicial Court has long held the view that Article XII's guarantee that "no subject shall be arrested, imprisoned, . . . or deprived of his life, liberty, or estate, but by the . . . law of the land" to embrace many due process and criminal procedure protections. In an 1857 case, Chief Justice Lemuel Shaw reasoned that "law of the land" cannot refer to such laws as the Legislature might pass and later alter; rather, the framers must have intended the phrase to refer to "the ancient established law and course of proceedings, by an adherence to which our ancestors in England, before the settlement of this country, and the emigrants themselves and their descendants, had found safety for their personal rights." *Jones v. Robbins* (1857). Among the protections included within the "law of the land" are protection against double jeopardy, the requirement of indictment by a grand jury for certain crimes, protection for incompetent individuals, and, not least, a presumption of innocence in criminal proceedings.

In respect to double jeopardy, the court observed in 1832 that, as a matter of common law, individuals ought not to be twice placed in jeopardy for the same offense. See *Commonwealth v. Roby* (1832). In *Commonwealth v. Forte* (1996), the court acknowledged that this protection has a constitutional dimension, noting that "[c]ertain double jeopardy concepts are no doubt embraced within the Massachusetts Constitution's due process of law provisions." Nonetheless, in effectuating the protection against double jeopardy in particular cases, the court has by and large followed the guidance of the U.S. Supreme Court's implementation of the Fifth Amendment's double jeopardy provision. See, e.g., *Powers v. Commonwealth* (1998) (following federal analysis for determining whether a particular punishment is civil or criminal for double jeopardy purposes).

From an early day, the court also concluded that the "law of the land" required that prosecutions of certain crimes be preceded by grand jury indictment. In *Jones v. Robbins*, the defendant challenged his conviction for theft as requiring a grand jury indictment because, upon conviction, he had been sentenced to time in the state prison. The court had little difficult locating the protection afforded by grand jury indictment within the "law of the land":

> The right of individual citizens to be secure from an open and public accusation of crime, and from the trouble, expense and anxiety of a public trial, before a probable cause is established by the presentment and indictment of a grand jury, in case of high offences, is justly regarded as on of the securities to the innocent against hasty, malicious and oppressive public prosecutions, and as one of the ancient immunities and privileges of English liberty.

Id. On the facts, the court held that a grand jury indictment would be required under the Massachusetts Constitution for those crimes involving high offenses and for which "infamous punishments" might be imposed, which punishments include a term in the state prison.

Further, the court has held that the "law of the land" requires that an accused be competent to stand trial and to consult effectively with his or her counsel. See *In re Hinnant* (1997). Here again, the court has applied the same analysis as the federal courts, seeking to ascertain whether a defendant has the ability to consult with a lawyer with a reasonable degree of rational understanding, as well as some understanding of the proceedings themselves. See *Commonwealth v. Hill* (1978).

Finally, the court has ruled that a presumption of innocence that attaches to an individual whose liberty is at stake in a criminal proceeding is part of the "law of the land." In *Fisher v. McGirr* (1854), a defendant challenged the requirements of a statute concerning the manufacture and sale of "spirituous and intoxicating liquors." Chief Justice Shaw, again writing for the court, reasoned that a prosecution for violation of such a statute could withstand constitutional scrutiny only if it did not abridge the dictates imposed by the "law of the land," which require that an accused stand trial at which he will enjoy the presumption of innocence unless and until "proofs are adduced against him to establish the crime or misdemeanor with which he is charged." *Id.* The Chief Justice continued: "Such a trial alone can satisfy . . . the Declaration of Rights, art. 12." *Id.*

ARTICLE XIII. Verification of Facts in Vicinity of the Crime
In criminal prosecutions, the verification of facts in the vicinity where they happen, is one of the greatest securities of the life, liberty, and property of the citizen.

This Article has not been amended.

This Article concerns an individual's right to be tried on criminal charges in the vicinity of the events leading to the prosecution. Fairness requires that defendants be tried where they may have access to witnesses and evidence, see *Commonwealth v. Brogan* (1993), and that "the proof of facts in criminal prosecutions should be in the vicinity or neighbourhood where they happened." *Commonwealth v. Parker* (1824). Whether the principle of fairness upon which Article XIII is premised has been violated—either by a judicial decision to try a defendant in a particular court, or a legislative determination that criminal trials be held in particular courts—has been examined in the few cases addressing Article XIII in light of an evolving understanding of the term "vicinity."

The Supreme Judicial Court has reasoned that the use by the framers of the term "vicinity," rather than the more precise term "county," indicates an intention to avoid a narrow, technical interpretation of the word. See *Opinion of the Justices* (1977). Accordingly, Article XIII does not prohibit trial in any county other than the one in which the crime allegedly occurred, and it does not provide a defendant a right to be tried in a particular county. Indeed, the court has interpreted the Article as essentially a "cautionary declaration," providing guidance as to where criminal cases may be tried, and not as prohibiting the Legislature or the courts from "causing trials to be had in adjoining counties when the public interest should demand it." *Parker*.

In view of this interpretation of Article XIII, the court concluded in an advisory opinion that proposed legislation giving the Chief Justice of the Supreme Judicial Court the authority to manage judicial resources by transferring criminal cases from one county to an adjoining county would be constitutional. The purpose of the transfer authority was to reduce caseloads and ensure prompt disposition of cases, both aims related to matters of public concern and the interests of justice, and therefore not inconsistent with the dictates of Article XIII. Similarly, in *Commonwealth v. Duteau* (1981), the court held that Article XIII poses no obstacle to the Legislature redrawing a grand jury or trial jury district within the Commonwealth.

The court has also relied upon a flexible understanding of Article XIII to uphold judicial orders concerning the venue of criminal trials. The court in *Commonwealth v. Brogan* (1993) held that a defendant may be tried in a court in a county adjoining the alleged locus of the crime. Given modern developments in communication and transportation, it was "neither mischievous nor unjust to try a person in Cambridge for contempt of a Middlesex Superior Court order committed in the abutting city of Boston or in the adjacent town of Brookline."

The court has held that, in addition to providing direction regarding the appropriate venue for criminal trials, Article XIII does not, in particular trials, preclude the admission of competent evidence "of facts occurring abroad, which are material to sustain a prosecution here for a crime committed here." *Commonwealth v. Holt* (1876). Accordingly, in a prosecution for adultery, the court upheld the admission of evidence of marriage occurring outside the Commonwealth. See *id.* At the same time, however, Article XIII provides protection to non-Massachusetts citizens from prosecution for conduct occurring outside the Commonwealth's borders. The events surrounding an allegation of criminal conduct must bear some connection to Massachusetts in order to be actionable by the Commonwealth; pursuant to Article XIII, the Legislature cannot "assume to regulate the conduct of citizens of foreign states who have never been within [the Commonwealth's] borders, and to punish them for acts which were lawful when they were done." *Bradley v. Burton* (1890).

ARTICLE XIV. Search and Seizure

Every subject has a right to be secure from all unreasonable searches, and seizures, of his person, his houses, his papers, and all his possessions. All warrants, therefore, are contrary to this right, if the cause or foundation of them be not previously supported by oath or affirmation; and if the order in the warrant to a civil Officer, to make search in suspected places, or to arrest one or more suspected persons, or to seize their property, be not accompanied with a special designation of the persons or objects of search, arrest, or seizure: and no warrant ought to be issued but in cases, and with the formalities prescribed by the laws.

This Article has not been amended.

Article XIV protects the privacy of individuals by establishing procedural guidelines with which government agents must comply before effecting a search or seizure of a person or property. Though Article XIV served as a model for the Fourth Amendment to the U.S. Constitution, the U.S. Supreme Court and the

Supreme Judicial Court have often diverged in their respective interpretations of the protection against unreasonable searches and seizures. When reviewing a claim under this Article, a court must first determine "whether the defendant had a subjective expectation of privacy which can be recognized as 'reasonable.'" *Commonwealth v. Pratt* (1990). A person, her home, and the areas around her home have been understood as inherently private, with any reasonable expectation of privacy declining as the person moves about in the world beyond the home. Nonetheless, even in respect to searches related to the home, courts also must evaluate whether particular expectations of privacy are objectively reasonable. In *Pratt*, for example, the court faced the question whether a defendant had a privacy interest in the contents of his trash bag. The court concluded that, because the bag was placed near the street in his driveway and exposed to the public, the defendant had no reasonable expectation of privacy in its contents—though such an expectation may well have been warranted had the bag not been placed curbside for collection.

If an individual has a reasonable expectation of privacy, a governmental search or seizure typically must be authorized by a legally effective, magistrate-issued warrant, unless the government action falls within a few well-defined categories exceptions to this rule. See, e.g., *Commonwealth v. Balicki* (2002). We proceed by addressing the requirements for searches and seizures with and without a warrant, as well as the standard under the Massachusetts Constitution for excluding at trial evidence seized in conjunction with an unconstitutional search or seizure. This chapter is not intended to be a comprehensive analysis of search-and-seizure law under either the state or federal constitutions; rather, it highlights the basic protections available to individuals under Article XIV and how the scope of those protections may differ from those available under the Fourth Amendment.

Warrant Requirements: Particularity and Probable Cause

In reviewing an application for a warrant, a magistrate must consider the information contained in the application and supporting affidavit in a commonsense, nonhypertechnical manner. See *Commonwealth v. Penta* (1996). Article XIV requires that a warrant contain a detailed description of the place to be searched and the persons or things to be seized; this is known as the particularity requirement. See *Commonwealth v. Rutkowski* (1990). In addition, the proposed search and seizure must be supported by probable cause—information sufficient for an impartial magistrate to believe that the object or objects to be seized under the warrant are in the place to be searched. See *Commonwealth v. Upton* (1985). Differing from the federal standard, Massachusetts courts have also required that the police actually have and exhibit the warrant at the time of the search, both to guide the police as to the permissible scope of the search, and to put an individual on notice of the authority to conduct the search and the reasons supporting the search. See *Commonwealth v. Guaba* (1994).

Particularity

Both the Fourth Amendment and Article XIV require that warrants particularly describe the places to be searched and the items sought in execution of a warrant. *Commonwealth v. McCarthy* (1999). This requirement defines the scope of the search to be conducted and protects Massachusetts residents against "general" searches—those standardless searches by government officials that the framers found to be a particularly odious invasion of individuals' rights of privacy and possession. *Commonwealth v. Pope* (1968). To satisfy Article XIV, the description of the place to be searched must be sufficiently particular so as to allow the executing officer to locate and identify the premises with reasonable effort, and to preclude the probability that another premises might be mistakenly searched. *Commonwealth v. Rugaber* (1976).

Beyond the places or items specifically listed, warrants authorizing the search of a residence include within their scope any areas owned or controlled by the owner of such residence, including automobiles, located within the curtilage of the premises at the time the warrant is executed. See *Commonwealth v. McCarthy* (1999). Following federal precedent, the Massachusetts courts have defined "curtilage" as an extension of the home which an individual reasonably may expect will be treated as the home itself, both for extending Fourth Amendment and Article XIV protections and for defining the scope of search warrants.

Probable Cause

To establish probable cause, a warrant's supporting affidavit must contain, at a minimum, information sufficient to support a disinterested magistrate's determination that the items related to the criminal activity being investigated reasonably may be expected to be found in the place to be searched at the time the warrant issues. See, e.g., *Commonwealth v. Byfield* (1992). Probable cause requires more than mere suspicion of criminal involvement, but less than that required to demonstrate, prima facie, the commission of a crime or to warrant a conviction. See *Commonwealth v. Spano* (1993). In reviewing a warrant application to determine whether probable cause to issue the warrant existed, the court must read the affidavits supporting the warrant as a whole, in an ordinary, commonsense manner. See *Commonwealth v. Blake* (1992). Only the facts revealed within the four corners of the affidavit, and any reasonable inferences to be drawn from those facts, are considered in determining whether a motion to suppress evidence seized should be allowed. See *Commonwealth v. Allen* (1990).

The Massachusetts courts have taken a different course than the federal courts in respect to information in a supporting affidavit provided by confidential informants. In *Commonwealth v. Upton* (1985), the Supreme Judicial Court of Massachusetts rejected the U.S. Supreme Court's adoption of a less strict, "totality of the circumstances" standard and instead retained the test enumerated in *Aguilar v. Texas* (1964) and *Spinelli v. United States* (1969). Under the

Aguilar-Spinelli test, the information provided by the confidential informant must possess a "basis of knowledge" and exhibit "veracity," either alone or with independent police corroboration. *Commonwealth v. Warren* (1994); *Upton*. The Supreme Judicial Court reasoned that this standard would encourage more careful police work and reduce the number of searches conducted in violation of Article XIV. See *Upton*.

The court has applied the *Upton* standard in numerous cases. In *Commonwealth v. Byfield* (1992), for instance, the court held the warrant issued by the magistrate supported by probable cause when the affidavit established that the informant's basis of knowledge was grounded upon personal observation of the defendant participating in a suspicious transaction, and that the informant's veracity was evidenced by previous credible information he had supplied on earlier occasions. In contrast, the court determined that the warrant challenged in *Commonwealth v. Allen* (1990) lacked probable cause when two of the three informants provided information gained through hearsay, an insufficient basis of knowledge, while the third informant lacked veracity because he remained anonymous. In addition, the police did not independently corroborate any of the information that might have possibly provided probable cause.

Probation Searches

As to searches of probationers, the Supreme Judicial Court has relaxed the requirement that a warrant be supported by probable cause. In *Griffin v. Wisconsin* (1987), the U.S. Supreme Court concluded that a search of a probationer's home need not be supported by probable cause and a warrant; rather, so long as a regulation governing such searches requires a probation officer to have reasonable grounds to search, the probationer can have no Fourth Amendment objection. Addressing the same issue in *Commonwealth v. LaFrance* (1988), the Supreme Judicial Court agreed that a reduced level of suspicion would justify a search of probationers and their premises, given the "need to supervise" probationers, "both to aid in [their] rehabilitation and to ensure . . . compliance with the conditions of probation." Importantly, however, the court concluded that the warrant requirement should not be eliminated; nothing about the circumstances of a probation search justifies abandoning a central protection of Article XIV—compelling a governmental actor to articulate the reasons that justify a search to a neutral magistrate, in order to deter "impulsive or arbitrary governmental conduct." *Id.* In short, the court held that Article XIV "bars the imposition on probationers of a blanket threat of warrantless searches." *Id.*

Warrantless Searches and Seizures

In the absence of a warrant, the Supreme Judicial Court has required that two conditions be met for a search or seizure to be considered constitutionally valid: there must be probable cause and the search or seizure must fall under a recognized exception to the warrant requirement. See *Commonwealth v. A Juvenile (No. 2)* (1991). The probable cause requirement is met when the police possess information sufficient to justify a reasonable person's belief that a crime has been or is being committed and that a suspect or evidence will be obtained in the course of the search. See *Commonwealth v. Motta* (1997). Because a search or seizure necessarily represents a serious invasion of privacy, there are only a limited number of circumstances in which an exception to the warrant requirement has been recognized, including: when objects are discovered in plain view, when a search is conducted incident to a lawful arrest, when a search is performed under exigent circumstances, and when the search qualifies as an inventory and storage space search. See *Horsemen's Benev. and Protective Ass'n, Inc. v. State Racing Com'n* (1989).

Objects in Plain View

Under Article XIV, if a governmental agent is lawfully in a position to view an object, the object's incriminating character is immediately apparent, and the object may be lawfully obtained, then it may be sized without a warrant. See *Commonwealth v. D'Amour* (1999); *Commonwealth v. Santana* (1995). In addition, unlike under the Fourth Amendment, the viewing must be inadvertent. By requiring inadvertence, the plain view doctrine under Article XIV ensures that law enforcement officers, having probable cause to believe that incriminating evidence is in a particular place, will obtain a warrant for its seizure rather than simply placing themselves where they will have plain view of the evidence. See *D'Amour*; *Commonwealth v. Moynihan* (1978).

Searches Incident to Lawful Arrest

Searches conducted incident to lawful arrest are valid for the purpose of seizing the fruits and instrumentalities of crime, as well as contraband and other evidence of the crime for which the arrest was made, in order to prevent destruction or concealment of such items. See *Commonwealth v. Elizondo* (1998). In *United States v. Robinson* (1973), the U.S. Supreme Court held that the Fourth Amendment also allows the use of evidence discovered during a search incident to arrest that incriminates the defendant in respect to unrelated criminal activity. In reaction to *Robinson*, the Massachusetts Legislature adopted G.L. c. 276, §1, which provides that evidence discovered during a search incident to arrest may be used at trial only if it relates to the crime for which the defendant was arrested. See *Commonwealth v. Toole* (1983).

Exigent Circumstances

A warrant is not required for a search conducted with probable cause in exigent circumstances. See *Commonwealth v. DeJesus* (2003). The standards for determining exigency are strict. See *Commonwealth v. Forde* (1975). The state's burden, therefore, is to show not only that circumstances made obtaining a warrant impractical but also that there was an imminent danger of either the suspect evading the police or destroying evidence.

In determining whether exigency exists, courts look to whether the crime involves violence, whether the suspect is armed, whether there is strong reason to believe the suspect is within a dwelling and may escape, whether the elapsed time to obtain a warrant would enhance the danger to the police or to other persons, and whether any delay related to the time necessary to obtain a warrant would facilitate destruction of evidence. Exigency requirements are applied less stringently for searches of automobiles, based upon a belief that cars are inherently mobility. See *Commonwealth v. Krisco Corp.* (1995). Though warrantless surveillance undertaken with the consent of one of the parties is considered to be reasonable under the Fourth Amendment, see *United States v. Caceres* (1979); *United States v. White* (1971), such surveillance is deemed to be a violation of Article XIV unless exigent circumstances. See *Commonwealth v. Blood* (1987).

Inventory and Storage Space Searches

Before an individual's incarceration, the police may inventory and retain all items on his or her person in order to safeguard property, protect the police from accusations of theft, and keep weapons and contraband out of the prison population. See *Commonwealth v. Seng* (2002). The permissible scope of a warrantless inventory search lies in distinguishing it from an investigative search which results in information used to further the criminal investigation against the defendant. Though the U.S. Supreme Court has held that the Fourth Amendment requires that inventory searches be conducted pursuant to standardized police procedures, to reduce the possibility that the police will use the inventory procedures as investigative searches, the Supreme Judicial Court has gone a step further by requiring that the standardized police procedures be in writing. See *Commonwealth v. Figueroa* (1992). Accordingly, Article XIV requires the exclusion of evidence seized during an inventory search not conducted pursuant to standardized, written guidelines, although minor variations from the protocols may not render the search unreasonable. See *Commonwealth v. Garcia* (1991).

Searches and Seizures Not Based on Probable Cause

The Supreme Judicial Court, like the U.S. Supreme Court, has recognized that government agents may effect certain searches and seizures absent probable cause and a warrant, so long as there exists some articulable, individualized suspicion to justify what is, in the event, a minimal intrusion on privacy. See, e.g., *Commonwealth v. Wilson* (2004) (police may make investigatory stop where suspicious conduct give officer "reasonable ground to suspect that a person is committing, has committed, or is about to commit a crime"). Areas in which the standards for these searches developed by the Supreme Judicial Court under

Article XIV have diverged from the U.S. Supreme Court's standards under the Fourth Amendment include those involving motor vehicle stops, roadblocks, and random drug testing.

Stops of motor vehicles, even for a brief period of time and whether on an individual basis or collectively at a roadblock, constitute a seizure. See *Commonwealth v. Rodriguez* (2000). Such stops, and consequent searches of the vehicle, the driver, or the passengers, may arise in a variety of ways. Ordinarily, government actors must possess at least an articulable suspicion before stopping a vehicle. The U.S. Supreme Court abandoned even this modest showing in *Pennsylvania v. Mimms* (1977), in which it held that a police officer may order a driver out of a vehicle that has been stopped for a traffic violation. In *Maryland v. Wilson* (1997), the high court extended this rule to include passengers. The Supreme Judicial Court in *Commonwealth v. Gonsalves* (1999) rejected this rule, holding that, under Article XIV, a police officer must have at least a reasonable suspicion of danger before ordering a driver to leave a motor vehicle. In other cases involving stops of individual motor vehicles, the court has provided protections that are not necessarily recognized under federal law. See, e.g., *Commonwealth v. King* (1983) (no basis to further investigate after police, making valid investigatory check of parked car at rest area, verified identification of driver and passenger and vehicle registration).

In respect to roadblocks, the U.S. Supreme Court's analysis has focused on the purpose of the roadblock; the court concluded, for example, that the roadblocks set up to detect drunk drivers in *Michigan Dep't of State Police v. Sitz* (1990), and to detect illegal aliens in *United States v. Martinez-Fuerte* (1976), were constitutional because their primary purpose was not a general interest in crime control. Under the Fourth Amendment, law enforcement officials may use roadblocks to detect drunk drivers so long as they develop and comply with a plan for the roadblock procedure that meets standard, neutral guidelines that constrain the exercise of police discretion. See *Commonwealth v. Trumble* (1985). Differing from the federal approach, the Supreme Judicial Court has added the requirement that the roadblock procedures be developed in advance; include the date, location, time, duration, and set pattern of cars to be stopped; be controlled by law enforcement supervisory personnel; and be directed toward areas with a recent history of accidents or drunken driving arrests. Law enforcement compliance with the plan has been deemed a sufficient substitute for individualized suspicion; importantly, the court has interpreted Article XIV to require full compliance with written guidelines to prevent any degree of police discretion in implementing the roadblock procedure. See *Commonwealth v. Cameron* (1990).

The U.S. Supreme Court has upheld warrantless, suspicionless searches in circumstances in which the government can demonstrate the existence of "special needs, beyond the normal need for law enforcement," that make warrant and probable-cause requirements impracticable and, on balance, outweigh any privacy concerns. See *Vernonia School District v. Acton* (1995). The court has held that such special needs include sustained drug tests for railway employees involved in train accidents, see *Skinner v. Railway Labor Executives Ass'n* (1989), and random drug tests for high school students participating in interscholastic sports. The Supreme Judicial Court, on the other hand, has not fully embraced the "special needs" exception under Article XIV. In *Guiney v. Police Commissioner of Boston* (1991), the court addressed the constitutionality of a Boston Police Department rule authorizing random drug testing of police officers. The court declined to adopt the U.S. Supreme Court special needs balancing test and held the testing an unreasonable search and seizure under Article XIV; the court concluded that, "[i]f such an intrusive testing process could ever be justified as reasonable in an art. 14 sense (barring the police officer's consent to the testing), the government would have to make a strong factual showing that a substantial public need exists for the imposition of such a process applicable to all police officers." *Id.*

Automatic Standing

Unlike the federal courts, Massachusetts courts have retained the rule of automatic standing, which allows an individual charged with a crime in which possession is an essential element automatic standing to challenge the legality of a search. See *Commonwealth v. Carter* (1997). In *United States v. Salvucci* (1980), the U.S. Supreme Court abandoned the automatic standing rule set out in *Jones v. United States* (1960), reasoning that defendant's dilemma—admitting to possession in order to challenge a search or seizure—and the unfair advantage created when a prosecutor may argue that the defendant had possession but no expectation of privacy, were eliminated by the court's decisions in *Simmons v. United States* (1968), in which the court proposed to avoid the self-incrimination issue by preventing the defendant's testimony in support of a motion to suppress from being admitted as evidence of his guilt at trial, and *Rakas v. Illinois* (1978), in which the court concluded that no legal contradiction lies in a prosecutor simultaneously arguing that a defendant criminally possessed a seized good, but was not subject to a Fourth Amendment deprivation.

Ten years after *Salvucci*, the Supreme Judicial Court rejected this reasoning and retained the automatic standing rule under Article XIV for searches of houses and automobiles, leaving for case-by-case determination other circumstances that involve possession crimes. In the court's view, the rationale behind adoption of the rule in *Jones* still obtained, and the fear of forcing a defendant to incriminate himself or herself in order to challenge a search, as well as the potential contradiction of a prosecutor arguing that the defendant had possession by no expectation of privacy, warranted stricter safeguards than provided by the U.S. Supreme Court's interpretation of the Fourth Amendment.

In *Commonwealth v. Frazier* (1991), the court expanded the automatic standing rule to include defendants not in actual possession of the item seized at the time of the search or present when the search occurred. One of the two defendants in *Frazier*, Donald Johnson, was charged with trafficking in cocaine even though he was not in actual possession of any cocaine at the time of arrest, and not present when the police, without a warrant, searched and found a large quantity of cocaine in a handbag belonging to his companion, Michele Frazier. The court ruled that, as possession—either actual or constructive—was an essential element of the trafficking indictment, Johnson had automatic standing to object to the warrantless search of Frazier's handbag under the same rationale that justified the automatic standing rule in cases involving allegations of actual possession.

Remedies

As a general matter, the fruits of an invalid search are inadmissible at trial. See *Commonwealth v. Marquez* (2001). In determining whether to suppress evidence illegally obtained, a court will examine the degree to which the violation undermined principles underlying governing rule of law, and the extent to which suppression will tend to deter such violations in the future. See *Commonwealth v. Frodyma* (1984). If the evidence would have been obtained by lawful means and the constitutional violation is not severe, the evidence may be admissible under the inevitable discovery exception. See *Commonwealth v. O'Connor* (1989).

The government may avoid suppression by demonstrating the inevitable discovery of evidence. The U.S. Supreme Court has held that, under the Fourth Amendment, the government need only demonstrate the evidence's inevitable discovery by a preponderance of the evidence. See *Nix v. Williams* (1984). The Supreme Judicial Court, by contrast, has adopted a more rigorous analysis under the inevitable discovery doctrine, requiring not only a showing of inevitability by a preponderance of the evidence, but also a demonstration with a high level of specificity and factual detail that the discovery was certain as a practical matter in light of the character of the police misconduct. See *Commonwealth v. Perrot* (1990).

ARTICLE XV. Right to a Jury Trial

In all controversies concerning property, and in all suits between two or more persons, except in cases in which it has heretofore been otherways and practiced, the parties have a right to a trial by jury; and this method of procedure shall be held sacred, unless, in causes arising on the highseas, and such as relate to mariners wages, the legislature shall hereafter find it necessary to alter it.

This Article has not been amended.

Article XV secures the common law right to a jury trial in all civil matters involving property and in all cases between two or more persons "as established and known at the time the Constitution was adopted in 1780." *Stonehill College v. Massachusetts Com'n Against Discrimination* (2004) (quotation omitted). The Seventh Amendment to the U.S. Constitution also secures citizens the right to a jury trial in civil cases, but the U.S. Supreme Court has held that this protection is not necessarily applicable to civil trials in state courts via the due process clause of the Fourteenth Amendment to the U.S. Constitution. The Supreme Judicial Court has nonetheless found Seventh Amendment jurisprudence instructive in interpreting Article XV's jury trial guarantee. *New Bedford Housing Authority v. Olan* (2001).

This Article operates to protect citizens from the arbitrary use of government power in resolving disputes by ensuring that cases will be decided by an impartial panel of fact-finders. See *Jamgochian v. Dierker* (1997). The Article also serves a democracy-reinforcing function, for "[t]he jury system, as the 'sacred' method for resolving factual disputes, is the most important means by which laypersons can participate in and understand the legal system." *Dalis v. Buyer Advertising, Inc.* (1994). Nonetheless, the courts have not interpreted Article XV inflexibly, but have viewed Article XV as articulating a "living principle capable of reasonable adaptation to a constantly changing society." *New Bedford Housing Authority*.

As an initial matter, a case will qualify for a jury trial if it concerns property, or is a suit between two or more persons. Either real or personal property must be at issue. See *Weeks v. Brooks* (1910); *Gardner v. Essex County Com'rs* (1903). This includes disputes over lawful possession of property. Suits involving rights incident to property ownership, however, generally concern the question of available remedies, making such cases more equitable in nature and not the kind of controversy "concerning property" contemplated by the framers of Article XV. See *Demoulas v. Demoulas Super Markets, Inc.* (1997). In addition to cases concerning property, the jury trial right extends to all civil cases involving suits between two or more persons. The disputes covered by Article XV accordingly include the enforcement of contractual and statutory rights. See *Nei v. Burley* (1983). And they include such modern causes of action as employment discrimination suits.

Regardless whether a suit concerns property or a dispute between two or more persons, it will not be eligible for trial by jury if the case "was one in which a court of equity would have exercised jurisdiction in 1780." *Dalis*. In determining whether Article XV applies, a court will examine whether a plaintiff's claim is analogous, in either its subject matter or in the remedy the plaintiff seeks, to cases that fell within the court's equity jurisdiction at the time the constitution was adopted. In *Dalis*, for example, the court reasoned that an action for employment discrimination was akin to an action sounding in tort or contract, for which money damages are available as a remedy. Thus, an employment discrimination claim is unlike a case traditionally heard in a court of equity, and the plaintiff in *Dalis* was entitled to a jury trial.

The court has been clear that the right to a jury trial may attach even to new causes of action, and the court has been wary of narrowing the right to a jury trial by expanding the boundaries of essentially equitable matters. The Legislature may not eliminate the right to a jury trial by changing a traditionally nonequitable action into an equitable one. It remains, however, that mixed equitable and legal claims brought in the same action may be separated, so that the equitable issues are not heard by the jury.

ARTICLE XVI. Liberty of the Press; Free Speech
The liberty of the press is essential to the security of freedom in a state: it ought not, therefore, to be restrained in this commonwealth. The right of free speech shall not be abridged.

This Article was amended in 1948 by Amendment LXXVII, which added the second sentence providing for the protection of freedom of speech. The right of freedom of association, which is protected by Article XIX, is often invoked in tandem with Article XVI. See *Bowe v. Secretary of the Com.* (1946). Together, these provisions protect the rights of free speech and assembly from infringement by the government. See *Commonwealth v. Noffke* (1978).

For the most part, the Supreme Judicial Court has not interpreted Part I, Article XVI independently of the First Amendment to the U.S. Constitution. Indeed, freedom of speech analysis under the Massachusetts state constitution often tracks federal analysis of First Amendment claims. See *Hosford v. School Committee of Sandwich* (1996); see also *George W. Prescott Pub. Co. v. Stoughton Div. of Dist. Court Dept. of Trial Court* (1998). Still, while the court has stated that its analysis of issues arising under Article XVI will parallel the analysis employed by the federal courts in considering an issue arising under the First Amendment, the court has maintained that it is not necessarily bound by any federal analysis. See *Bowe* ("Upon [a] question of Massachusetts law, Federal decisions are persuasive, but not controlling."). In this chapter, we focus on particular instances in which the Supreme Judicial Court has, in respect to a specific issue, sought to provide guidance as to the reach and scope of Article XVI.

Rationales Underlying Freedom of Speech and Liberty of the Press

Because analysis of claims raising Article XVI so often parallel analysis under the First Amendment, an understanding of the philosophical and normative rationales for protecting freedom of speech and liberty of the press may provide some guidance in understanding Article XVI. Jurists and commentators have developed a number of premises upon which the guarantees of freedom of speech and liberty of the press may be based. Like the U.S. Supreme Court in respect to the First Amendment, the Supreme Judicial Court has on occasion expressly or implicitly invoked one or more of these rationales when interpreting the scope of protection afforded under Article XVI. The court has, for example, endorsed the notion that freedom of speech should be understood to protect a "marketplace of ideas." On this view, protection for speech is warranted because "the best test of truth is the power of . . . thought to get itself accepted in the competition of the market." *Abrams v. United States* (1919) (Holmes, J., dissenting). In addressing the constitutionality of a proposed law that would materially restrict the use of corporate funds to oppose or support ballot questions, the court opined that such a restriction would "operate[] at the very heart of the right to free speech" under Article XVI. *Associated Ind. of Mass. v. Attorney General* (1994). "Free speech freedoms are founded," the court continued, "on the idea that a full airing of views fosters competition in the marketplace of political ideas." *Id.*

The court has also referred to the self-governance rationale as animating its interpretation of Article XVI. This rationale suggests that a well-informed citizenry is essential to a properly functioning constitutional democracy. In *Associated Industries,* the court expressed a similar view, remarking that, when there is competition in the marketplace of ideas, arguments about political questions will be communicated to the citizenry, and "[w]hen that is done, the people, properly informed, will make the right decision or will have no one to blame but themselves." And the court has opined that liberty of the press, too, serves essentially to inform "political discussion of men and measures, in order that the electorate at the polls may express the genuine and informed will of the people." *Bowe.*

These rationales support the court's expansive view of the range of expressive activities protected under Article XVI. The court has made clear that Article XVI's protections concern "the communication of ideas," regardless of the form that communication takes. *Aristocratic Restaurant of Massachusetts, Inc. v. Alcoholic Beverages Control Commission* (1978). The range of expression protected under Article XVI accordingly includes such diverse activities as picketing, see *Saveall v. Demers* (1947), and nude dancing, see *Commonwealth v. Sees* (1978).

Content-based Speech Restrictions and Prior Restraints on Speech

Only in 1994 did the Supreme Judicial Court expressly hold the compelling interest standard applicable to content-based speech restrictions—that is, to restrictions aimed at the content of speech, or at particular speakers—under Article XVI. In *Associated Industries of Massachusetts v. Attorney General,* the court reasoned that a proposed law regulating corporate speech would burden the free speech rights of a corporation to "speak out in favor of or in opposition to a ballot question that materially affects it," a burden that would have to be justified by a compelling state interest. The court suggested that there might be a compelling interest in restricting the use of corporate funds on ballot questions, but it declined to resolve that issue in the circumstances presented. This was the first explicit articulation of the compelling interest standard for speech restrictions under the state constitution. Importantly, the court noted that, while "[t]he identity of the standard does not . . . mean that this court's conclusions on applying the compelling State interest standard will invariably be the same as those of the Supreme Court of the United States." *Id.*

The compelling interest standard has been specifically applied in the context of governmental efforts to prevent speakers from exercising their Article XVI rights, popularly referred to as "prior restraints." Indeed, in 1825 the court held that Article XVI was intended to prevent prior restraints "as had been practised by other governments, and in early times here, to stifle the efforts of patriots towards enlightening their fellow subjects upon the rights and duties of rulers." *Commonwealth v. Blanding* (1825). As the court put it almost one hundred seventy years later, "[a]n injunction that forbids speech activities is a classic example of a prior restraint." *Care and Protection of Edith* (1996). The court explained in *Care and Protection of Edith* that prior restraints must be justified by a compelling governmental interest, and be no greater than necessary to secure that interest. In the circumstances of the case, the lower court had entered an order in a care and protection proceeding enjoining the father from discussing any aspects of the proceeding with members of the media. The court held that, absent evidence and findings as to what effect the disclosure of names of particular children, or the comments about the proceedings, might have on the children, the Commonwealth had failed to demonstrate a compelling interest.

The Supreme Judicial Court has also held that the converse of a prior restraint—compelled speech—does not necessarily offend Article XVI. The court, in *In the Matter of Enforcement of a Subpoena* (2002), ruled that compelled speech in the context of judicial or quasi-judicial proceedings does not abridge an individual's speech rights. In that case, the Commonwealth's Commission on Judicial Conduct subpoenaed the spouse of a judge to produce documents concerning a matter before the commission. The witness refused to produce the requested documents, and the commission sought and obtained a judicial enforcement order. On appeal, the witness claimed that the subpoena infringed upon his speech rights under Article XVI. The court concluded that the order did not violate the state constitution: witnesses in a variety of proceedings are requested to give evidence concerning matters of historical fact, and the court saw no chilling effect where the witness could not be subject to disciplinary action by the commission. The court noted that, even if the witness's speech rights were implicated by the subpoena, there existed a compelling interest in "the thorough investigation and fair resolution of allegations of judicial misconduct." *Id.*

Vagueness and Overbreadth Challenges

Laws affecting speech and expression are often challenged as constitutionally vague or overbroad—as being susceptible, in certain circumstances, to discriminatory and selective enforcement. Though they are related, vagueness and overbreadth represent distinct challenges. An overbroad law is one that encompasses more speech or conduct than may be constitutionally proscribed; in *Houston v. Hill* (1987), for example, the U.S. Supreme Court invalidated, on overbreadth grounds, a law that prohibited any person to "assault strike or in any manner oppose, molest, abuse or interrupt any policeman in the execution of his duty." The Court concluded that the law was overbroad because "the First Amendment protects a significant amount of verbal criticism and challenge directed at police officers." *Id.* A law is vague, on the other hand, when persons "of common intelligence must necessarily guess at its meaning and differ as to its application." *Connally v. General Construction Co.* (1926) (defining vagueness in the context of a due process challenge).

The Supreme Judicial Court has recognized that challenges can be made to laws affecting speech under Article XVI on the grounds that they are either vague or overbroad. Further, the court has endorsed an overbreadth exception to the traditional requirement of standing (though it has not done so in respect to vagueness challenges). Thus, an individual may assert the rights of others to challenge the constitutionality of government action under Article XVI "in a manner similar to that in which overbreadth arguments have been advanced under the First Amendment." *Aristocratic Restaurant.* To have standing to assert a facial overbreadth challenge, a party must show that the governmental action at issue cannot appropriately be limited to unprotected speech, and that the deterrent effect the action has on speech is both "real and substantial." *Id.* (quotation omitted). On the facts presented in *Aristocratic Restaurant,* the court concluded, among other things, that the plaintiffs lacked standing to challenge a regulation limiting entertainers from mingling with patrons in places of entertainment because they failed to demonstrate that the law would have acted as a real and substantial deterrent on protected speech activities.

Liberty of the Press

The Supreme Judicial Court has taken seriously Article XVI's promise that liberty of the press ought not be restrained. Protection of the press was originally conceived as freedom from the requirement of a license imposed on the press in Europe, and the court early on interpreted the constitution to bar prior restraints on publication, and thus Article XVI serves to contribute to the enlightenment of the people "upon their rights and the duties of rulers." *Blanding.* "Liberty of the press" has grown to encompass pamphlets and leaflets as well as newspapers; "the press" includes "every sort of publication which affords a vehicle of information and opinion." *Bowe*. The court has recognized that the liberty to publish affords scant protection without the corresponding liberty to circulate the published ideas.

In particular cases, the court has further defined the liberty that the press enjoys under the state constitution. In an *Opinion of the Justices* (1973), for example, the court examined the question whether, if a newspaper or other general circulation publication published a paid political advertisement, it would be a constitutional violation to compel the publication of a paid advertisement espousing a contrary view. The court concluded that Article XVI does not exempt the press from reasonable regulation, but it does forbid regulation of the expression of political views. In this case, the court saw no legislative findings or other evidence that there existed an overriding governmental interest in compelling the publication of responsive paid advertisements of any nature or size.

Further, while there is no provision in the Massachusetts Constitution corresponding to the right to a "public trial" under the Sixth Amendment to the U.S. Constitution, the Supreme Judicial Court has acknowledged that there does exist under the state constitution "the general principle of publicity." *Ottaway Newspapers, Inc. v. Appeals Court* (1977). Expanding on this principle in *Boston Herald v. Superior Court Dep't* (1995), the court held that the general right of public access to judicial proceedings requires the trial court, prior to closing a proceeding, to consider reasonable alternatives, and to tailor any order of closure as narrowly as possible.

ARTICLE XVII. The Right to Keep and Bear Arms

The people have a right to keep and to bear arms for the common defence. And as, in time of peace, armies are dangerous to liberty, they ought not to be maintained without the consent of the legislature; and the military power shall always be held in an exact subordination to the civil authority, and be governed by it.

This Article has not been amended.

Consistent with the language of this Article, as well as the historical circumstances surrounding the adoption of many states' constitutional provisions dealing with the right to keep and bear arms, the Massachusetts courts have interpreted Article XVII narrowly. The Supreme Judicial Court has held that the right to keep and bear arms relates to the common defense, and, in particular, to service in an organized militia—"civilians primarily, soldiers on occasion." *Commonwealth v. Davis* (1976) (quotation omitted). The court has interpreted "the people" to refer to "the aggregate of citizens." *Id.* Thus, the Article does not guarantee a private right to own or possess weapons, and reasonable regulation of arms is constitutionally permissible. *Chief of Police of Shelburne v. Moyer* (1983).

The Supreme Judicial Court elaborated its understanding of the right to keep and bear arms in *Commonwealth v. Davis*, in which the defendant challenged his conviction for illegal possession of a shotgun with a barrel less than eighteen inches long. The defendant argued that the statute under which he was convicted violated his rights under Article XVII. The Supreme Judicial Court noted that the Article was not intended to guarantee individual ownership or possession of weapons, and concluded that the statute at issue was "part of a large regulatory scheme to promote the public safety" and, therefore, constitutional. *Id.* Nothing in the common law or the language of the Article, the court continued, "suggest[s] that . . . due regulation of possession or carrying of firearms, short of some sweeping prohibition, would have been thought to be an improper curtailment of individual liberty or to undercut the militia system." *Id.*

The Court of Appeals addressed the reach of Article XVII in *Chief of Police of Shelburne v. Moyer*. In *Moyer*, the defendant was denied a license to carry firearms based on a prior conviction for marijuana possession. The appeals court held that, because private citizens have no right to keep and bear arms under Article XVII, the denial was proper. Further, the court confirmed that it is not unconstitutional to require a citizen to have a license to keep and bear arms.

ARTICLE XVIII. Fitness of Lawgivers and Magistrates

A frequent recurrence to the fundamental principles of the constitution, and a constant adherence to those of piety, justice, moderation, temperance, industry, and frugality, are absolutely necessary to preserve the advantages of liberty, and to maintain a free government. The people ought, consequently, to have a particular attention to all those principles, in the choice of their officers and representatives: and they have a right to require of their lawgivers and magistrates, an exact and constant observance of them, in the formation and execution of the laws necessary for the good administration of the commonwealth.

This Article has not been amended.

The first sentence of this Article announces a statement of ideals, an admonition to the people of Massachusetts to respect "the fundamental principles" of the constitution, as well as certain values—piety, justice, moderation, temperance, industry, and frugality—that the framers apparently believed citizens ought to heed in order to "preserve the advantages of liberty, and to maintain a free government." In the second sentence, this Article initially suggests that, in addition to honoring both the fundamental principles of the constitution and the enumerated extra-constitutional values, the people should expect their governmental representatives and officials to respect those values most acutely in performing their duties as lawmakers and administrators. This part of the second sentence in effect establishes criteria for the people to keep in mind when assessing the performance of their governmental representatives and officials, and the latter part of the sentence establishes a right of the people to demand of those representatives and officials "an exact and constant observance" of both fundamental constitutional principles and the enumerated extra-constitutional values.

The Supreme Judicial Court has not stated definitively whether this right of the people is enforceable in the courts, or whether it represents another instance in which the framers sought to use the constitutional text as a means to educate the people (under the assumption that the text would be widely read) about what they should expect from their government, and what criteria they should consider most relevant in selecting and evaluating its members. In *Manning v. Municipal Court* (1977), the court addressed a claim by an individual citing to this Article. In that case, the plaintiff sought an order to a municipal court judge to find probable cause to pursue an assault and battery charge against an individual who had allegedly struck the plaintiff. The plaintiff in *Manning* claimed his right to relief rested "on a right to just, fair and equal treatment under the laws . . . as provided in arts. 10, 11, 18 and 19." *Id.* The court concluded otherwise, holding that the plaintiff had no such right, and no right "to direct the conduct of a public prosecutor." *Id.*

ARTICLE XIX. Right to Instruct Representatives and Petition the Legislature

The people have a right, in an orderly and peaceable manner, to assemble to consult upon the common good: give instructions to their representatives, and to request of the legislative body, by the way of addresses, petitions, or remonstrances, redress of the wrongs done them, and of the grievances they suffer.

This provision has not been amended. Article XIX protects the rights of citizens to assemble peaceably, to instruct Representatives, and to request of the Legislature the redress of wrongs and grievances. The right of freedom of expression, which is protected by Article XVI, is often invoked in tandem with Article XIX. See *Bowe v. Secretary of the Com.* (1946). Together, these provisions protect the rights of free speech and association from infringement by the government. See *Commonwealth v. Noffke* (1978). As with Article XVI, the Supreme Judicial Court has stated that the scope of protection afforded by Article XIX generally extends no further than that of the First Amendment to the U.S. Constitution. See *Opinion of the Justices* (2000).

Article XIX has long been regarded as critical to the proper functioning of representative democracy in Massachusetts. As Chief Justice Lemuel Shaw put it in *Commonwealth v. Porter* (1854), the rights of suffrage "assume and are founded on the right of voters to have the fullest and freest discussion and consultation upon the merits and qualifications of candidates, for their information and the means of exercising a sound and enlightened judgment in regard to public men and political measures." *Id.* The right to assemble also includes the right of association, which guarantees "an opportunity for people to express their ideas and beliefs through membership or affiliations with a group." *Caswell v. Licensing Com'n for Brockton* (1983). In claiming that associational activity is protected by Article XIX, it must be shown that an identifiable group exists and that a gathering of its members would advance the social, legal, or economic benefits of the group. In *Caswell v. Licensing Com'n for Brockton*, for instance, the court concluded that the right of association did not extend to a potential group of patrons of a video game arcade when that group could not be specifically identified and, even if it did, their gathering would not benefit them in a way contemplated by Article XIX.

The right to assemble or to associate is not unlimited. The court has indicated that it "cannot be exercised at times and places and in circumstances in conflict with the enjoyment of other well-recognized rights of individuals or the public." *Commonwealth v. Surridge* (1929). In *Surridge*, for example, the court concluded that making a speech from atop a box to attract a crowd is inconsistent with an easement of travel acquired by the layout of a highway. See *id.* In addition to restriction of the right of assembly due to conflict with private property rights, the government may, as with the right to free expression under Article XVI, regulate associational interests upon the showing of a compelling interest justifying the restriction, along with narrowly tailored means for achieving that interest. See *Associated Indus. of Massachusetts v. Attorney General* (1994).

Article XIX, in addition to establishing the right to assembly and association, protects the right of the people to instruct their Representatives, as well as the right to seek redress from the Legislature for wrongs and grievances. There are no cases elaborating the meaning of these provisions. By statute, Massachusetts citizens may seek to place on the ballot "non-binding 'questions of instructions' to senators and representatives relative to public policy under G.L. c. 53, § 19," *New England Christian Action Council, Inc. v. Sec'y of the Commonwealth* (1989), and it has been argued that there also exists a constitutional right of instruction, which entitles citizens to tell their legislators how to vote. Indeed, in the *New England Christian Action Council* case, the court suggested that the constitutional right "to give instructions to . . . representatives" may be one that citizens could invoke in particular circumstances, though the court did not explain what those circumstances might entail.

Of course, the text of Article XIX plausibly can be read as suggesting that, when the people invoke their right to assemble and "consult upon the common good," an expected result will be either advice to their Representatives in respect to public policy issues, or a request of those representatives to address issues of popular concern. This reading finds support in the long-standing view, discussed above, that the right of assembly is related to the optimal functioning of representative democracy. On this reading, Article XIX complements Article V, which provides that the people's representatives are merely agents who act in their behalf of the people, and that they should limit the exercise of their powers to those actions that the people themselves would sanction. And the people's representatives will learn of the people's wishes, presumably, through such means as elections and the formal results of public assembly, including those "instructions" given via "questions of instruction" from the voting public. See Mass. G.L. c. 53, sec. 19 (concerning questions of instruction by ballot).

ARTICLE XX. Legislative Suspension of the Laws
The power of suspending the laws, or the execution of the laws, ought never to be exercised but by the legislature, or by authority derived from it, to be exercised in such particular cases only as the legislature shall expressly provide for.

This Article has not been amended.

The historical basis of this provision may be traced to the framers' concern with contemporary attempts by the Crown to suspend laws or their operation without Parliament's consent. See *Holden v. James* (1815). Article XX permits the Legislature to suspend a law or its execution, or to authorize another governmental body to do so, but only in particular cases. Thus, the Legislature may, through the normal process of lawmaking, pass a law that suspends another law or its execution, but it must justify the exercise of this power, or the delegation of this power, with particularity. Absent a particularized authorization from the Legislature, no power exists to suspend a law or its operation. See *Massachusetts Bay Trans. Advisory Bd. v. Massachusetts Bay Trans. Auth.* (1981) (concluding that the Governor could not, absent legislative authorization, suspend the operation of a particular law).

As the Supreme Judicial Court has interpreted Article XX, only the Legislature is empowered to suspend an existing law or its operation, or to authorize another governmental body to do the same. See *Commissioner of Public Health v. Bessie M. Burke Mem. Hosp.* (1975). Further, the court has held that the language referring to "particular cases" means particular laws, "and not particular individuals or matters within a class governed by a given law." *Id.* In an *Opinion of the Justices,* the court opined that a statutory grant of authority to the Governor to exercise any authority over persons and property necessary for addressing a war-related emergency did not include the specific authority to alter the date of state primary elections. See *Opinion of the Justices* (1944). The Governor lacked authority to alter the primary dates, the court concluded, because the Legislature had not provided for the suspension of the particular law at issue in its statutory grant of authority, as required by Article XX.

The reach of the Legislature's power under Article XX has rarely been tested in the courts. In *Gorman v. City of Bedford* (1981), the plaintiffs challenged special acts by the Legislature authorizing the voters of the City of Bedford to decide the question whether the public water supply should continue to be fluoridated. The court rejected the argument that Article XX invalidated such acts: because the Legislature specifically authorized the city's voters to resolve the fluoridation issue, it was the Legislature—and not the municipality's voters—that had ultimately authorized a potential suspension of the fluoridation law, thus satisfying Article XX's particularity requirement in respect to delegation of the suspension power.

ARTICLE XXI. Legislative Speech and Debate

The freedom of deliberation, speech and debate, in either house of the legislature, is so essential to the rights of the people, that it cannot be the foundation of any accusation or prosecution, action or complaint, in any other court or place whatsoever.

This Article has not been amended.

This Article serves to protect the people's interest in having their representatives in the Legislature "execute the functions of their office, without fear of prosecutions, civil or criminal." *Coffin v. Coffin* (1808). Like its counterpart in the U.S. Constitution, see U.S. Const. Art. 1, § 6, cl. 1, Article XXI reflects a concern to prevent the use of the judicial process to put untoward pressure on legislators. See *United States v. Gillock* (1980). Article XXI's grant of immunity may be invoked only by members of the Legislature; the Supreme Judicial Court has held, for example, that the Article's protections do not extend to officials in the executive branch of government. See *Babets v. Sec'y of the Executive Office of Human Services* (1988).

In determining whether this Article's immunity from civil or criminal prosecution applies in a particular case, the proper inquiry focuses on whether an individual was acting as a representative while "executing the duties of his office." *Coffin*. The Supreme Judicial Court has taken a liberal view of the protection afforded by this provision, extending its reach to such legislative activities as "the giving of a vote," "the making of a written report," and "to every other act resulting from the nature, and in the execution, of the office." *Id.* But the protection available to legislators is not unlimited. In *Coffin v. Coffin*, for instance, the court concluded that the defendant, a member of the House of Representatives, could not invoke Article XXI immunity against a defamation claim because his allegedly slanderous remarks, while made in the Legislature and to another legislator, did not involve a matter at the time under debate.

Few cases concerning the scope of Article XXI have been reported. In *Irvin v. McGee* (1993), the defendant, a member of the House of Representatives, claimed immunity from suit by a former employee who claimed he had been unlawfully terminated from his position as an administrative assistant. The Superior Court ruled that such immunity was not available because personnel decisions are "anything but legislative." *Id.* Further, relying upon federal case law interpreting the federal constitution, the court concluded that, because the plaintiff's position involved clerical work and not policymaking, the defendant could not rely on Article XXI to avoid any potential liability for his discharge.

ARTICLE XXII. Assembly of the Legislature

The legislature ought frequently to assemble for the redress of grievances, for correcting, strengthening and confirming the laws, and for making new laws, as the common good may require.

This Article has not been amended.

On its face, this provision of the Declaration of Rights appears to reflect a concern that the Legislature might choose not to meet often enough to engage in the processes of lawmaking and, thereby, represent the interests of the people. See *In re Municipal Suffrage to Women* (1894) (describing the characteristic feature of post-Revolutionary state constitutions as the establishment of "government by representatives of the people"). There are historical reasons why the framers would have been concerned that legislative sessions would be suspended; the Crown, for example, had more than a few times suspended Parliament in England and legislatures in the colonies. Thus the language of Article XXII creates at least an expectation that legislators will regularly meet to fulfill the duties of their office: to discuss, debate, and, perhaps, pass legislation on such matters as the redress of grievances, the efficacy and utility of existing laws in the Commonwealth, or the need to draft new laws to address such problems as affect "the common good." It is not clear from the text of Article XXII how the "redress of grievances" might differ, in either form or substance, from either the "correcting, strengthening and confirming [of] the laws," or the "making [of] new laws." Article XIX also speaks of the right of the people to assemble and to request of their legislative body the redress of grievances. See Mass. Const., pt. I, art. XIX (providing a right "to request of the legislative body, by way of addresses, petitions or remonstrances, redress of the wrongs done them, and of the grievances they suffer").

So understood, the dictates of Article XXII serve to illuminate the broad discretionary authority granted the Legislature in Part II of the Massachusetts Constitution—namely, the power and authority to, "from time to time, . . . make, ordain, and establish, all manner of wholesome and reasonable Orders, laws, statutes, and ordinances, directions and instructions, either with penalties or without." Part II, c. I, § I. To the extent the Constitution—and the Declaration of Rights in particular—may be viewed as a vehicle through which the framers sought to educate the citizenry of the Commonwealth about how to ensure the proper functioning of their government, the expectation articulated in Article XXII provides the people some guidance as to how often ("frequently") and for what reasons ("for the redress of grievances," etc.) the legislators should meet together as a lawmaking body.

By comparison, on the subject of legislative assembly the U.S. Constitution provides only that "[t]he Congress shall assemble at least once in every year, and such meeting shall be on the first Monday in December, unless they shall by law appoint a different day." U.S. Const. art I, § 4, cl 2. This provision was amended to provide that "[t]he Congress shall assemble at least once in every year, and such meeting shall begin at noon on the 3d day of January, unless they shall by law appoint a different day." U.S. Const. Amend. XX, § 2. That amendment coordinates legislative sessions with the changes to the term of the President and Vice President, which end on January 20, and the terms of members of Congress, which end on January 3.

There are no reported cases interpreting Article XXII.

ARTICLE XXIII. No Taxation Without Consent of the People

No subsidy, charge, tax, impost, or duties, ought to be established, fixed, laid, or levied, under any pretext whatsoever, without the consent of the people or their representatives in the legislature.

This Article has not been amended.

This Article confirms that "the power to raise money, levy taxes and control the expenditure of public funds is vested in the General Court." *Opinion of the Justices* (1936). This authority includes the power to attach conditions to expenditures appropriated by the Legislature. The Supreme Judicial Court has been careful to distinguish appropriations from expenditures. While the Legislature cannot delegate its authority to appropriate money, it can, within reasonable limits, leave to executive officers or boards "the question of administration as to the means by which the object of an appropriation may be accomplished." *Opinion of the Justices* (1939).

In one of the few cases raising Article XXIII concerns, *Baker v. Commonwealth* (1942), individuals who had completed repair work on two of the Commonwealth's armories sued to collect payment owed them. The plaintiffs argued that they should have been paid from the quartermaster's unexpended balance. But that balance existed—to the extent it existed at all—as a result of a transfer of funds between departments of the state government. The Supreme Judicial Court affirmed the lower court's judgment for the Commonwealth, reasoning that, because the power to appropriate funds lies exclusively in the Legislature, one department of the government cannot transfer funds appropriated it to another department. To allow such transfers would be to divest the Legislature of its constitutional responsibility for managing the financial affairs of the Commonwealth.

For additional provisions related to taxation, see Pt. II, c. 1, § 1, art. 4; Amendment XLIV.

ARTICLE XXIV. Ex Post Facto Laws

Laws made to punish for actions done before the existence of such laws, and which have not been declared crimes by preceding laws, are unjust, oppressive, and inconsistent with the fundamental principles of a free government.

This Article has not been amended.

Like its counterparts in the U.S. Constitution, which prohibit the state and federal governments from enacting any ex post facto law, see U.S. Const. Art. 1, §§ 9(3), 10(1), Article XXIV of the Massachusetts Declaration of Rights prohibits "[l]aws made to punish for actions done before the existence of such laws." In interpreting Article XXIV, the Supreme Judicial Court has viewed the reach of the state and federal ex post facto clauses as identical. See *Santiago v. Commonwealth* (1998). Indeed, the court has adopted the U.S. Supreme Court's definition of an ex post facto law as one which makes criminal an act that was not so when it was performed; or which increases the punishment for an activity already declared criminal; or which alters the situation of a party to a criminal proceeding to his disadvantage, as a change in the rules of evidence might. See *Commonwealth v. Phelps* (1911). Ex post facto laws accordingly are those that alter or affect an individual's substantive rights, as opposed to law concerning exclusively procedural issues, such as requirements relating to the persons to whom notice of hearing must be sent. See *Stewart v. Chairman, Massachusetts Parole Board* (1994).

Article XXIV, in short, prohibits those laws that operate retrospectively "and to the detriment of the defendant." *Commonwealth v. Fuller* (1995). Importantly, this Article prohibits "only after the fact legislative change of the criminal consequences of prior actions." *Gaffney v. Contributory Retirement Appeal Board* (1996). Further, courts should presume that the Legislature did not intend a law to operate retroactively absent clear language to the contrary.

ARTICLE XXV. Conviction of Treason or Felony by the Legislature
No subject ought, in any case, or in any time, to be declared guilty of treason or felony by the legislature.

This Article has not been amended.

The Supreme Judicial Court has interpreted Article XXV as a prohibition on bills of attainder. See *Sheridan v. Gardner* (1964). Article XXV accordingly complements Article 1, Section 10(1) of the U.S. Constitution, which provides that "[n]o state shall . . . pass any Bill of Attainder," and Article 1, Section 9(3) of the U.S. Constitution, which prohibits the U.S. Congress from passing any federal bill of attainder. The drafters of the Declaration of Rights elected to spell out their understanding of bills of attainder in the constitutional text, rather than simply referring to a general prohibition on such bills, by stating that the Legislature could not declare individuals guilty, "in any case, or in any time." The court has interpreted this language as proscribing "the substitution of a legislative for a judicial determination of guilt." *Sheridan* (quotation omitted). In determining whether an act violates this Article, the court has sought to ascertain whether the Legislature intended "to declare guilt or to impose punishment." *Id.*

In the few cases addressing arguments raised under Article XXV, the court upheld the legislative acts in question. In *Sheridan v. Gardner*, the plaintiffs challenged the qualifications for members of a state crime commission; the qualifications precluded from service those persons who, among other things, had been convicted of felonies, gaming offenses, and misdemeanors involving moral turpitude. Because the Legislature intended such qualifications to instill confidence by the public in the commission's independence and integrity, and because other classes of persons were also excluded from service, the court concluded the legislation manifested no intent essentially to declare guilt in respect to the plaintiffs.

In *Administrative Justice of the Housing Court Department v. Commissioner of Administration* (1984), the plaintiff claimed that the alteration of the terms, conditions, and nature of his commission by the Legislature amounted to an unlawful bill of attainder. Because the only evidence of punitive intent that the plaintiff could produce were statements by legislators indicating a punitive motive, the court concluded that the plaintiff has failed to state a basis for his argument. Only the statutory text and official legislative records, the court noted, could be considered "appropriate source[s] from which to discover the intent of legislation." *Id.* See also *Bessette v. Commissioner of Public Works* (1965) (if abolition of a governmental office is within the Legislature's power, there is "no basis for concluding that the change was made for any reason other than the public interest").

ARTICLE XXVI. Cruel or Unusual Punishment

No magistrate or court of law, shall demand excessive bail or sureties, impose excessive fines, or inflict cruel or unusual punishments. No provision of the Constitution, however, shall be construed as prohibiting the imposition of the punishment of death. The general court may, for the purpose of protecting the general welfare of the citizens, authorize the imposition of the punishment of death by the courts of law having jurisdiction of crimes subject to the punishment of death.

In the Massachusetts Constitution of 1780, Article XXVI contained only the first sentence; the remaining portions of this Article, concerning the death penalty, were added by Amendment CXVI in 1982. The first sentence of this Article essentially mirrors the Eighth Amendment to the U.S. Constitution, which provides that "Excessive bail shall not be required, nor excessive fines imposed, nor cruel and unusual punishments inflicted." U.S. Const., Amend. VIII. The differences in wording are minor: the state constitution prohibits "cruel or unusual" punishment, as opposed to the federal constitution's prohibition of "cruel and unusual" punishment. The distinctions have not, in most instances, been deemed significant by the Supreme Judicial Court, as the court has faithfully interpreted Article XXVI as proscribing excessive bails, sureties and fines, as well as cruel or unusual punishments.

Excessive Bail, Sureties, or Fines

"The purpose of bail is to ensure the defendant's appearance in court." *Commonwealth v. Ray* (2001). The ability to ensure the defendant's appearance is essential to the proper functioning of the judiciary and the service of justice. See *Querubin v. Commonwealth* (2003). In situations in which the imposition of bail would not reasonably ensure a defendant's appearance in court, the judge has the discretion to deny bail. And, while "[f]reedom from physical restraint is a fundamental right," see *Commonwealth v. Bruno* (2003), a prisoner may be detained prior to trial without violating that right. See *Querubin*.

The Supreme Judicial Court has held that judges and magistrates have wide discretion to set bail based upon the totality of the facts of a case, including the seriousness of the charge or charges, the wealth of the defendant, and the defendant's past criminal history, including attempts at escape or record of defaults. See, e.g., *Preston v. Commonwealth* (1984). Once bail is set by a judge or magistrate, it will stand as valid unless a higher court finds an error of law or abuse of discretion on appeal. Thus defendants must bear a heavy burden; for example, in *Leo v. Commonwealth* (2004), the supreme judicial court determined that $500,000 was not excessive bail despite the fact that the defendant could not post it. If bail is not posted the defendant remains in custody until trial, alleviating any flight risk.

The Legislature has the authority to determine how criminal conduct should be punished. See *Commonwealth v. Dane Entertainment Services* (1985). The Legislature may establish fines as punishment for criminal conduct, and the courts have interpreted the Legislature's discretion in that regard broadly. For example, the court has found no constitutional violation in requiring a defendant convicted of illegal gambling to "forfeit double the value" of his winnings. *Commonwealth v. Novak* (1930).

Cruel or Unusual Punishment

The Legislature's authority to define crimes and punishments is not entirely unlimited. See *McDonald v. Commonwealth* (1899). Any punishment established by the Legislature is subject to judicial review upon a claim that that the punishment is cruel or unusual. The court has held that Article XXVI's prohibition against cruel or unusual punishments "must draw its meaning from the evolving standards of decency that mark the progress of a maturing society." *Michaud v. Sheriff of Essex County* (1983). What may have been standard practice in the past may now be considered "cruel or unusual" by modern standards. In general, if the punishment is so disproportionate to the offense that it "shocks the conscience and offends fundamental notions of human dignity," it is "cruel or unusual." *Commonwealth v. Alvarez* (1992) (quotation omitted).

The term "cruel or unusual" often implies punishment that is inherently barbaric, inhumane, or "involve[s] the wonton infliction of pain," but terms of incarceration "grossly disproportionate to the severity of the crime" may also be considered "cruel or unusual." *Michaud*. In a claim that the punishment imposed for a crime is "cruel or unusual" the defendant has the burden of proof. This burden is heavy considering the presumption of validity afforded to the Legislature; the punishment will pass scrutiny unless it shocks the conscious or is grossly disproportionate to the crime. The exact test employed by the court to evaluate a claim of cruel or unusual punishment will vary depending on the exact nature of the claim.

When faced with a claim that punishment is "cruel or unusual" because it is disproportionate to the crime committed, the court will consider: "(1) the nature of the offender and the offense in light of the degree of harm to society; (2) sentencing provisions in other jurisdictions for similar offenses; and (3) sentences for more severe offenses within the Commonwealth." *Alvarez*. A punishment may be disproportionate to the offense due to its length or its nature. *Commonwealth v. Jackson* (1976).

Applying this standard, Massachusetts courts have resisted arguments that mandatory prison sentences of various lengths for various crimes constitute cruel or unusual punishment. See *Alvarez* (mandatory minimum of imprisonment for not less than two years for drug-dealing offenses committed within 1,000 feet of a school not cruel or unusual); *Commonwealth v. Jackson* (1976) (mandatory one-year sentence for carrying an unlicensed firearm not cruel or unusual).

Once imprisoned, defendants still may raise challenges under this Article. When the court is asked to evaluate prison conditions or a like claim, it will consider: (1) whether the condition or situation "poses a substantial risk of harm"; and (2) if the facts establish that a prison official "has knowledge of the situation and ignores it." *Torres v. Commissioner of Corrections* (1998). These challenges are generally brought by a prisoner claiming the conditions of a prison are so inhumane as to constitute cruel or unusual punishment. In general, if prisoners are provided with adequate food, clothing, sanitation, medical care, and communication with others, the court will not find the prison conditions cruel or unusual. See *Libby v. Commissioner of Correction* (1982). The court has declined to hold that claims of "isolation" and "loneliness" are, in and of themselves, cruel or unusual.

Prison conditions have, in some cases, been successfully challenged. For example, in *Michaud*, prisoners brought a class action suit challenging the sanitary conditions of their prison facility. The cells at the Essex County House of Correction and Jail had no flushing toilets, sinks, or running water. Prisoners were instead provided with five-gallon metal or plastic containers, which were kept, often uncovered, in the prisoner's cells and emptied only once per twenty-four hour period, by the prisoners themselves. In addition, each cell housed at least two and sometimes four prisoners. The Supreme Judicial Court held that the conditions at the correctional facility were "inconsistent with evolving standards of human decency" and thus "clearly unacceptable" under Article XXVI.

Prior to the amendment of Article XXVI in 1982, the Supreme Judicial Court found the death penalty in violation of the prohibition on cruel or unusual punishment. See, e.g., *District Attorney v. Watson* (1980). Though the court acknowledged that, at the time it was framed, Article XXVI would allow capital punishment, it explained that circumstances had changed, and the understanding of what conduct constituted cruel or unusual punishment under the Massachusetts Constitution must evolve: what may have been valid when the constitution was written may become invalid with the passage of time. The *Watson* court concluded that, when subjected to contemporary standards, the death penalty could only be considered cruel. The inevitable finality of the punishment of death frustrates justice, the court reasoned, by preventing "relief in light of later developments in the law or the evidence." *Id.* In addition, the court found that the death penalty is also cruel to the extent that it inflicts an unimaginable amount of pain, both physical and mental.

The Supreme Judicial Court concluded that the death penalty is cruel or unusual notwithstanding that the U.S. Supreme Court has held the death penalty constitutional under the Eighth Amendment to the U.S Constitution. See *Gregg v. Georgia* (1976). This would seem to indicate that "cruel or unusual" under Article XXVI means something different than "cruel and unusual" under the Eighth Amendment, though the court did not fully explore the basis for that difference. It is possible that the Supreme Judicial Court would have upheld the death penalty had evidence been available to suggest that it "performed some legitimate State function more effectively than life imprisonment." *Opinion of the Justices* (1977). In the absence of that evidence, the court has referred to the death penalty as a "pointless infliction of excessive punishment." *Id.*

In response to the Supreme Judicial Court's invalidation of the death penalty, Article XXVI was amended via Amendment CXVI, ratified in 1982, to provide:

> No provision of the Constitution, however, shall be construed as prohibiting the imposition of the punishment of death. The general court may, for the purpose of protecting the general welfare of the citizens, authorize the imposition of the punishment of death by the courts of law having jurisdiction of crimes subject to the punishment of death.

Despite the apparent intent of the amendment to reinstate the death penalty in Massachusetts, in 1984 the Supreme Judicial Court invalidated yet another death penalty statute. *Commonwealth v. Colon-Cruz* (1984). In *Colon-Cruz*, the court held the statute at issue to impermissibly burden a defendant's Article XII rights against self-incrimination and to a jury trial because the death penalty could only be imposed following a jury trial, and not if the defendant chose to plead out. Essentially, the statute rewarded a defendant for pleading guilty, thereby influencing defendants to waive their rights to a jury trial. The court reasoned that invalidating the statute did not run afoul of the amended Article XXVI because its ruling did not amount to a judicial decree prohibiting the Legislature from devising an acceptable death penalty regime. As the court put it, "nothing in the new language of art. 26" prevents a Massachusetts court "from invalidating a particular death penalty statute under the Massachusetts Constitution on a ground other than that the imposition of the punishment of death is forbidden." *Id.*

ARTICLE XXVII. Quartering of Soldiers

In time of peace, no soldier ought to be quartered in any house without the consent of the owner; and in time of war, such quarters ought not to be made but by the civil magistrate, in a manner ordained by the legislature.

This Article has not been amended.

This Article establishes a property-based privacy interest enforceable under the state constitution. The Article provides, first, that, in a time of peace, the government may not quarter soldiers in any house absent the owner's consent. Second, it provides that, in a time of war, the government may quarter soldiers in houses, contingent upon the enactment by the Legislature of appropriate laws authorizing civil magistrates to conduct the quartering of soldiers. This Article thus complements Part I, Article XIV, in placing limits on the extent to which privacy—in particular, physical, spatially-oriented privacy—may be invaded by the state or its agents. Left undefined in the text is the meaning of critical terms, like "soldier," "house," "peace," and "war."

The Massachusetts courts have provided no guidance as to the meaning of these terms, or how the requirements of this provision should be implemented. Indeed, Massachusetts courts have not had occasion to consider this Article, and the federal courts have only rarely addressed its quite similar federal counterpart, the Third Amendment to the U.S. Constitution, which states that "No soldier shall, in time of peace be quartered in any house, without the consent of the Owner, nor in time of war, but in a manner to be prescribed by law." Those few cases in which the federal courts have addressed the Third Amendment may offer some guidance as to how Massachusetts courts would interpret Article XXVII.

In *Engblom v. Carey* (1982), the U.S. Court of Appeals for the Second Circuit considered whether National Guardsmen are "soldiers" and how ownership should be defined under the Third Amendment. The court concluded that National Guardsmen are soldiers for constitutional purposes, and that they are also state employees under the control of a state's governor, except when "federalized" under federal law. The court rejected the argument that the meaning of "owner" should be restricted to those individuals who are fee simple owners of houses. Rather, the court took the view that the property-based privacy interest protected by the Third Amendment extends to those interests "recognized and permitted by society as founded on lawful occupation or possession with a legal right to exclude others." *Id.* The *Engblom* court accordingly held that the plaintiffs, striking corrections officers who had been residing in staff housing, had a tenancy interest in their housing and, therefore, standing to seek the protection of the Third Amendment when they were evicted and their residences used to house National Guardsmen.

ARTICLE XXVIII. Application of Martial Law

No person can in any case be subject to law-martial, or to any penalties or pains, by virtue of that law, except those employed in the army or navy, and except the militia in actual service, but by authority of the legislature.

This Article has not been amended.

This Article establishes an individual right to be free from martial law, except if a person is employed by one of the armed services, serving in the militia, or if martial law is authorized by the Legislature. While there is no equivalent provision in the U.S. Constitution, a Massachusetts court interpreting Article XXVIII today would likely rely upon federal law to inform its understanding of the Article's reach. The U.S. Constitution, adopted nine years after the Massachusetts Constitution, in 1789, provides for the national defense by granting the Congress the authority to "declare War," U.S. Const. art. I, sec. 8, cl. 11, "raise and support Armies," U.S. Const. art I, sec. 8, cl. 12, and "provide and maintain a Navy," U.S. Const. art. I, sec. 8, cl. 13. It follows that the terms "army" and "navy" in Article XXVIII likely would be interpreted as referring to the national armed forces, as to whose employees the dictates of the state constitution would not apply under the Supremacy Clause of the federal constitution. See U.S. Const., art. VI, cl. 2. Further, federal case law has defined members of the National Guard—the modern militia—as both soldiers for constitutional purposes and state employees under the control of the Commonwealth's governor, except when "federalized" pursuant to federal law. See *Engblom v. Carey* (1982). When considered to be state employees, members of the Massachusetts National Guard would be subject to the requirements of Article XXVIII.

Those Massachusetts citizens who are not either employees of one of the armed forces, or actually serving in the National Guard, may not, under this Article, be subject to martial law except when the Legislature duly enacts a law authorizing the imposition of martial law. In this way, the framers placed their confidence in the ordinary processes lawmaking process, and the participation of citizens in that process, to protect individuals from the arbitrary imposition of martial law by the government of the Commonwealth.

ARTICLE XXIX. Impartiality of Judges; Judges of the Supreme Judicial Court

It is essential to the preservation of the rights of every individual, his life, liberty, property, and character, that there be an impartial interpretation of the laws, and administration of justice. It is the right of every citizen to be tried by judges as free, impartial and independent as the lot of humanity will admit. It is, therefore, not only the best policy, but for the security of the rights of the people, and of every citizen, that the judges of the supreme judicial court should hold their offices as long as they behave themselves well; and that they should have honorable salaries ascertained and established by standing laws.

This Article has not been amended.

Article XXIX establishes an independent and impartial judiciary. To this end, justices of the Supreme Judicial Court cannot be removed from office, so long as "they behave themselves well." This provision also provides that justices should have honorable salaries—presumably, salaries sufficient to enable them to satisfy the demands of impartiality associated with an independent judiciary. Further, Article XXIX assigns the judicial power exclusively to the courts. See *Opinion of the Justices* (1932). The text of Article XXIX assumes that the judicial power includes the authority to interpret the laws—in other words, to say what the law is, which necessarily requires the court to exercise some form of judicial review over the acts of the coordinate branches of government, the executive and the legislature. This stands in contrast to the U.S. Constitution, which does not expressly confer on the U.S. Supreme Court the power of judicial review, though the federal high court has long exercised some form of judicial review—and did so even before the authority to do so was confirmed in *Marbury v. Madison* (1803).

The judicial power under Article XXIX also includes the inherent authority to prescribe the qualifications of those individuals to be admitted to the practice of law in the courts of the Commonwealth, and "to do whatever may be done under the general principles of jurisprudence to insure to the citizen a fair trial, whenever his life, liberty, property or character is at stake." *Crocker v. Justices of the Superior Court* (1911). While the exercise of this authority relates primarily to adjudicatory matters, it may also involve such functions as rulemaking and judicial administration, "which are essential if the courts are to carry out their constitutional mandate." *O'Coins v. Treasurer of Worcester County* (1972). The courts accordingly have the power to prevent the impairment of their functions due to inadequate facilities or a failure of resources, and a judge, to prevent such impairment, may obtain the necessary goods or services by suitable means, even absent statutory authorization. This authority, the Supreme Judicial Court has warned, must be exercised with caution and appropriate consideration of choices made by one of the coordinate branches of government.

Beyond assigning the judicial power to the courts, Article XXIX establishes an individual right to be tried, in either a civil or criminal matter, by as impartial and independent a judge "as the lot of humanity will allow." The judicial officers to whom this provision applies include presiding judges and also county commissioners and jurors, *Hall v. Thayer* (1870), as well as masters and auditors, *Frade v. Costa* (1961). Indeed, the Supreme Judicial Court has suggested that the provision should be "broadly applied to all classes of cases where one is appointed to decide the rights of his fellow-citizens." *Hall.* It has yet to be resolved whether Article XXIX establishes a more stringent standard of impartiality for judicial officers than the due process provisions of either the state or federal constitutions. See *Varga v. Bd. of Registration of Chiropractors* (1991).

The Supreme Judicial Court has observed that "[a] rigid adherence to the principle" of impartiality embraced by Article XXIX "is essential to the maintenance of free institutions." *Thomajanian v. Odabashian* (1930). At a minimum, a person acting in a judicial capacity must be free from bias. *Id.* Bias requiring disqualification will typically arise from an extrajudicial source. See *Commonwealth v. Gogan* (1983). A judge has discretion to determine whether disqualification is appropriate. That determination requires the judge to consult his own conscience and emotions, and to "attempt an objective appraisal" of whether his impartiality might reasonably be questioned in the proceeding at hand. *Id.* Jurors may be disqualified when responses to material questions on voir dire reveal bias. See *Commonwealth v. Emerson* (1999).

Importantly, "an earlier expression of opinion as to a matter to be decided does not disqualify a judge or indicate want of competency to hear fairly and decide impartially all issues." *King v. Grace* (1936). Indeed, even knowledge of "damaging information" about a defendant does not automatically disqualify a judge from sitting on a case. See *Howe v. Prokop* (1985). Judges, moreover, are not expected to refrain from participating in all aspects of civic life. In *Frade v. Costa*, for example, the court determined that a contribution made by a judicial master to the defendants' counsel's campaign for district attorney did not evince an interest in the outcome of the litigation.

Once a judge determines that grounds for disqualification exist, he must "completely disassociate himself from participating in the case." *Parenteau v. Jacobson* (1992). It is not sufficient simply to order a jury trial, as the trial court judge in *Parenteau* did, for a judge presiding over a jury trial still exercises discretion over matters that might affect the jury's judgment. *Id.* Simply put, "a courtroom has no place for a judge whose impartiality may be reasonably questioned." *Id.*

ARTICLE XXX. Separation of Powers

In the government of this commonwealth, the legislative department shall never exercise the executive and judicial powers, or either of them: the executive shall never exercise the legislative and judicial powers, or either of them: the judicial shall never exercise the legislative and executive powers, or either of them: to the end it may be a government of laws and not of men.

This article has not been amended.

Through Article XXX the Massachusetts Constitution, unlike a majority of state constitutions and the U.S. Constitution, explicitly provides for separation of powers. *Opinion of the Justices* (1974). The plain text of Article XXX "calls for complete and rigid division of all powers among the three branches." *Id.* To ensure the practical functioning of the government, the prevailing interpretation of the Article demands flexible separation of powers rather than strict division. The Supreme Judicial Court in myriad cases has held that, though the limitation of Article XXX "must be scrupulously observed . . . such an absolute division is neither possible nor always desirable." *Opinion of the Justices* (1977). The separation of powers does not require "three watertight compartments" within the Massachusetts government. See *Commonwealth v. Gonslaves* (1989).

This chapter addresses the powers attributed to each branch of government by Article XXX and the extent to which each may exercise the power of another. Each branch of government may properly exercise those powers granted it by Part the Second (Part II) of the Massachusetts Constitution. The legislative and executive branches may also exercise those powers incidental to the accomplishment of the charges of Part II. *Opinion of the Justices* (1975); *Opinion of the Justices* (1939). The executive and legislative branches may exercise incidental powers in a manner commonly attributed to another branch. The judicial branch may exercise inherent powers essential to its functioning, to the maintenance of its authority, or to its capacity to decide cases in order to fulfill the guarantees of Article XXIX. See *First Justice v. Clerk-Magistrate* (2003). The Supreme Judicial Court has held that a violation of Article XXX occurs when an act of one branch of government "unduly restricts" a coordinate branch from performing its core functions—those necessary to the existence of that branch. See *Chief Admin. Justice v. Labor Relations Comm'n* (1989); *New Bedford Standard Times Pub. Co. v. Clerk* (1979).

Legislative Power

The Massachusetts Constitution confers on the General Court certain powers, which the Legislature may exercise and may not abandon. See Mass. Const. Pt. II, ch. I; *Opinion* of the Justices (1939). The General Court may also exercise those powers incidental to carrying out the powers conferred upon it in Part II of the Massachusetts Constitution. *Opinion of the Justices; Attorney Gen. v.*

Brissenden (1930). These incidental powers or ancillary duties may be delegated to committees and individuals in an executive or judicial manner, but the General Court may not delegate any power expressly conferred upon it by the Massachusetts Constitution. Among the powers expressly delegated the General Court are: the power to make laws, the power to create public offices, and the power to establish courts subordinate to the Supreme Judicial Court. See Mass. Const. Pt.II, ch. I, § I, Art. III, IV.

The General Power to Make Laws

Part II of the Massachusetts Constitution confers upon the Legislature the general power to make laws "for the good and welfare of [the] Commonwealth[.]" *Opinion of the Justices* (1978). For the General Court to successfully execute its lawmaking powers, it must have the authority to exercise other powers ancillary or incidental to its lawmaking power and also the authority to delegate certain duties. Incident to the General Court's power to make laws is the authority to conduct investigations relating to the enactment of proposed legislation or the amendment of existing legislation. In *Attorney General v. Brissenden*, for example, the Supreme Judicial Court considered whether the authorization of the Attorney General to conduct such an investigation was a proper delegation of legislative authority and was aiding the legislative process. The General Court had statutorily directed the Attorney General to investigate the circumstances surrounding a pension award to a Boston police officer. The court held that when a resolve explicitly stated the legislative purpose for an executive officer performing an investigation, there was little or no question as to whether the act was permissible under Article XXX; the court also held that even when a resolve does not cite a legislative purpose, it must be presumed to aid the legislative process.

Also incident to its lawmaking power, the General Court has the authority to determine what conduct is punishable and to prescribe penalties. See *Commonwealth v. Jackson* (1976). This is illustrated in *Commonwealth v. Jackson*, in which the defendant was sentenced to one year in a house of correction for illegal possession of a firearm, pursuant to a statute mandating a one-year minimum sentence for such offenses. He argued that the statute interfered with the inherent judicial power to defer the imposition of sentence and, therefore, violated Article XXX. The Supreme Judicial Court concluded that the ability to defer the imposition of sentence was a valuable feature of the legal system, but not necessary to the very existence of a court and, accordingly, not an inherent judicial power. The court also reasoned that, taken to its logical extreme, the unfettered ability to defer the imposition of sentence would strip all legislative power from the General Court, contrary to the Constitution. Because the court did not recognize the power to defer the imposition of sentence as inherently judicial, the statute prescribing mandatory minimums for illegal gun possession did not represent a violation of Article XXX.

Included in the power to establish criminal penalties is the authority of the Legislature to define methods of criminal practice and procedure. See *Commonwealth v. Pyles* (1996). In *Commonwealth v. Pyles,* the Commonwealth appealed the judge's disposition of Pyles's case on grounds that the disposition intruded on the executive power of the district attorney. Pyles had allegedly cocked and pointed a handgun at his twelve-year-old nephew. He entered a plea of guilty and the judge ordered the case continued for one year and then dismissed on conditions that Pyles enter a substance abuse treatment program and pay certain expenses to the victim's mother. Because the statute only established methods of criminal practice and procedure, the Legislature did not intrude upon the district attorney's authority: "[t]he disposition provided for in [the statute] flow[ed] from, and [was] encompassed within, the Legislature's broad authority to classify criminal conduct, to establish criminal penalties, and to adopt rules of criminal practice and procedure." *Id.*

The General Court may delegate, to a board or officer of the executive branch, the authority to implement a legislatively adopted policy. See *Constr. Ind. v. Comm'r of Labor* (1993). In 1984, the court adopted a three-part test for determining the propriety of a legislative delegation of power: (1) The Legislature may not delegate the making of fundamental policy decisions but may delegate the implementation of legislatively determined policy; (2) the legislative act must "provide adequate direction for implementation, either in the form of statutory standards or," if the party delegated to "is to develop standards, sufficient guidance . . . to do so"; and (3) "the act [must] provide safeguards such that abuses of discretion can be controlled." *Chelmsford Trailer Park, Inc. v. Town of Chelmsford* (1984). Applying this test in *Chelmsford Trailer Park,* the Supreme Judicial Court held valid an act enabling towns to adopt by-laws to control rents and evictions in mobile home parks. The court reasoned that when the policy and purpose of the Legislature are clearly expressed, the absence of detailed standards would not itself render an act invalid. The court also concluded that the absence of a list enumerating reasons for eviction did not render the statute invalid; such a list was also absent from other statutes governing evictions of tenants in mobile home parks. Finally, the act guarded against abuses of discretion by providing an opportunity for judicial review, thus making the delegation of legislative power valid.

The power of appropriation is implicitly granted to the General Court by the general power to legislate expressed in Part the Second, Chapter I, Section I, Article IV. The court has defined the power of appropriation as the authority "to set apart from the public revenue a certain sum of money for a specified object, in such manner that the executive officers of the government are authorized to use that money, and no more, for that object and for no other." *New England Div. of Amer. Cancer Soc. v. Comm'r of Admin.* (2002). There is a difference between the power of appropriation and the power to spend appropriated funds; the power to appropriate funds, reserved to the General Court, is the power to determine the purposes for which funds will be expended. *Amer. Cancer Soc. v. Comm'n of Admin.* (2002). The activity of spending money or the power to determine the "extent of expenditures committed to a particular purpose" is executive in nature.

The General Court, incidental to the power of appropriation, may "prescribe in detail the particular purposes for which money appropriated shall be expended or permit executive or administrative officers to exercise judgment and discretion within a wide field in the expenditure of money appropriated for a given object to accomplish the general purposes of the appropriation." *Opinion of the Justices* (1939). In a 1939 advisory opinion, the Supreme Judicial Court held valid a statute authorizing the Governor, with the consent of a special recess commission, to transfer funds from the general fund in the case of an emergency. Because the Governor's role amounted only to exercising the power of expenditure under the statute, the court found no abandonment of the General Court's appropriation power. See also *Amer. Cancer Soc. v. Comm'n of Admin.* (2002) (concluding that the General Court's authorization to the Governor, to reduce allotments for expenditure appropriated in 2002 for smoking prevention and multiple sclerosis, was a valid exercise of the Governor's spending power and not an abandonment of the General Court's power of appropriation).

The Power to Create Public Offices

The General Court under Part II, ch. I, § I, art. IV, has the express power to create public offices. Incidental to creating public offices, the General Court may confer the power of appointment upon the executive branch, make a public official an automatic member of a newly created commission, and remove public officers from a statutorily created office. *Collins v. Selectmen of Brookline* (1950). In *Sheridan v. Gardner* (1964), for example, the Supreme Judicial Court held valid statutory provisions creating the Massachusetts Crime Commission and authorizing the executive branch to appoint members to the commission.

The General Court possesses the incidental power to remove a public officer from an office statutorily created. See *Collins v. Selectmen of Brookline* (1950). It may delegate this power to an executive officer or board as it sees fit, provided the delegation is "reasonably necessary for the proper performance of the executive or administrative duty entrusted to it." *Id.* In *Collin v. Selectmen of Brookline,* the petitioner, a member of the Brookline Housing Authority, challenged the constitutionality of the Town Selectman's authorization to remove him from Housing Authority. The power to remove members of the housing authority on grounds of inefficiency, neglect of duty and misconduct in office was conferred upon the Selectman by statute. Because the power to remove a public officer was incidental to another legislative power, the court held that the General Court could confer the power upon an executive officer or board.

The Power to Establish Subordinate Courts

Part II, ch. I, § I, art. III, expressly confers upon the General Court the power to establish courts subordinate to the Supreme Judicial Court. Incidental to this power is the authority to "modify, enlarge, diminish, or abolish" the jurisdictions of all courts subordinate to the Supreme Judicial Court. See *Opinion of the Justices* (1943). This also includes the authority, when the Legislature has an enumerated power as to the subject matter of a particular case or set of cases, to establish rules for, and limit the power of, the courts. See *Russell Box Co. v. Comm'r of Corps. & Taxation* (1950). For example, in *Russell Box Co.*, the Supreme Judicial Court upheld a statute requiring corporations to remain as corporations for the purposes of prosecuting and defending suits for three years after it their dissolution. Because the dissolution of corporations was a matter of legislative cognizance, the General Court had the authority to pass the statute and to set rules for courts to follow in that area. The Legislature may also delegate, to a judicial officer, the authority to fix, limit, or change the jurisdiction of courts subordinate to the Supreme Judicial Court.

More recent cases indicate that the General Court may delegate its legislative power to a judicial officer only if the judicial officer—through the delegation—would be performing an act closely related to customary judicial activities. For example, in a 1977 advisory opinion, the Supreme Judicial Court upheld a statute authorizing the Chief Justice of the Supreme Judicial Court to "establish, revise or abolish divisions of the Superior or District Courts." *Opinion of the Justices* (1977). According to the court, when determining the constitutionality of a statute like the one in question, the test is "whether the statute authorizes the courts to perform a function so closely connected with and so far incidental to strictly judicial proceedings that the courts in obeying the statute would not be exercising executive or nonjudicial powers." *Id.* Because the ability to establish, revise, or abolish divisions of the Superior or District Courts was so strongly implicated in judicial administration, delegating that power to the Chief Justice was constitutional under Article XXX.

The General Court also has the incidental power to establish standards of conduct for officers of the courts. In a 1978 advisory opinion, the Supreme Judicial Court held that the General Court could require judicial officers, other than judges, to annually file financial interest statements that would be subject to public inspection. *Opinion of the Justices* (1978). The court reasoned that, although the judicial department had the authority to establish standards of conduct for judicial employees or officers, the General Court could establish complementary standards.

The General Court has the power to establish the rules controlling the admission and removal of attorneys at law. *In re Keenan* (1941). In *In re Keenan*, the petitioner, after having been previously disbarred, sought admission to the bar. The relevant statute provided that a U.S. citizen over the age of twenty-one could file a petition in the Supreme Judicial Court or Superior Court to be examined for admission and, if qualified, admitted as an attorney at law. Since controlling the conduct of attorneys is an inherent judicial power, the court construed the statute as in aid of judicial powers. The court found the petitioner's argument, that exclusive jurisdiction for these types of cases rested with the Supreme Judicial Court, unpersuasive. The General Court could authorize Superior Court jurisdiction over these types of cases provided the Supreme Judicial Court retained the power to review lower court dispositions.

Executive Power

Part II of the Massachusetts Constitution charges the Governor with executing the laws of the Commonwealth. See Mass. Const. Pt. 2, Ch. 2, § 1, art. I; Mass. Const. Pt. 2, Ch. 2, § 1, art. IV. The executive, like the legislative branch, possesses those powers incidental to executing the laws of the Commonwealth. Included in the executive's express powers is the power to appoint public officers and employees, the discretion to prosecute criminal cases, the power to execute judicial orders and the power to spend.

The Power to Execute Judicial Orders

Through its general power to execute the laws, the executive is responsible for executing a judicial order pursuant to those laws. See *In re Ierardi* (1973). In *Ierardi*, the petitioner challenged the governor's order to extradite him to Florida pursuant to a Massachusetts statute. See *id.* The petitioner claimed that the Governor did not have the power to send him to Florida because doing so would nullify a judicial order—his sentence. The Supreme Judicial Court concluded that the execution of a sentence is attributable to the executive branch; moreover, laws granting the executive branch authority over the terms of a sentence and in effect at the time sentencing must be viewed as part of the sentence. Because the petitioner's extradition was allowed by statute, it did not amount to nullification of a judicial order; it only served to delay the execution of the sentence.

The executive also enjoys the incidental power to determine the manner in which a judicial order, pursuant to the laws of the Commonwealth, is executed. For example, in *Gray v. Dept. of Revenue* (1996), the Supreme Judicial Court held that the Department of Revenue may seize the bank and credit card accounts of an obligor ordered—by the Probate Court—to pay child support arrearages. The plaintiff claimed that the Department of Revenue had violated Article XXX by seizing his bank and credit union accounts in order to force his compliance with the child support order. The court held that the Department, by levying Gray's property, did not unconstitutionally modify a judicial order; it only determined the manner of its enforcement.

The Power to Appoint and to Remove Public Officials

The creation of public offices is the responsibility of the General Court. But the Constitution confers upon the Governor, with the advice and consent of the Executive Council, the power to appoint certain public officials, including judicial officers, to the public offices created by the General Court. See Mass. Const. Pt. 2, Ch. II, § I, art. IX. The Governor has the discretion to choose the method by which he will carry out appointments. In a 1975 advisory opinion, for example, the Supreme Judicial Court held that the Governor could create a judicial nominating commission to advise him in appointing judges. See *Opinion of the Justices* (1975). The creation of a judicial nominating commission falls within the ambit of the executive's incidental power; further, because the commission had no sovereign power to select judges and was created by a revocable executive order, the court determined that the Governor had not abandoned his power of appointment. As well, the executive possesses the incidental power to remove a public officer from his position. See *Opinion of the Justices* (1939) ("The power to appoint and the power to remove officers are in their nature executive powers.").

The Power of the Executive in Criminal Matters

The executive, through the action of a district attorney or other attorney authorized by an executive, has discretion in prosecuting a criminal case, see *Commonwealth v. Gordon* (1991), including the power to participate in probation hearings, the power to execute criminal sentences, and the power to enter or deny a *nolle prosequi*. See *Commonwealth v. Dascalakis* (1923). The executive has the power to pardon for criminal offenses. *Opinion of the Justices* (1938). The Governor, with the advice of the Executive Counsel, is explicitly granted the power to pardon those not convicted before the Senate by impeachment of the House by Part II, Chapter II, Section I, Article VIII. In a 1938 advisory opinion, the Governor and Executive Council asked the Supreme Judicial Court whether "the Governor by and with the advice of the Executive Council [has] power to pardon for criminal contempt of court . . ." Although the power to punish for contempt is inherently judicial and may not be restricted by the Legislature, the court held that the executive may pardon those convicted of criminal contempt just as it may do so in connection with all other crimes.

The Power to Spend Appropriated Funds

Part II, Chapter II, Section I, Article XI, confers upon the executive branch the power to direct the spending of appropriated funds; the power to determine the "extent of expenditures committed to a particular purpose" is executive in nature. But the Governor may not spend funds for any purpose other than the one for which they are appropriated, though he or she may use his or her discretion in respect to the amount of appropriated funds spent. See *Opinion of the Justices* (1978). The Supreme Judicial Court has concluded that it would be unconstitutional to require the Governor to spend the full amount of appropriated funds. The Governor must be allowed to "make[] a reasonable determination that the full legislative purpose can be accomplished by spending less than the legislative forecast or estimate represented by an appropriation." *Id.* While the Governor may decide to spend less than the full amount of money appropriated for a certain purpose, he or she may not withhold funds altogether; the Governor has an obligation to carry out the legislative purpose.

The Governor also has the negative power of appropriation before a bill is enacted. The governor has general veto power over proposed bills transmitted to him by the General Court. See Mass. Const. Pt. 2, Ch. 1, § 1, Art. II. In addition, Section V of Article LXIII of the Articles of Amendment to the Constitution, as amended by Article XC, provides that the "governor may disapprove or reduce items or parts of items in any bill appropriating money." Mass. Const. Amend. Art. XC. This power is illustrated in *Barnes v. Sec. of Admin.*, in which the plaintiffs claimed that, by reducing the appropriation for a certain program, the Governor had violated Article XXX. See *Barnes v. Sec. of Admin.* (1992). The court held that the Governor's negative power of appropriation under Section V of Article LXIII was coextensive with that of the Legislature and thus no violation had occurred.

Judicial Power

In addition to those powers expressly conferred by Part II, ch. II, the judicial branch possesses inherent powers "which regarded by themselves in the abstract, might be deemed legislative or executive [but are] considered proper to be exercised by the courts because they were intimately connected with and necessary or auxiliary to the exercise of strictly judicial powers." *LaChapelle v. United Shoe Mach. Co.* (1945). Inherent powers concern not only adjudication but also include ancillary functions essential for the courts to carry out their constitutional mandate. *Opinion of the Justices* (1977). The General Court may recognize inherent judicial powers but they exist without statutory authorization and cannot be restricted or abolished by the Legislature. *Diluzo v. United Elec., Radio & Mach.* (1984). Inherent powers are those essential to the functioning of the judicial department, the maintenance of its authority or its capacity to decide cases. See *First Justice of the Bristol Div. of the Juvenile Ct. Dept. v. Clerk-Magistrate of the Bristol Div. of the Juvenile Ct. Dept.* (2003).

The concept of inherent judicial powers flows from the principles stated in Articles XXIX and XI, as discussed above. Inherent judicial powers include the authority to make rules governing the internal organization of courts and to control the practice of law. See *Collins v. Godfrey* (1949). In *Collins v. Godfrey*, the plaintiff, an attorney and special justice of the District Court of Springfield who had given advice on the defendant's intestate, disputed the validity of a rule adopted by the court providing that special justices would not be retained or employed or practice as attorneys on the criminal side of any court in the Commonwealth. The Supreme Judicial Court held that it was an inherent power of the court to establish such rules and there had been no violation of Article XXX.

Closely related is the inherent power to control and supervise personnel within the judicial system. This includes the ability to control the admission to the bar of persons found qualified to be attorneys and the removal of those once admitted and "found to be unfaithful to their trust." *Opinion of the Justices* (1939). The Supreme Judicial Court has the inherent power to supervise and discipline judges and lesser functionaries, including clerks, though they may be elected, because they are essential to the function of a court in the proper performance of their duties. This power also applies to probation officers, whose work is intimately connected to the function of the judiciary.

Judges have the authority to control judicial proceedings, the conduct of participants, officers of the court, and the general environment of the courtroom. *Chief Admin. Justice v. Labor Rel. Comm'n* (1989). This includes the authority to hold a defendant without bail. See *Querubin v. Commonwealth* (2003). Similarly, courts have the inherent power to punish for contempt. See *Opinion of the Justices* (1943).

A judge has the inherent power to enter a finding of not guilty immediately following a prosecutor's opening statement subject to certain qualifications. See *Commonwealth v. Lowder*. Doing so is proper where the statement by the prosecutor clearly admits a fact which necessarily precludes a conviction or requires an acquittal, or includes all operative facts and is insufficient to sustain a claim for relief. Further, where finding of not guilty seems proper, two procedural safeguards must be followed: "(1) counsel must be given full opportunity to be heard and (2) the trial judge must give careful consideration to alternatives." *Id.*

An officer of the judicial branch may enter into a voluntary agreement with the executive branch where there is no interference with legislative or executive authority. See *Clerk of the Super. Ct. v. Treasurer* (1982). *Clerk of the Superior Court v. Treasurer* concerned a situation in which the Chief Administrative Justice and Treasurer and Receiver General by voluntary agreement implemented a program by which the chief directed that monies received by the Superior Court would be consolidated and invested for the benefit of the Commonwealth. Because, the court held, each branch participated voluntarily and there was no danger of interference by either branch with the other, the system did not violate Article XXX.

Separation of Powers Issues

Though the lines between the three branches of government in the Commonwealth may seem clear, it is not uncommon for one branch to interfere with another branch's powers. This interference is generally an unintended effect of each branch attempting to carry out its powers.

Legislative Interference with the Executive's Powers and Duties

The General Court may not statutorily convey the general executive power to itself. In a 1986 advisory opinion, the Supreme Judicial Court considered questions propounded by the Senate regarding the constitutionality of Senate No. 1763. The bill, stating that there was an urgent need to establish a program for the management and disposal of low-level radioactive waste, gave the executive branch the authority to establish criteria for selecting a location for the proposed waste management facility. *Opinion of the Justices* (1986). The bill also provided that once the Department of Public Health issued a license for the facility, a vote by each House would approve or disapprove the proposed site and the "technology or means to be utilized at the . . . facility" there. *Id.* The Supreme Judicial Court held that the final vote by the Legislature, approving or disapproving the waste facility, was an unconstitutional interference with the executive branch. Because the bill provided that one House of the Legislature alone could—by disapproval—effectively veto the executive decision to grant a license, there was an interference with the executive power to execute the laws of the Commonwealth.

The Legislature may not confer the power of appointment on its own members. *Opinion of the Justices* (1974); *Opinion of the Justices* (1939). In a 1939 advisory opinion, the Senate propounded the question of whether a bill establishing a special recess commission to be appointed "by the President of the Senate and the Speaker of the House of Representatives of three and five persons, respectively" would violate Article XXX. Because the function of those appointed would be to spend appropriated funds and not to exercise some power incidental to the legislative or appropriation power, appointments could not be constitutional as legislative delegations of power. The Supreme Judicial Court held that members of the General Court could exercise the power to create public offices but could not appoint individuals to fill those offices, as that is an executive function. Because the President of the Senate and Speaker of the House were members of the General Court, the statutory provision for appointment of the commission was an unconstitutional interference by the legislative with the executive branch. The Legislature also may not confer the power of appointment on a member of the Supreme Judicial Court, where making the appointment is not judicial in nature, as it is an interference with the executive branch.

Abandoning powers by conferring them upon another branch of government will also be considered interference by the Legislature. For example, the Legislature may not delegate its appropriation power to the executive branch because doing so would constitute abandonment of that power. A 1999 advisory opinion considered questions propounded by the Senate regarding a bill creating the Commonwealth Stabilization Fund and prohibiting the General Court from appropriating from the fund unless "[t]he Governor first makes a finding of a defined fiscal emergency." *Opinion of the Justices* (1999). The Senate asked whether making an appropriation contingent on a determination made by the Governor violated Article XXX. Although the bill provided standards to guide the Governor in his determination, this was not a determination made regarding the power to spend, it was one restricting the General Court from its core function of appropriating funds. The Supreme Judicial Court stated, "By conferring on the Governor the exclusive power to initiate a law making and appropriation from the fund beyond that stated in art. 63, the proposed bill would deprive the Legislature of its full authority to pass laws making appropriation." *Id.* Article LXIII gives the Governor the power to "disapprove or reduce items or parts of items in any bill appropriating money" subject to the Legislature's power to overrule his veto by a two-thirds vote of each house. Mass. Const. Articles of Amendment LXIII § 5; Mass. Const. Pt. 2, Ch. 1, § 1, art. 2. The court ruled the Governor's power in the proposed bill went beyond that granted by Article LXIII.

Legislative Interference with the Judiciary's Powers and Duties

Just as the General Court cannot convey the general executive power to itself, it cannot usurp or regulate the powers of the judicial branch. In a 1943 advisory opinion, the Supreme Judicial Court held that a bill by the House of Representatives that sought to provide an automatic appeal and a stay of the sentence for anyone found guilty of criminal contempt violated Article XXX. *Opinion of the Justices* (1943). The court stated that the General Court could not take or hinder the free exercise of a judge's power to punish for contempt. The court highlighted a distinction between the Massachusetts and U.S. Constitutions. Under the U.S. Constitution, Congress created the Federal District and Circuit Courts, therefore, the U.S. Supreme Court held that Congress could restrict the courts' power to punish for criminal contempt. The Massachusetts Constitution, on the other hand, explicitly provides for separation of powers in Article XXX. For that reason the Massachusetts Legislature could not abrogate or render inoperative the courts' power to punish for criminal contempt.

The court has also held the Legislature's statutory authorization of re-litigation of criminal complaints that had been previously dismissed with prejudice to violate Article XXX of the Massachusetts Constitution. In *Department of Revenue v. LaFratta* (1990), the Supreme Judicial Court dealt with the re-litigation of a paternity suit previously dismissed with prejudice. In June, 1983, the Department of Public Welfare brought a criminal complaint against LaFratta on behalf of a mother who claimed he was the father of her child. LaFratta paid $3,000 to the Department of Public Welfare and the case was dismissed with prejudice In 1987, the mother brought her own action seeking a paternity determination and child support under a statute not in effect in 1983, which provided: "No proceeding hereunder shall be barred by a prior finding or adjudication under any repealed sections of chapter two hundred and seventy-three . . ." *Id.* The court held that because a dismissal with prejudice "constitutes an adjudication on the merits as fully and completely as if the order had been entered after trial," and because Article XXX "prohibits any legislative attempt to grant a new trial or rehearing in a cause in the courts, or to declare ineffective or reverse, annual, change, modify or affect the judgment of the court," the law was unconstitutional.

As the Legislature cannot authorize the re-litigation of a case where a court has made a judgment, it also may not nullify a court judgment through legislation. In *Spinelli v. Commonwealth* (1984), the Supreme Judicial Court considered an eminent domain case—once dismissed by the Superior Court and dormant for many years—restored by plaintiff's motion and made inactive again by an order vacating the granting of plaintiff's motion. The Legislature had passed a 1982 statute providing, "[n]otwithstanding any provision of law or judicial decision to the contrary, the civil case of Anthony Spinelli v. Commonwealth of Massachusetts, docket number 28087 of the superior court of Barnstable County shall be restored to the status of said case of March thirty-first, nineteen hundred and sixty-five in said court." *Id.* Because the statute superseded a judgment of the court, which "must stand as final" and be "reversed, modified or superceded only by judicial process" it violated Article XXX. *Id.*

The Legislature also may not vest control over the judiciary in an executive commission. See *Opinion of the Justices* (1974). In an advisory opinion concerning the establishment of a Data Processing and Telecommunications Commission, the Supreme Judicial Court held that the Legislature had authorized an executive commission to interfere with judicial functions. Concerned with the degree of control the commission would over the use of data gathered by the judiciary, the court held the creation of the commission would violate Article XXX. The court emphasized that its decision did not preclude the judiciary from voluntarily participating in the sharing of data-processing facilities and services.

Unconstitutional Legislative Delegation of Power

The Legislature my not abandon the general legislative power granted it by Part the Second, Chapter I, Section I, of the Massachusetts Constitution. The Supreme Judicial Court found such abandonment when the House of Representatives asked whether it was "constitutionally competent for the General Court to provide that any town that had adopted a town manager form of government may make amendments in such form of government without enabling legislation being enacted by the General Court." *Opinion of the Justices* (1952). The General Court holds the power to prescribe, regulate, or alter municipal governments; it may not transfer that power to cities, towns, or their inhabitants. The court concluded that allowing the municipal governments to make amendments where the Legislature had not laid down guidelines as to what amendments could be made was essentially handing the municipal governments the legislative power to establish and maintain uniformity in the form of municipal governments in the Commonwealth. The court stated that the General Court may delegate to municipal governments the power to "fill[] in . . . the details of a board policy laid down by the Legislature[,]" but because the proposed bill would have the General Court wholly abandon its power to establish the form of municipal governments, it violated Article XXX. *Id.*

Executive Interference

In addition to the violations and executive interferences discussed above, officers of the executive branch may not deny rights in violation of a court order. In *Hoffer v. Comm'r of Corr.* (1986), the Commissioner challenged a single judge's order barring him, the Department of Corrections and Department employees from withdrawing—without the approval of the court—the right of Massachusetts Correctional Legal Services (MCLS) staff attorneys and paralegals to meet with inmates confined at the Massachusetts Correctional Institution at Cedar Junction and elsewhere. In holding that a government official violates Article XXX when it denies rights in violation of a court order, it found that the Department of Corrections violated Article XXX when it refused to allow a MCLS paralegal access to inmates.

Judicial Interferences with the Legislature's Powers and Duties

Because the Legislature holds the power of appropriation, the Judiciary violates Article XXX when it forces the executive to make an appropriation not approved by the Legislature. *Opinion of the Justices* (1939). In *Bromfield v. Treasurer and Receiver-General* (1983), the Supreme Judicial Court held that, where plaintiffs were owed just compensation pursuant to Article X of the Massachusetts Declaration of Rights in an eminent domain action, a court could not issue a mandamus compelling the Treasurer to make payment. Additionally, absent an unreasonable delay in payment, a court may not compel the Legislature to fulfill an obligation to a landowner in an eminent domain action. Although the court held a mandamus inappropriate in *Bromfield*, it did suggest that a court could later order recovery of the property to the plaintiffs by imposing a constructive trust on it. A court could also enjoin the agency responsible for the taking from taking any other land until the dispute with the plaintiffs is settled.

In a similar case, *Bates v. Dir. of Office of Campaign and Political Finance* (2002), the plaintiffs were owed money under the clean elections law. Because the executive officer in charge of the funds could not release them without direction from the Legislature, the Supreme Judicial Court held that it could not enjoin the office in an effort to force the release of the funds to the plaintiffs. Recognizing that the plaintiffs' judgment might remain unsatisfied, the court stated that a single justice would have broad discretion to prescribe other remedies, although those remedies were not identified.

Judicial Interferences with the Executive's Powers and Duties

The judicial branch may not perform a function assigned to the executive branch by the Legislature without specific authorization by the Legislature. See *Brach v. Chief Justice of the Dist. Ct. Dept.* (1982). *Brach* concerned the validity of an administrative regulation promulgated by the Chief Justice of the District Court Department requiring those convicted of certain motor vehicle offenses to surrender their driver's licenses to the court. Because the Legislature had assigned the subject of license revocation to the executive, a judge would violate Article XXX by exercising the revocation power under the administrative regulation.

Part the Second, Chapter II, Section I, Article II, as amended by Amendment LXXXV, provides: "Each branch of the legislature, as well as the governor or the council, shall have authority to require the opinions of the justices of the supreme judicial court, upon important questions of law, and upon solemn occasions," Mass. Const. Pt. 2, Ch.2, § 1, Art. 2. When there is no present duty, there is no solemn occasion, and the justices may not render an advisory opinion. The Supreme Judicial Court may not answer hypothetical or abstract questions of law in an advisory opinion.

Finally, a judge may violate Article XXX if she dismisses a case, in the interest of public justice, over the Commonwealth's objection. See *Commonwealth v. Cheney* (2003). In *Commonwealth v. Gordon,* the defendant was charges with two counts of murder in the first degree. Prior to trial, the defendant indicated a willingness to plead guilty to murder in the second, and, over the Commonwealth's objections, the judge accepted the pleas. On appeal, the Supreme Judicial Court held that dismissing prior to a verdict, finding, or plea without an evidentiary hearing and over the Commonwealth's objection, had the effect of entering a *nolle prosequi*—a province of the executive branch. A court may dismiss a case only when there is a legal basis; in the absence of a legal basis, a judge may not accept a plea to a lesser offense, thereby precluding the Commonwealth from submitting its case to a jury.

The Frame of Government

PART THE SECOND: THE FRAME OF GOVERNMENT

The people inhabiting the territory formerly called the Province of Massachusetts Bay, do hereby solemnly and mutually agree with each other, to form themselves into a free, sovereign, and independent body politic, or state by the name of "THE COMMONWEALTH OF MASSACHUSETTS."

CHAPTER I. THE LEGISLATIVE POWER

SECTION I. THE GENERAL COURT

ARTICLE I. Legislative Department
The department of legislation shall be formed by two branches, a Senate and House of Representatives: each of which shall have a negative on the other. The legislative body shall assemble every year [on the last Wednesday in May, and at such other times as they shall judge necessary; and shall dissolve and be dissolved on the day next preceding the said last Wednesday in May;] and shall be styled, The General Court of Massachusetts.

This Article was amended by Amendment X in 1831, to provide that "the general court assemble every year on the first Wednesday of January instead of the last Wednesday of May" and "dissolve on the next day preceding the first Wednesday of January."

This Article establishes a bicameral legislative department, consisting of a Senate and a House of Representatives. Because each branch "shall have a negative on the other," a bill must pass both the Senate and the House of Representatives, independently, before submission to the Governor. *Opinion of the Justices* (1939). A law may be enacted only when "one body conscious that the other has taken action and intending to agree with it expresses its approval." *Openshaw v. City of Fall River* (1934). In addition to lawmaking powers through the bicameral process, the Senate and House of Representatives respectively possess unicameral powers to establish internal rules of procedure. *Paisner v. Att'y General* (1983). Those powers are exclusively granted to the Senate and the House of Representatives through various provisions of Chapter I.

This Article also sets forth when the General Court will convene and grants the General Court the power to convene when it shall judge necessary, so that the Legislature could convene in cases of emergency and to address situations arising unexpectedly. *Opinion of the Justices* (1936). The General Court is not restricted as to the subjects it may consider when it self-convenes. *Id.*

ARTICLE II. Approval of Bill or Resolve by Governor; Veto; Passage over Veto; Failure of Governor to Return Bill or Resolve

No bill or resolve of the senate or house of representatives shall become a law, and have force as such, until it shall have been laid before the governor for his revisal; and if he, upon such revision, approve thereof, he shall signify his approbation by signing the same. But if he have any objection to the passing of such bill or resolve, he shall return the same, together with his objections thereto, in writing, to the senate or house of representatives, in whichsoever the same shall have originated; who shall enter the objections sent down by the governor, at large, on their records, and proceed to reconsider the said bill or resolve. But if after such reconsideration, two thirds of the said senate or house of representatives, shall, notwithstanding the said objections, agree to pass the same, it shall, together with the objections, be sent to the other branch of the legislature, where it shall also be reconsidered, and if approved by two thirds of the members present, shall have the force of a law: but in all such cases, the votes of both houses shall be determined by yeas and nays; and the names of the persons voting for, or against, the said bill or resolve, shall be entered upon the public records of the commonwealth.

And in order to prevent unnecessary delays, if any bill or resolve shall not be returned by the governor within [five] days after it shall have been presented, the same shall have the force of a law.

This Article was amended by Amendment XC, to allow the Governor ten days instead of five to approve or veto a bill or resolution and to return it to the legislative branch from which it originated.

This Article establishes a gubernatorial check on the Legislature. The Governor has the power to veto a bill or resolution after both branches of the General Court have approved it, at which point the bill or resolution is sent back to the branch in which it originated with the Governor's comments. If the Governor fails to return the bill or resolution within ten days, it will become a law as then written. *Opinion of the Justices* (1868). The Governor personally holds the duty of revisal; therefore, the bill or resolution must be presented to him personally, or to the person acting as Governor at the time, in order for the bill or resolution to become a law. *Id.* The Governor's veto power does not include the ability to veto part of a bill or resolution and approve the remaining portion; he must approve or veto the bill or resolution in its entirety. *Opinion of the Justices* (1936). The Governor retains his veto power in respect to laws proposed through initiative petition. *Opinion of the Justices* (1976).

The gubernatorial veto may be overturned by a vote of "two thirds" of the members present in both branches of the General Court, starting with the branch the bill or resolution originated in. The Supreme Judicial Court has made it clear that the vote need only be two-thirds of the members present for the vetoed bill or resolution to become a law. *Kay Jewelry Co. v. Bd. of Regist. in Optometry* (1940).

ARTICLE III. Power of General Court to Constitute Courts and Judiciaries; Power of Courts and Judiciaries to Administer Oaths or Affirmations

The general court shall forever have full power and authority to erect and constitute judiciaries and courts of record, or other courts, to be held in the name of the commonwealth, for the hearing, trying, and determining of all manner of crimes, offences, pleas, processes, plaints, actions, matters, causes and things, whatsoever, arising or happening within the commonwealth, or between or concerning persons inhabiting, or residing, or brought within the same, whether the amse be criminal or civil, or whether the said crimes be capital or not capital, and whether the said pleas be real, personal, or mixed; and for the awarding and making out of execution thereupon. To which courts and judicatories are hereby given and granted full power and authority, from time to time, to administer oaths or affirmations, for the better discovery of truth in any matter in controversy or depending before them.

This provision has not been amended.

The Supreme Judicial Court is the only court expressly created by the constitution of the Commonwealth. *Walton Lunch Co. v. Kearney* (1920). This Article grants power to the Legislature to create all other courts in the Commonwealth. *Opinion of the Justices* (1977). With that power the Legislature may and has created courts of general jurisdiction and courts of special jurisdiction, such as the Land, Probate, and Housing Court. *Id.* The Legislature also has the power to change the jurisdiction of or abolish existing courts as it sees fit. *Commonwealth v. Leach* (1923). In addition to creating courts, the Legislature may reorganize, enlarge, reduce, or in any other way alter the power of judicial officers provided the changes do not result in a demotion of the officer in violation of the constitutional provision on judicial tenure. *Opinion of the Justices* (1977).

The Legislature's powers under this Article are not unlimited, however. *Leach*. Other provisions of the constitution restrict the Legislature in various ways. For example, judges are to be appointed by the Governor only. *Id.* The Legislature may not establish courts whose judges can be removed during periods of good behavior. *Id.* See *infra* part 2, ch. 3, art. 1. Because the Supreme Judicial Court was created by the constitution as a co-ordinate department of government, the Legislature holds no power to alter its jurisdiction to modify its structure. *Russell v. Howe* (1858).

ARTICLE IV. Power of General Court to Enact Laws, etc.; Valuation of Estates

And further, full power and authority are hereby given and granted to the said general court, from time to time, to make, ordain, and establish, all manner of wholesome and reasonable orders, laws, statutes, and ordinances, directions and instructions, either with penalties or without; so as the same be not repugnant or contrary to this constitution, as they shall judge to be for the good and welfare of this commonwealth, and for the government and ordering thereof, and of the subjects of the same, and for the necessary support and defence of the government thereof; and to name and settle annually, or provide by fixed laws, for the naming and settling all civil officers within the said commonwealth; the election and constitution of whom are not hereafter in this form of government otherwise provided for; and to set forth the several duties, powers, and limits, of the several civil and military officers of this commonwealth, and the forms of such oaths or affirmations as shall be respectively administered unto them for the execution of their several offices and places, so as the same be not repugnant or contrary to this constitution; and to impose and levy proportional and reasonable assessments, rates, and taxes, upon all the inhabitants of, and persons resident, and estates lying, within the said commonwealth, except that, in addition to the powers conferred under Articles XLI and XCIX of the Amendments, the general court may classify real property according to its use in no more than four classes and to assess, rate and tax such property differently in the classes so established, but proportionately in the same class, and except that reasonable exemptions may be granted; and also to impose and levy, reasonable duties and excises, upon any produce, goods, wares, merchandise, and commodities, whatsoever, brought into, produced, manufactured, or being within the same; to be issued and disposed of by warrant, under the hand of the governor of this commonwealth for the time being, with the advice and consent of the council, for the public service, in the necessary defense and support of the government of the said commonwealth, and the protection and preservation of the subjects thereof, according to such acts as are or shall be in force within the same.

And while the public charges of government, or any part thereof, shall be assessed on polls and estates, in the manner that has hitherto been practiced, in order that such assessments may be made with equality, there shall be a valuation of estates within the commonwealth taken anew once in every ten years at least, and as much oftener as the general court shall order.

Amendment CXII, ratified in 1978, inserted in the first paragraph: "except that, in addition to the powers conferred under Articles XLI and XCIX of the Amendments, the general court may classify real property according to its use in no more than four classes, and to access, rate and tax such property differently in the classes so established, but proportionately in the same class, and except that reasonable exemptions may be granted."

This article grants to the Legislature the power to make all laws wholesome and reasonable for the good of the Commonwealth. *Hingham & Quincy Bridge & Tpk. Corp. v. County of Norfolk* (1863). "One of the main purposes of this general grant of power was to vest in the legislature a superintending and controlling authority, under and by virtue of which they might enact all laws not repugnant to the constitution, of a police and municipal nature, and necessary to the due regulation of the internal affairs of the commonwealth." *Id.* When using this law-making power—often referred to as "the police power"—the Legislature must have a reasonable basis for passing a law, rationally connected to the promotion of public health, safety, morals and the general welfare. *Zayre Corp. v. Att'y General* (1977); *Wyeth v. Thomas* (1909).

This Article grants the Legislature the power to impose and levy "proportional and reasonable assessments, rates, and taxes" upon the residents and property within the Commonwealth. See *Opinion of the Justices* (1929). For purposes of setting tax rates on property, the Legislature may establish no more than four classes with which to categorize all property in the Commonwealth. See *Salem & Beverly Water Supply Bd. v. Bd. of Assessors* (2005). In establishing the principle of uniformity of taxation of property, this Article mandates that taxes may be assessed differently among the four classes of property, but must they must be proportionate within each class. *Carr v. Assessors of Springfield* (1959). This Article also establishes the excise tax, placing the following two limitations upon it: (1) it must be reasonable, and (2) it must only be levied upon produce, goods, wears, merchandise, and commodities.

This Article also provides the Legislature the power to appoint officers and to settle the election of officers not expressly provided for by the constitution; and to set forth the duties, powers, and limits of the civil and military officers of the Commonwealth. With those powers the Legislature may enact laws relative to the holding of primaries and elections, including laws regarding the time for state primaries. *Opinion of the Justices* (1944). Though the power to appoint and remove officers is inherently executive in nature, the Supreme Judicial Court has held that this Article permits the Legislature to name annually all civil officers within the Commonwealth. *Opinion of the Justices* (1939).

SECTION II. THE SENATE

ARTICLE I. Election of Councillors and Senators; Number; Districts

[There shall be annually elected, by the freeholders and other inhabitants of this commonwealth, qualified as in this constitution is provided, forty persons to be councillors and senators for the year ensuing their election; to be chosen by the inhabitants of the districts, into which the commonwealth may from time to time be divided by the general court for that purpose: and the general court in assigning the numbers to be elected by the respective districts, shall govern themselves by the proportion of the public taxes paid by the said districts; and timely make known to the inhabitants of the commonwealth, the limits of each district, and the number of councillors and senators to be chosen therein; provided that the number of such districts shall never be less than thirteen; and that no district be so large as to entitle the same to choose more than six senators.

And the several counties in this commonwealth shall, until the general court shall determine it necessary to alter the said districts, be districts for the choice of councillors and senators, (except that the counties of Dukes County and Nantucket shall form one district for that purpose) and shall elect the following number for councillors and senators, viz.—

Suffolk	**Six**
Essex	**Six**
Middlesex	**Five**
Hampshire	**Four**
Plymouth	**Three**
Barnstable	**One**
Bristol	**Three**
York	**Two**
Dukes County and Nantucket	**One**
Worcester	**Five**
Cumberland	**One**
Lincoln	**One**
Berkshire	**Two]**

This Article was superseded by amendments XVI, XLIV, and CI.

ARTICLE II. Manner of Choosing Senators; "Inhabitant" Defined

The senate shall be the first branch of the legislature; and the senators shall be chosen in the following manner, viz. there shall be a meeting on the [first Monday in April,] [annually,] forever, of the inhabitants of each town in the several counties of this commonwealth; to be called by the selectmen, and warned in due course of law, at least seven days before the [first Monday in

April,] for the purpose of electing persons to be senators and councillors; [and at such meetings every male inhabitant of twenty-one years of age and upwards, having a freehold estate within the commonwealth, of the annual income of three pounds, or any estate of the value of sixty pounds, shall have a right to give in his vote for the senators for the district of which he is an inhabitant.] And to remove all doubts concerning the meaning of the word "inhabitant" in this constitution, every person shall be considered as an inhabitant, for the purpose of electing and being elected into any office, or place within this state, in that town, district or plantation where he dwelleth, or hath his home.

The selectmen of the several towns shall preside at such meetings impartially; and shall receive the votes of all the inhabitants of such towns present and qualified to vote for senators, and shall sort and count them in open town meeting, and in presence of the town clerk, who shall make a fair record, in presence of the selectmen, and in open town meeting, of the name of every person voted for, and of the number of votes against his name: and a fair copy of this record shall be attested by the selectmen and the town clerk, and shall be sealed up, directed to the secretary of the commonwealth for the time being, with a superscription, expressing the purport of the contents thereof, and delivered by the town clerk of such towns, to the sheriff of the county in which such town lies, thirty days at least before [the last Wednesday in May] [annually;] or it shall be delivered into the secretary's office seventeen days at least before the said [last Wednesday in May:] and the sheriff of each county shall deliver all such certificates by him received, into the secretary's office, seventeen days before the said [last Wednesday in May.]

[And the inhabitants of plantations unincorporated, qualified as this constitution provides, who are or shall be empowered and required to assess taxes upon themselves toward the support of government, shall have the same privilege of voting for councillors and senators in the plantations where they reside, as town inhabitants have in their respective towns; and the plantation meetings for that purpose shall be held annually [on the same first Monday in April], at such place in the plantations respectively, as the assessors thereof shall direct; which assessors shall have like authority for notifying the electors, collecting and returning the votes, as the selectmen and town clerks have in their several towns, by this constitution. And all other persons living in places unincorporated (qualified as aforesaid) who shall be assessed to the support of government by the assessors of an adjacent town, shall have the privilege of giving in their votes for councillors and senators in the town where they shall be assessed, and be notified of the place of meeting by the selectmen of the town where they shall be assessed, for that purpose accordingly.]

The only portion of this Article which remains intact is the first sentence, stating that "the Senate shall be the first branch of the legislature." The portions dealing with the election of officers including Senators and Councillors has been amended by Amendments II, XV, XVI, LXIV, and CI. The portions dealing with the qualifications of voters and voting in general were amended by Amendments X, XX, XXX, XXXI, XXXII, XLV, XCIII, XCIV, and C.

ARTICLE III. Examination of Returned Copies of Records; Issuance of Summons to Persons Elected

And that there may be a due convention of senators on the [last Wednesday in May] annually, the governor with five of the council, for the time being, shall, as soon as may be, examine the returned copies of such records; and fourteen days before the said day he shall issue his summons to such persons as shall appear to be chosen by [a majority of] voters, to attend on that day, and take their seats accordingly: provided nevertheless, that for the first year the said returned copies shall be examined by the president and five of the council of the former constitution of government; and the said president shall, in like manner, issue his summons to the persons so elected, that they may take their seats as aforesaid.

Amendment X changed the date of convention from the last Wednesday in May to the first Wednesday of January. Amendment XIV removed the term "majority" and states that the official with the "highest number of votes shall be deemed and declared to be elected." This Article establishes a formal procedure for counting votes. It also provides that the Governor along with five Council members are to issue a summons to each elected official fourteen days before the convention of Senators so each shall appear and take their seats on the first Wednesday of January.

ARTICLE IV. Senate as Final Judge of Elections; Returns and Qualifications of their Own Members; Vacancies

The senate shall be the final judge of the elections, returns and qualifications of their own members, as pointed out in the constitution; and shall, [on the said last Wednesday in May] [annually,] determine and declare who are elected by each district, to be senators [by a majority of votes; and in case there shall not appear to be the full number of senators returned elected by a majority of votes for any district, the deficiency shall be supplied in the following manner, viz.: The members of the house of representatives, and such senators as shall be declared elected, shall take the names of such persons as shall be found to have the highest number of votes in such district, and not elected, amounting to twice the number of senators wanting, if there be so many voted for; and out of these shall elect by ballot a number of senators sufficient to fill up the vacancies in such district; and in this manner all such vacancies shall be filled up in every district of the commonwealth; and in like manner all vacancies in the senate, arising by death, removal out of the state, or otherwise, shall be supplied as soon as may be, after such vacancies shall happen.]

This Article was modified by the Amendments X and XIV, which changed the time for determining and declaring election results from the last Wednesday in May to the first Wednesday in January and declared the person having the highest number of votes to be the "elected." Amendments LXXX and LXXXII provide that Senators shall be elected biennially and Amendment XXIV requires that "Any vacancy in the senate shall be filled by election by the people of the unrepresented district, upon the order of a majority of senators elected."

This Article grants to the Senate the broad authority to regulate the election process of its own members. *Opinion of the Justices* (1978). With this power, the Senate has the final authority to judge the qualifications of its members. *Id.* In exercising this authority, however, the Senate may not "impede[] the right of the voter to exercise freely his choice of candidates or measures." *Id.* And all legislation aimed at the election process must be "reasonably necessary to achieve legitimate public objectives," for example legislation aimed at exposing conflicts of interest between candidates and the public interest. *Id.*

ARTICLE V. Qualifications of a Senator

Provided nevertheless, that no person shall be capable of being elected as a senator, [who is not seised in his own right of a freehold within this commonwealth, of the value of three hundred pounds at least, or possessed of personal estate to the value of six hundred pounds at least, or of both to the amount of the same sum, and] who has not been an inhabitant of this commonwealth for the space of five years immediately preceding his election, and at the time of his election, he shall be an inhabitant in the district for which he shall be chosen.

Following the ratification of Amendment XIII in 1840, a candidate for Senator no longer has to be "seised" of a freehold estate. The remaining portions of this Article were ultimately superseded by Amendment CI, requiring that Senators be residents of the Commonwealth for at least five years immediately prior to their election and that they be inhabitants of the districts they represent at the time of their election.

Although the "right to hold office is not necessarily co-extensive with the right to vote," a question was asked of the Supreme Judicial Court regarding the effect of the passage of the Nineteenth Amendment to the U.S. Constitution on the right of women in the Commonwealth to serve in political office. *Opinion of the Justices* (1922). Because the Nineteenth Amendment removed the word "male" from all constitutions in this country in respect to voting rights, and because "there ha[d] been, under the Massachusetts Constitution and under Massachusetts custom, equality among qualified voters as to eligibility for such officers as are recognized or created by the Constitution[,]" the court held women in the Commonwealth should have the right to run for political office. *Id.*

ARTICLE VI. Adjournments

The senate shall have power to adjourn themselves, provided such adjournments do not exceed two days at a time.

This Article authorizes the Senate to adjourn itself while it is in session provided the adjournment does not last longer than two days. *Opinion of the Justices* (1939).

ARTICLE VII. President; Officers; Rules of Proceedings

The senate shall choose its own president, appoint its own officers, and determine its own rules of proceedings.

This Article broadly empowers the Senate to establish rules regarding its own workings and to elect its own officers, including its President. *Paisner v. Att'y General* (1983). When the Senate establishes a rule of internal procedure, it need not seek approval of the House of Representatives or the executive; neither is it bound by actions taken by a prior Legislature—rules adopted in one session will not be binding upon later sessions. *Id.* In respect to electing officers of the Senate, the constitution does not specify the length of the term. The Supreme Judicial Court stated in an advisory opinion that the Senate may set the term for its officials, provided that term is not longer than the two-year life of each Senate. *Opinion of the Justices* (1921).

ARTICLE VIII. Impeachments

The senate shall be a court with full authority to hear and determine all impeachments made by the house of representatives, against any officer or officers of the commonwealth, for misconduct and mal-administration in their offices. But previous to the trial of every impeachment the members of the senate shall respectively be sworn, truly and impartially to try and determine the charge in question, according to evidence. Their judgment, however, shall not extend further than to removal from office and disqualification to hold or enjoy any place of honor, trust, or profit, under this commonwealth: but the party so convicted, shall be, nevertheless, liable to indictment, trial, judgment, and punishment, according to the laws of the land.

This Article authorizes the Senate to try all impeachments for misconduct or maladministration made by the House of Representatives against officers of the Commonwealth. Only officers of the Commonwealth can be impeached; therefore, it is important to determine who qualifies as an officer of the Commonwealth. *Opinion of the Justices* (1897). Not all civil officers are considered officers of the Commonwealth for impeachment purposes. *Id.* The Supreme Judicial Court has adopted the following test to determine impeachability: "Officers elected by the people at large, or provided for in the constitution, for the administration of matters of general or state concern, are subject to impeachment." *Id.*

For example, county commissioners, *Opinion of the Justices, supra,* district attorneys, *Attorney General v. Pelletier* (1922), and clerks of the district courts, *In re Dugan* (1994), are not officers of the Commonwealth for impeachment purposes. The Councillor, however, is an officer of the Commonwealth because the office is provided for in the constitution and the duties performed are for the administration of matters of general or state concern. *Opinion of the Justices* (1941). An officer of the Commonwealth may only be impeached for misconduct *or* maladministration in office. Activities outside his or her duties are not grounds for impeachment. *Id.* The Senate, with its impeachment powers, may remove an officer and disqualify that person from holding office for the remainder of the term. *Id.* Impeached officers may also face criminal penalties. *Opinion of the Justices* (1938).

ARTICLE IX. Quorum
[Not less than sixteen members of the senate shall constitute a quorum for doing business.]

This Article was superseded by Amendment XXXIII, ratified in 1891, defining a quorum as a majority of the Senate members.

SECTION III. THE HOUSE OF REPRESENTATIVES

ARTICLE I. Representation of the People
There shall be, in the legislature of this commonwealth, a representation of the people, [annually] elected, and founded upon the principle of equality.

This Article was amended by Amendments LXXX and LXXXII, ratified in 1950 and 1964, respectively, providing that the members of the House of Representatives be elected on a biennial basis. Because this Article provides that the election of Representatives is based on the principle of equality, each member of the House will represent the people of the Commonwealth equally; none will have a larger role than the other members.

ARTICLE II. Election of Representatives
[And in order to provide for a representation of the citizens of this commonwealth, founded upon the principle of equality, every corporate town containing one hundred and fifty ratable polls, may elect one representative: every corporate town, containing three hundred and seventy-five ratable polls may elect two representatives: every corporate town containing six hundred ratable polls, may elect three representatives: and proceeding in that manner, making two hundred and twenty-five ratable polls, the mean increasing number for every additional representative.

Provided nevertheless, that each town now incorporated, not having one hundred and fifty ratable polls, may elect one representative: but no place shall

hereafter be incorporated with the privilege of electing a representative, unless there are within the same one hundred and fifty ratable polls.]

And the house of representatives shall have power from time to time to impose fines upon such towns as shall neglect to choose and return members to the same, agreeably to this constitution.

This Article was superseded by Amendments XXXV and CI, ratified in 1893 and 1974, respectively. Amendment CI establishes that the House of Representatives shall have 160 members, each of which will represent an equal number of inhabitants as determined by the federal census. The only provision remaining from the original Article is: "The house of representatives shall have power from time to time to impose fines upon such towns as shall neglect to choose and return members to the same, agreeably to this constitution." This provision allows the House to fine towns that fail to elect Representatives in accordance with constitutional parameters.

ARTICLE III. Election by Written Votes

Every member of the house of representatives shall be chosen by written votes; [and for one year at least next preceding his election, shall have been an inhabitant of, and have been seised in his own right of a freehold of the value of one hundred pounds within the town he shall be chosen to represent, or any ratable estate to the value of two hundred pounds; and he shall cease to represent the said town immediately on his ceasing to be qualified as aforesaid.]

The original version of this Article included residency requirements which were annulled and superseded multiple times by various Articles of Amendment. Amendment CI provides for the establishment of legislative districts by using federal census information. The original property requirements of this Article were abolished by the Amendment XIII, ratified in 1840. The first sentence of this Article is the only provision currently in force, providing for written votes. The requirement that the vote be "written" does not preclude the use of voting machines. *In re House Bill No. 1291* (1901).

ARTICLE IV. Qualifications of a Voter

[Every male person, being twenty-one years of age, and resident in any particular town in this commonwealth for the space of one year next preceding, having a freehold estate within the same town, of the annual income of three pounds, or any estate of the value of sixty pounds, shall have a right to vote in the choice of a representative, or representatives for the said town.]

This Article was superseded by various Amendments. Age and residence requirements for voters are found in Article III, which itself has been amended multiple times. Article XX imposes limited literacy requirements. Article XXVIII as amended addresses the voting rights of veterans. Article XXX provides for change of residence as it relates to voter qualifications. Amendment XLV as amended empowers the general court to provide for absentee voting.

ARTICLE V. Time of Electing Representatives

[The members of the house of representatives shall be chosen annually in the month of May, ten days at least before the last Wednesday of that month.]

The subject matter of this Article is now addressed by Amendment XV, ratified in 1855, which provides in part that the meeting for the choice of Senators and Representatives shall be held on the Tuesday after the first Monday in November.

ARTICLE VI. Grand Inquest; Impeachments

The house of representatives shall be the grand inquest of this commonwealth; and all impeachments made by them, shall be heard and tried by the senate.

This provision allows the House of Representatives to impeach officers of misconduct or maladministration. After the House determines that a state officer should be impeached, the impeachment is handed to the Senate to be heard. *Opinion of the Justices* (1939). A state officer need only be accused of misconduct or maladministration, not both, before an impeachment is brought before the Senate. *Opinion of the Justices* (1941).

ARTICLE VII. Money Bills

All money bills shall originate in the house of representatives; but the senate may propose or concur with amendments, as on other bills.

Before enactment, money bills must pass both the House of Representatives and the Senate; however, they must originate in the House. Money bills are defined as those that call for appropriation of funds raised through taxation instead of appropriation of funds from the treasury. *Opinion of the Justices* (1958). "[T]he exclusive constitutional privilege of the House of Representatives to originate money bills is limited to bills that transfer money or property from the people to the State, and does not include bills that appropriate money from the Treasury of the Commonwealth to particular uses of the government." *Opinion of the Justices* (1878).

ARTICLE VIII. Adjournment

The house of representatives shall have power to adjourn themselves; provided such adjournment shall not exceed two days at a time.

This Article authorizes the House of Representatives to adjourn itself where it sees fit, provided the adjournment does not last more that two days.

ARTICLE IX. Quorum

[Not less than sixty members of the house of representatives, shall constitute a quorum for doing business.]

The original provisions of this Article are inoperative. The subject matter of this amendment is now covered by Amendment XXXIII, ratified in 1891, which provides that a majority of the members of each branch of the General Court shall constitute a quorum.

ARTICLE X. House as Judge of Returns; Elections and Qualifications of Its Members; Officers; Rules; Punishment for Offenses; Privileges of Members

The house of representatives shall be the judge of the returns, elections, and qualifications of its own members, as pointed out in the constitution; shall choose their own speaker; appoint their own officers, and settle the rules and orders of proceeding in their own house: They shall have authority to punish by imprisonment, every person, not a member, who shall be guilty of disrespect to the house, by any disorderly, or contemptuous behavior, in its presence; or who, in the town where the general court is sitting, and during the time of its sitting, shall threaten harm to the body or estate of any of its members, for any thing said or done in the house; or who shall assault any of them therefor; or who shall assault, or arrest, any witness, or other person, ordered to attend the house, in his way in going or returning; or who shall rescue any person arrested by the order of the house. And no member of the house of representatives shall be arrested, or held to bail on mesne process, during his going unto, returning from, or his attending the general assembly.

This Article authorizes the House of Representatives to exclusively judge elections and returns of its own members. *Dinan v. Swig* (1916). No other department has the power to make any decision on the subject nor does the House of Representatives have the power to delegate the power to any other branch of government. *Id.* Consequently, the Supreme Judicial Court has no authority to review a House decision to seat, or not seat, an individual. *Wheatley v. Secretary of the Commonwealth* (2003).

This provision also authorizes the House of Representatives to imprison nonmembers for contempt of, or disrespect to, the House. *Burnham v. Morrissey* (1859). This power does not extend to "contemptuous acts committed outside of the house before any commission composed of members of the house and others[,]" it reaches only to the "internal affairs of the house itself." *Opinion of the Justices* (1954). Disobedience of a House order warrants arrest and appearance before the House. *Id.* Further disobedience may result in imprisonment. *Id.*

The House is not all powerful in these matters; the Supreme Judicial Court may inquire into the legality of any such order for imprisonment. *Burnham*.

The House of Representative also possesses the power of expulsion. The Supreme Judicial Court has stated that "there is a marked difference between the power of punishment and the power of expulsion." *Hiss v. Bartlett* (1855). Although this Amendment does not expressly state that the House has the power to expel a member, "the power of expulsion is a necessary and incidental power, to enable the house to perform its high functions, and is necessary to the safety of the State" *Id.* This Article also prohibits a member of the House of Representatives from being arrested on his or her way to or from or during general assembly.

ARTICLE XI. Power of Senate, Governor, and Council to Punish; Power of Senate and House to Try Cases Concerning Their Rights and Privileges

The senate shall have the same powers in the like cases; and the governor and council shall have the same authority to punish in like cases. Provided that no imprisonment on the warrant or order of the governor, council, senate, or house of representatives, for either of the above described offences, be for a term exceeding thirty days.

And the senate and house of representatives may try, and determine, all cases where their rights and privileges are concerned, and which, by the constitution, they have authority to try and determine, by committees of their own members, or in such other way as they may respectively think best.

The Article provides the Senate, the Governor, and the Council with power similar to that of the House of Representatives in respect to punishing its members. It does not, however, contain a similar arrest clause. It is possible, but not clear, that the drafters intended to provide the Senate the same privilege with respect to arrest. *Luscomb v. Bowker* (1956). This Article, unlike Article X, limits imprisonment for any of the described offenses to a term of thirty day.

CHAPTER II. EXECUTIVE POWER

SECTION I. GOVERNOR

ARTICLE I. Supreme Executive Magistrate; Title

There shall be a supreme executive magistrate, who shall be styled, THE GOVERNOR OF THE COMMONWEALTH OF MASSACHUSETTS; and whose title shall be—HIS EXCELLENCY.

This Article establishes the Governor as the "supreme executive magistrate" of the Commonwealth. In carrying out the duties of that office, the Governor has the broad discretion to employ the "energies of the executive branch and the resources of the Commonwealth," as he or she sees fit. *Opinion of the Justices* (1978). For example, the Governor has the power to create a Judicial Nominating Committee, charged with advising the Governor with respect to the appointment of judges. See *Opinion of the Justices* (1975).

ARTICLE II. Term; Eligibility

The governor shall be chosen [annually:] and no person shall be eligible to this office, unless at the time of his election, he shall have been an inhabitant of this commonwealth for seven years next preceding; [and unless he shall declare himself to be of the Christian religion.]

Amendment VII, ratified in 1821, provides that no oath, declaration, or subscription shall be required of the Governor to qualify him to perform the duties of the office. Amendment LXIV, as amended, provides that the governor shall be elected quadrennially. Originally, only men were eligible to hold the office of Governor because one had to have the right to vote to hold office. *Opinion of the Justices* (1922). When the Nineteenth Amendment to the U.S. Constitution was ratified, making it illegal to prohibit someone from voting based on gender, the Supreme Judicial Court held that women in the Commonwealth had the right to hold political office, including the office of Governor. *Id.*

ARTICLE III. Election of Governor

Those persons who shall be qualified to vote for senators and representatives within the several towns of this commonwealth, shall, at a meeting to be called for that purpose, on the [first Monday of April] [annually,] give in their votes for a governor, to the selectmen, who shall preside at such meetings; and the town clerk, in the presence and with the assistance of the selectmen, shall, in open town meeting, sort and count the votes, and form a list of the persons voted for, with the number of votes for each person against his name; and shall make a fair record of the same in the town books, and a public declaration thereof in the said meeting; and shall, in the presence of the inhabitants, seal up copies of the said list, attested by him and the selectmen, and transmit the same to the sheriff of the county thirty days at least before the [last Wednesday in May]; and the sheriff shall transmit the same to the secretary's office, seventeen days at least before the said [last Wednesday in May]; or the selectmen may cause returns of the same to be made to the office of the secretary of the commonwealth, seventeen days at least before the said day; and the secretary shall lay the same before the senate and the house of representatives, on the [last Wednesday in May], to be by them examined: and in case of an election by a [majority] of all the votes returned, the choice shall be by them declared and published. [But if no person shall have a [majority] of votes, the house of representatives shall, by ballot, elect two out of four persons who had the

highest number of votes, if so many shall have been voted for, but, if otherwise, out of the number voted for; and make return to the senate of the two persons so elected; on which the senate shall proceed, by ballot, to elect one, who shall be declared governor.]

The original meeting dates in this Article were amended at various times. Amendment XV, ratified in 1855, provides for meeting on the Tuesday after the first Monday in November. The provision for meeting annually was superseded and annulled by several Amendments and eventually replaced by Amendment LXXXII, which provides that the Governor shall be elected quadrennially. The provisions for the performance of certain acts on or before the "last Wednesday in May" were superseded in 1855 by Amendment XIV, which requires that such acts be performed on the "first Wednesday in January." Finally, the provisions for election by a majority were superseded in 1855 by Amendment XIV, which provides for election of the person having the highest number of votes. Amendment XXXVIII allows for the use of voting machines or other mechanical devises during elections.

ARTICLE IV. Power of Governor and of Governor and Council
The governor shall have authority from time to time, at his discretion, to assemble and call together the councillors of this commonwealth for the time being; and the governor with the said councillors, or five of them at least, shall, and may, from time to time, hold and keep a council, for the ordering and directing the affairs of the commonwealth, agreeably to the constitution and the laws of the land.

This Article authorizes the Governor to call together the Council, which consists of the Governor, Lieutenant Governor, and eight persons elected biennially. *Pineo v. Executive Council* (1992). There are two situations in which the Council may act. *Opinion of the Justices* (1906). The first is when the Governor and the Council act together as an executive board and the other is when the Governor is acting alone, as the supreme executive magistrate, but with the "advice and consent" of the Council. *Id.* Whether the Council acts as an equal, together with the Governor, or whether it acts as advisory board, is determined by statute. *Murphy v. Casey* (1938). Because the Council meets at the discretion of the Governor, it is not subject to the open meeting law, and any attempt by the Legislature to control its internal affairs is a violation of separation of powers. *Pineo*.

ARTICLE V. Power to Adjourn or Prorogue General Court; Power to Convene General Court; Place of Convening
The governor, with advice of council, shall have full power and authority, during the session of the general court to adjourn or prorogue the same to

any time the two houses shall desire; [and to dissolve the same on the day next preceding the last Wednesday in May;] and, in the recess of the said court, to prorogue the same from time to time, not exceeding ninety days in any one recess; and to call it together sooner than the time to which it may be adjourned or prorogued, if the welfare of the commonwealth shall require the same: and in case of any infectious distemper prevailing in the place where the said court is next at any time to convene, or any other cause happening whereby danger may arise to the health or lives of the members from their attendance, he may direct the session to be held at some other, the most convenient place within the state.

[And the governor shall dissolve the said general court on the day next preceding the last Wednesday in May.]

The provisions of this Article relating to dissolution were superseded in 1831 by Amendment X, which provides that the General Court shall be dissolved on the day next preceding the first Wednesday of January, without any proclamation or other act of the Governor. This Article authorizes the Governor, with the advice of his or her Council, to call together the General Court before it is scheduled to convene, and to adjourn or prorogue (defer, suspend, or discontinue) the General Court during a scheduled session when both Houses agree. There is no express procedure that the Governor must use when calling the General Court together. When the Governor has called the General Court together, and the members of the General Court have complied with that order, the Supreme Judicial Court has stated that it "should not disturb the procedure adopted by the Governor and accepted by the Legislature." *Backman v. Secretary of the Commonwealth* (1982). The court further explained: "Where . . . the Constitution does not prescribe the procedures to be followed, this court should not reject the means selected by the Governor to achieve a constitutionally permissible end where the Legislature acquiesced in his determination." *Id.*

ARTICLE VI. Power to Adjourn or Prorogue General Court in Case of Disagreement Between Houses with Respect to Adjournment or Prorogation

In cases of disagreement between the two houses, with regard to the necessity, expediency or time of adjournment, or prorogation, the governor, with advice of the council, shall have a right to adjourn or prorogue the general court, not exceeding ninety days, as he shall determine the public good shall require.

This Article allows the Governor, with advice of Council, to adjourn or prorogue the General Court when it is to the benefit of the public good. The Governor possesses this power regardless of the agreement, or lack there of, between the two houses of the General Court. There is a limit of ninety days on any action taken by the Governor under this Article.

ARTICLE VII. Military and Naval Forces; Commander-in-Chief

The general court shall provide by law for the recruitment, equipment, organization, training and discipline of the military and naval forces. The governor shall be the commander-in-chief thereof, and shall have power to assemble the whole or any part of them for training, instruction or parade, and to employ them for the suppression of rebellion, the repelling of invasion, and the enforcement of the laws. He may, as authorized by the general court, prescribe from time to time the organization of the military and naval forces and make regulations for their government.

The text of this Article reflects the complete revision effected by Amendment LIV, and establishes the Governor as the Commander-in-Chief of the military and naval forces of the Commonwealth. It also authorizes the General Court to establish laws for the recruitment, organization, training, and maintenance of those forces. The power to determine who shall comprise the militia is exclusively granted to the federal government by the U.S. Constitution, therefore, "the legislature of this commonwealth cannot constitutionally provide for the enrollment in the militia of any persons, other than those enumerated in the act of congress of May 1792, ['an act more effectually to provide for the national defence by establishing an [*sic*] uniform militia throughout the United States']." *Opinion of the Justices* (1859).

Included in its powers under this Article, the General Court may provide for the construction of armories. *Hodgdon v. City of Haverhill* (1907). "[T]he legislature may reasonably treat the construction of armories as necessary for the maintenance of the militia in suitable efficiency, and accordingly it may order public money raised by taxation to be applied for this purpose." *Id.* In raising the money to construct and support an armory, the General Court may put a heavier tax burden on the town in which the armory is situated. *Id.*

ARTICLE VIII. Pardons

The power of pardoning offences, except such as persons may be convicted of before the senate by an impeachment of the house, shall be in the governor, by and with the advice of council, provided, that if the offence is a felony the general court shall have power to prescribe the terms and conditions upon which a pardon may be granted; but no charter of pardon, granted by the governor, with advice of the council before conviction, shall avail the party pleading the same, notwithstanding any general or particular expressions contained therein, descriptive of the offence or offences intended to be pardoned.

This Article was annulled by Amendment LXXIII, ratified in 1944, which added the provision giving the General Court the power to stipulate the terms and conditions of a pardon for a felony. This Article provides that the Governor shall possess the power to pardon; however, he or she must act with the advice of Council. *Ladetto v. Commissioner of Correction* (1977). Unless the Governor submits the pardon to the Council for advice, the pardon will not become effective. *Opinion of the Justices* (1906). In issuing a pardon, the Governor may hold the convict to conditions which, if violated, would result in the convict being returned to prison for the remaining part of his or her sentence. *Kennedy's Case* (1883). The Governor may also issue a pardon in the form of a reduced criminal sentence, for example reducing a death sentence to one of life imprisonment. *Commonwealth v. Arsenault* (1972).

ARTICLE IX. Nomination and Appointment of Judicial Officers and Certain Others

All judicial officers, [the attorney-general,] the solicitor-general, [all sheriffs,] coroners, [and registers of probate,] shall be nominated and appointed by the governor, by and with the advice and consent of the council; and every such nomination shall be made by the governor, and made at least seven days prior to such appointment.

This Article was amended by Amendment XIX, ratified in 1855, which provided for the election of sheriffs and registers of probate by the people of the several counties. The Amendment XVII, also ratified in 1855, removed "attorney-general" from this Article.

This article authorizes the Governor to nominate and appoint all judicial officers, the solicitor general, and the coroners with the advice and consent of council. In nominating and making appointments under this Article, the Governor "has broad discretion to select the means he will use." *Opinion of the Justices* (1975). For example, the Supreme Judicial Court held that the Governor was acting within his constitutional authority when he created the executive nominating commission to advise him with respect to the appointment of judicial officers. *Id.* The court concluded the Governor had not delegated his constitutional duty to nominate and appoint judicial officers, but had simply enlisted counsel. *Id.*

ARTICLE X. Military and Naval Officers

All military and naval officers shall be selected and appointed and may be removed in such manner as the general court may by law prescribe, but no such officer shall be appointed unless he shall have passed an examination prepared by a competent commission or shall have served one year in either the federal or state militia or in military service. All such officers who are entitled by law to receive commissions shall be commissioned by the governor.

The current version of this Article was ratified in 1918 as Amendment LIII. The Article authorizes the General Court to select, appoint, and remove military and naval officers. The General Court may prescribe by law the method by which it will carry out these duties. Because this Article does not establish a term of office for military and naval officers, the power to do so falls to the General Court. *Opinion of the Justices* (1914).

ARTICLE XI. Manner of Drawing Money from the Treasury; Purposes
No moneys shall be issued out of the treasury of this commonwealth, and disposed of (except such sums as may be appropriated for the redemption of bills of credit or treasurer's notes, or for the payment of interest arising thereon) but by warrant under the hand of the governor for the time being, with the advice and consent of the council, for the necessary defence and support of the commonwealth; and for the protection and preservation of the inhabitants thereof, agreeably to the acts and resolves of the general court.

This Article addresses withdrawals from the state treasury. "Because the activity of spending money is essentially an executive task," any disbursement of money from the treasury requires a warrant by the Governor, with the advice and consent of Council. *Opinion of the Justices* (1978). The Treasurer may not disburse any money from the treasury in the absence of a warrant from the Governor, nor may a court of law order the Treasurer to disburse money when the Governor has not issued a warrant. *Bromfield v. Treasurer & Receiver General* (1983).

Funds disbursed from the treasury must be spent on the necessary defense and support of the commonwealth. *Duffy v. Burrill* (1919). Because the money in the state treasury is raised by taxation, it may only be used for public purposes. *Opinion of the Justices* (1943). Although the Governor is obligated to issue warrants for disbursements of money appropriated by the General Court, the Governor is not obligated to spend money "foolishly or needlessly," or when the disbursement is not in accordance with the law. *Opinion of the Justices* (1978). It is also within the Governor's discretion to disburse less than the full amount of funds appropriated by the General Court if he or she "makes a reasonable determination that the full legislative purpose can be achieved by spending less than the legislative forecast or estimate represented by an appropriation." *Opinion of the Justices* (1978).

ARTICLE XII. Accounting by Public Boards and Officers, Letters, etc. of a Public Nature
All public boards, [the commissary-general,] all superintending officers of public magazines and stores, belonging to this commonwealth, and all commanding officers of forts and garrisons within the same, shall once in every three months, officially, and without requisition, and at other times, when required by the governor, deliver to him an account of all goods, stores, provisions, ammunition, cannon with their appendages, and small arms with their accoutrements, and of all other public property whatever under their care respectively; distinguishing the quantity, number, quality and kind of each, as particularly as may be; together with the condition of such forts and garrisons

and the said commanding officer shall exhibit to the governor, when required by him, true and exact plans of such forts, and of the land and sea or harbor or harbors adjacent.

And the said boards, and all public officers, shall communicate to the governor, as soon as may be after receiving the same, all letters, despatches, and intelligences of a public nature, which shall be directed to them respectively.

Amendment LIII eliminated the position of Commissary-General. This Article mandates that all public boards and public officials provide a quarterly accounting to the Governor. If at any time the Governor should request additional accounting from any public board or public officer, the same must comply with the request. The second paragraph of this Article requires public boards and public officers to report any and all information they receive that is of a public nature to the Governor promptly.

ARTICLE XIII. Salary of the Governor, Salaries of Justices of Supreme Judicial Court

As the public good requires that the governor should not be under the undue influence of any of the members of the general court by a dependence on them for his support, that he should in all cases, act with freedom for the benefit of the public, that he should not have his attention necessarily diverted from that object to his private concerns—and that he should maintain the dignity of the commonwealth in the character of its chief magistrate, it is necessary that he should have an honorable stated salary, of a fixed and permanent value, amply sufficient for those purposes, and established by standing laws: and it shall be among the first acts of the general court, after the commencement of this constitution, to establish such salary by law accordingly.

Permanent and honorable salaries shall also be established by law for the justices of the supreme judicial court.

And if it shall be found that any of the salaries aforesaid, so established, are insufficient, they shall, from time to time be enlarged as the general court shall judge proper.

This Article directed the first General Court to establish the Governor's salary and the salary of the justices sitting on the Supreme Judicial Court. The salaries were to be of a fixed value, established by law. By this Article, the General Court may increase the salaries of both the Governor and the Supreme Judicial Court justices if at any time the values are found to be insufficient.

SECTION II. LIEUTENANT GOVERNOR

ARTICLE I. Election of Lieutenant Governor; Title; Qualifications

There shall be [annually] elected a lieutenant governor of the commonwealth of Massachusetts, whose title shall be, HIS HONOR and who shall be qualified,

in point of [religion,] [property,] and residence in the commonwealth, in the same manner with the governor: and the day and manner of his election, and the qualifications of the electors, shall be the same as are required in the election of a governor. The return of the votes for this officer, and the declaration of his election, shall be in the same manner: and if no one person shall be found to have [a majority] of all the votes returned, the vacancy shall be filled by the senate and house of representatives, in the same manner as the governor is to be elected, in case no one person shall have [a majority] of the votes of the people to be governor.

The Lieutenant Governor is no longer elected annually, as this requirement was annulled by Amendment LXIV, ratified in 1918, which itself was annulled and replaced by Amendment LXXXII. The qualifications regarding religion and property were eliminated by the same Amendments, which did so for the position of Governor as well. The provision requiring election by a majority was superseded in 1855 by Amendment XIV, providing for election of the person having the highest number of votes.

This Article establishes the office of the Lieutenant Governor. The qualifications required to hold the office of the Lieutenant Governor are the same as those required of the Governor. By this Article, the Senate is authorized to fill any vacancies that may arise in the office of the Lieutenant Governor in the same manner it would fill vacancies in the office of the Governor. As with the office of the Governor, prior to 1922, when the Nineteenth Amendment to the U.S. Constitution was adopted, the office of Lieutenant Governor was held by a male. *Opinion of the Justices* (1922). After the Nineteenth Amendment gave women the right to vote, the Supreme Judicial Court held that women could not be prohibited from holding office. *Id.*

ARTICLE II. President and Member of Council

The governor, and in his absence the lieutenant governor, shall be president of the council, but shall have no vote in council: and the lieutenant governor shall always be a member of the council except when the chair of the governor shall be vacant.

This Article establishes the Governor as the president of the Council. As the president, the Governor does not have a vote in the Council. This Article also establishes that the Lieutenant Governor will always be a voting member of the Council, except in the Governor's absence. In that event, the Lieutenant Governor will take the seat of the Governor as the president of the Council and will not vote.

ARTICLE III. Acting Governor

Whenever the chair of the governor shall be vacant, by reason of his death, or absence from the commonwealth, or otherwise, the lieutenant governor, for

the time being, shall, during such vacancy, perform all the duties incumbent upon the governor, and shall have and exercise all the powers and authorities, which by this constitution the governor is vested with, when personally present.

This Article establishes that, in the event the Governor's chair becomes vacant, due to his or her death or absence from the state, all the powers and responsibilities of the Governor pass to the Lieutenant Governor.

SECTION III. COUNCIL, AND THE MANNER OF SETTLING ELECTIONS BY THE LEGISLATURE

ARTICLE I. Creation of Council; Membership; Meetings; Powers
There shall be a council for advising the governor in the executive part of government, to consist of [nine] persons besides the lieutenant governor, whom the governor, for the time being, shall have full power and authority, from time to time, at his discretion, to assemble and call together. And the governor, with the said councillors, or five of them at least, shall and may, from time to time, hold and keep a council, for the ordering and directing the affairs of the commonwealth, according to the laws of the land.

Amendment XVI, ratified in 1855, changed the number of Councillors from nine to eight. This Article creates the Executive Council as a part of the executive branch, the primary duty of which is to advise the Governor. Councillors need not be inhabitants of the district they are elected to represent. *Bigney v. Secretary of the Commonwealth* (1938). If the Council is to operate as an advisory body only, the Governor's decision on a given matter is his or her own to make and the Council's role is strictly to advise. *Id.* "Whether the Governor takes advice or not, his [or her] conclusion must rest finally upon his [or her] own judgment." *Id.* In giving its "advise and consent," the Council may hold a hearing at which witnesses will be called. *Murphy v. Casey* (1938). The Council may not, however, be compelled to hold a hearing. *Id.*

ARTICLE II. Number; Election
[Nine councillors shall be annually chosen from among the persons returned for councillors and senators, on the last Wednesday in May, by the joint ballot of the senators and representatives assembled in one room: and in case there shall not be found upon the first choice, the whole number of nine persons who will accept a seat in the council, the deficiency shall be made up by the electors aforesaid from among the people at large; and the number of senators left shall constitute the senate for the year. The seats of the persons thus elected from the senate, and accepting the trust, shall be vacated in the senate.]

This entire article was superseded by Amendment XVI in 1855. That article provides for eight Councillors and the manner of their election.

ARTICLE III. Rank of Councillors

The councillors, in the civil arrangements of the commonwealth, shall have rank next after the lieutenant governor.

This Article establishes the rank of Councillors in the hierarchy of state government, just below the Lieutenant Governor.

ARTICLE IV. Election by District

[Not more than two councillors shall be chosen out of any one district of this commonwealth.]

This Article was superseded by Amendment XVI, ratified in 1855, which provides that the Commonwealth be divided into eight districts and that one Councillor be elected from each district.

ARTICLE V. Register of Council

The resolutions and advice of the council shall be recorded in a register, and signed by the members present; and this record may be called for at any time by either house of the legislature; and any member of the council may insert his opinion, contrary to the resolution of the majority.

This Article "discloses the intent that the Council shall act in a formal manner upon matters coming before it, and that an official record of such acts shall be kept." *Scullin v. Cities Service Oil Co.* (1939). The register of Council is the only constitutional requirement in connection with the meeting of Councillors. *Pineo v. Executive Council* (1992).

ARTICLE VI. Succession in Case of Vacancy in Offices of Governor and Lieutenant Governor

Whenever the offices of governor and lieutenant-governor shall both be vacant, by reason of death, absence from the commonwealth, or otherwise, then one of the following officers, in the order of succession herein named, namely, the secretary, attorney-general, treasurer and receiver-general, and auditor, shall, during such vacancy, have full power and authority to do and execute all and every such acts, matters and things as the governor or the lieutenant-governor might or could lawfully do or execute, if they, or either of them, were personally present.

This Article established the order of succession should the offices of both the Governor and Lieutenant Governor become vacant. The original—providing that the Council assume the powers and duties of the Governor and Lieutenant Governor in the case of vacancy—was annulled in 1918 by Amendment LV, and replaced by the current Article.

ARTICLE VII. Adjournment of Elections; Order of Elections

[And whereas the elections appointed to be made by this constitution, on the [last Wednesday in May annually,] by the two houses of the legislature, may not be

completed on that day, the said elections may be adjourned from day to day until the same shall be completed. And the order of elections shall be as follows: [the vacancies in the senate, if any, shall first be filled up;] the governor and lieutenant governor shall then be elected, provided there should be no choice of them by the people: and afterwards the two houses shall proceed to the election of the council.]

The time for elections is fixed by Amendment X, ratified in 1831, which provides that the General Court shall assemble annually on the first Wednesday in January. Amendment LXIV, as originally ratified in 1918 and as subsequently amended, provides for the election of Councillors biennially. The procedure for filling vacancies in the Senate is prescribed by Amendment XXIV, ratified in 1860. Succession in the case of vacancy in the offices of Governor and Lieutenant Governor is covered by Part II, Chapter 2, § 3, Article 6, as amended. The election of Councillors is now prescribed by Amendments XVI and CI. The procedure for filling vacancies in the Council is found in Amendment XXV, ratified in 1860.

SECTION IV. SECRETARY, TREASURER, COMMISSARY, ETC.

ARTICLE I. Election; Eligibility

[The secretary, treasurer and receiver-general, and the commissary-general, notaries public, and naval officers, shall be chosen annually, by joint ballot of the senators and representatives in one room. And that the citizens of this commonwealth may be assured, from time to time, that the moneys remaining in the public treasury, upon the settlement and liquidation of the public accounts, are their property, no man shall be eligible as treasurer and receiver-general more than five years successively.]

This Article has been entirely replaced by certain Amendments. Amendments IV, LVII, and LXIX relate to the appointment of notaries public. The provisions of this Article which provided for a Commissary-General were originally superseded by the third paragraph of Amendment IV in 1821. That paragraph was annulled by Amendment LIII in 1918, which adopted the provisions currently governing the appointment of military and naval officers. The provision regarding successive terms for Treasurer and Receiver General was amended such that no person would be eligible for more than three successive terms. The Amendments dealing with this provision are the XVII and LXIV, as modified by Amendments XVIII and LXXXII.

ARTICLE II. Records of Commonwealth; Duties of Secretary; Deputies

The records of the commonwealth shall be kept in the office of the secretary, who may appoint his deputies, for whose conduct he shall be accountable, and he shall attend the governor and council, the senate and house of representatives, in person, or by his deputies, as they shall respectively require.

This Article establishes the Secretary as the custodian of the records of the Commonwealth. The Secretary may appoint a deputy of whose conduct the Secretary will be held accountable. Both the Secretary and any appointed deputies must answer to the Governor, Council, Senate, and House of Representatives at those branches' request.

CHAPTER III. JUDICIARY POWER

ARTICLE I. Tenure of Commission Officers; Term of Judicial Officers, Retirement

The tenure, that all commission officers shall by law have in their offices, shall be expressed in their respective commissions. All judicial officers, duly appointed, commissioned and sworn, shall hold their offices during good behavior, excepting such concerning whom there is different provision made in this Constitution; provided, nevertheless, the governor, with the consent of the council, may remove them upon the address of both houses of the legislature; and provided, also, that the governor, with the consent of the council, may after due notice and hearing retire them because of advanced age or mental or physical disability; and provided further, that upon attaining seventy years of age said judges shall be retired. Such retirement shall be subject to any provisions made by law as to pensions or allowances payable to such officers upon their voluntary retirement.

Amendment XCVIII, ratified in 1972, added the portion of this Article mandating that judges retire at the age of seventy. Amendment LVIII, ratified in 1918 added the "provided also" clause of this Article.

In the Commonwealth, only judges are considered judicial officers. *In re Dugan* (1994). This Article fixes the tenure for all judges in all courts in the Commonwealth, with an exception pertaining only to justices of the peace. *Opinion of the Justices* (1930). Judges are to hold office in good behavior and the General Court is powerless to prescribe otherwise. *Id.* Although judges in the Commonwealth hold office during good behavior, the Governor, upon the address of both houses of the General Court, may remove a judge from office for any cause deemed sufficient. *Commonwealth v. Harriman* (1883). This was intended to place a check on the judicial branch. *Id.* Although not expressed in this Article, the Supreme Judicial Court also has the power to hear and rule upon the misconduct of judicial officers. *In re DeSaulnier* (1972).

Because judicial officers may only be removed from office for cause, the General Court may not reorganize the courts in the Commonwealth in such a way as to demote any judge or to leave him or her without a position equal to his or her position prior to the reorganization. *Opinion of the Justices* (1977). A consolidation of the courts will not violate this Article, provided all judges affected or transferred maintain their office after the consolidation. *Id.* In 1972, the people of the Commonwealth voted to amend this Article, adding the provision that judges must retire upon reaching the age of seventy. The amendment has been upheld as valid under the Federal Age Discrimination in Employment Act. *Apkin v. Treasurer & Receiver General* (1988).

ARTICLE II. Opinions of the Justices of the Supreme Judicial Court
Each branch of the legislature, as well as the governor or the council, shall have authority to require the opinions of the justices of the supreme judicial court, upon important questions of law, and upon solemn occasions.

The original article was annulled by Amendment LXXXV in 1964 and the current text adopted. The Amendment substituted "governor or the council" for "governor and council."

This Article expressly authorizes the Supreme Judicial Court to render advisory opinions in very specific instances when requested by the other branches of government. *Answer of the Justices* (1913). Indeed, if such an instance exists, the justices have a duty to render an opinion. *Answer of the Justices* (1973). The purpose for this provision "is to enable the Justices to give such advise to the Legislature, the Governor and the Council as would be necessary to enable these departments to perform their duties in a manner consistent with [the Massachusetts] Constitution." *Answer of the Justices* (1977). Opinions issued under this Article are not binding; they are "open to argument in any judicial proceeding regularly brought before the courts" despite being accorded weight "as indicating what the law is." *Answer of the Justices to the Governor* (1913).

The Supreme Judicial Court may only answer important questions of law which are presented in the context of solemn occasions. *Answer of the Justices* (2005). This jurisdictional boundary ensures that separation of powers, established in Article XXX of the Massachusetts Declaration of Rights, is maintained. *Id.* A solemn occasion exists "when the Governor or either branch of the Legislature, having some action in view, has serious doubts as to their power and authority to take such action, under the Constitution, or under existing statutes." *Answer of the Justices* (1973). When an opinion by the justices would not aid the requesting body in carrying out a present duty, the Supreme Judicial Court is constitutionally prohibited from issuing an opinion. *Id.* In addition to the requirement that there be a present duty, the justices are further restricted from answering "abstract questions of law or hypothetical questions." *Id.* All questions propounded to the Supreme Judicial Court must contain a "definite statement of the point of difficulty." *Opinion of the Justices* (1982). If such a statement is absent or the justices are unable to ascertain what the important questions of law are, they may not issue an opinion.

Questions regarding the "effect or construction of a [current] statute" are not important questions of law or are they solemn occasions. *Opinions of the Justices* (1981). The justices of the Supreme Judicial Court have, on occasion, issued advisory opinions in cases where solemn occasions are not present. *Answer of the*

Justices (2005). In those instances, the justices generally make clear that their willingness to provide an advisory opinion stems from the specific circumstances presented and in no way does their action "establish[] a practice or depart[] from prior constitutional constraint." *Id.*

ARTICLE III. Commissions of Justices of the Peace; Expiration
In order that the people may not suffer from the long continuance in place of any justice of the peace, who shall fail of discharging the important duties of his office with ability or fidelity, all commissions of justices of the peace shall expire and become void, in the term of seven years from their respective dates; and upon the expiration of any commission, the same may, if necessary, be renewed, or another person appointed, as shall most conduce to the well-being of the commonwealth.

This provision establishes a seven-year term of office for justices of the peace, after which their commissions expire. All other court officers hold their office during good behavior, without a set termination date.

ARTICLE IV. Times and Places for Holding Probate Courts
The judges of probate of wills, and for granting letters of administration, shall hold their courts at such place or places, on fixed days, as the convenience of the people shall require; and the legislature shall, from time to time, hereafter appoint such times and places; until which appointments, the said courts shall be holden at the times and places which the respective judges shall direct.

Pursuant to this provision, notice must be given to interested parties that a petition in the Probate Court will be heard in a specific Probate Court, on a specific day and at a specific time. *Goodrich v. Hanson* (1921). In 1977, the Legislature passed a bill which combined the Probate Court, Land Court, Housing Court, and Superior Court. The Supreme Judicial Court approved this reorganization of the trial court, holding that it did not violate any constitutional provision. *Opinion of the Justices* (1977). The Probate Court is now referred to as the Probate and Family Court Department of the Massachusetts Trial Court.

ARTICLE V. Causes of Marriage, Divorce, and Alimony, and Appeals from Judges of Probate
All causes of marriage, divorce, and alimony, and all appeals from the judges of probate shall be heard and determined by the governor and council, until the legislature shall, by law, make other provision.

This provision vests the power to hear cases of marriage, divorce, and alimony in the Governor and Governor's Council. This was a temporary entrustment in the Governor and Council, most likely because the Province

Charter vested the power in this manner. *Sparhawk v. Sparhawk* (1874). This provision allowed the Legislature time to establish another arrangement under the law. *Id.* By 1869, the Legislature had taken steps such that all cases involving marriage, divorce, and alimony, and appeals from decisions thereof, were within the jurisdiction of the Probate Court. *White v. White* (1870). Neither the Governor nor the Governor's Council has the authority to hear such cases at this writing.

CHAPTER IV. DELEGATES TO CONGRESS

[The delegates of this commonwealth to the congress of the United States, shall, some time in the month of June annually, be elected by the joint ballot of the senate and house of representatives, assembled together in one room; to serve in congress for one year, to commence on the first Monday in November then next ensuing. They shall have commissions under the hand of the governor, and the great seal of the commonwealth; but may be recalled at any time within the year, and others chosen and commissioned, in the same manner, in their stead.]

This Chapter was annulled by the U.S. Constitution.

CHAPTER V. THE UNIVERSITY AT CAMBRIDGE, AND ENCOURAGEMENT OF LITERATURE, ETC.

SECTION I. THE UNIVERSITY

ARTICLE I. Harvard College

Whereas our wise and pious ancestors, so early as the year one thousand six hundred and thirty-six, laid the foundation of Harvard College, in which university many persons of great eminence have, by the blessing of GOD, been initiated in those arts and sciences, which qualified them for public employments, both in church and state: and whereas the encouragement of arts and sciences, and all good literature, tends to the honor of GOD, the advantage of the Christian religion, and the great benefit of this and the other United States of America—it is declared, that the PRESIDENT AND FELLOWS OF HARVARD COLLEGE, in their corporate capacity, and their successors in that capacity, their officers and servants, shall have, hold, use, exercise and enjoy, all the powers, authorities, rights, liberties, privileges, immunities and franchises, which they now have or are entitled to have, hold, use, exercise and enjoy: and the same are hereby ratified and confirmed unto them, the said president and fellows of Harvard College, and to their successors, and to their officers and servants, respectively, forever.

This Article establishes Harvard College, the undergraduate and oldest school of Harvard University.

ARTICLE II. Confirmation of Gifts, Grants, Etc.
And whereas there have been at sundry times, by divers persons, gifts, grants, devises of houses, lands, tenements, goods, chattels, legacies and conveyances, heretofore made, either to Harvard College in Cambridge, in New England, or to the president and fellows of Harvard College, or to the said college, by some other description, under several charters successively: it is declared, that all the said gifts, grants, devises, legacies and conveyances, are hereby forever confirmed unto the president and fellows of Harvard College, and to their successors in the capacity aforesaid, according to the true intent and meaning of the donor or donors, grantor or grantors, devisor or devisors.

This Article confirms that any and all gifts, grants, conveyances, etc. to Harvard College or to the president and fellows in their capacity as officials of Harvard College belong to the school.

ARTICLE III. Overseers of Harvard College; Alterations in Government
[And whereas, by an act of the general court of the colony of Massachusetts Bay passed in the year one thousand six hundred and forty-two, the governor and deputy-governor, for the time being, and all the magistrates of that jurisdiction, were, with the president, and a number of the clergy in the said act described, constituted the overseers of Harvard College: and it being necessary, in this new constitution of government to ascertain who shall be deemed successors to the said governor, deputy-governor and magistrates; it is declared, that the governor, lieutenant governor, council and senate of this commonwealth, are and shall be deemed, their successors, who with the president of Harvard College, for the time being, together with the ministers of the congregational churches in the towns of Cambridge, Watertown, Charlestown, Boston, Roxbury, and Dorchester, mentioned in the said act, shall be, and hereby are, vested with all the powers and authority belonging, or in any way appertaining to the overseers of Harvard College; provided, that] nothing herein shall be construed to prevent the legislature of this commonwealth from making such alterations in the government of the said university, as shall be conducive to its advantage and the interest of the republic of letters, in as full a manner as might have been done by the legislature of the late Province of the Massachusetts Bay.

This Article provides that the Legislature may alter the government of the university provided it is in the university's best interest.

SECTION II. THE ENCOURAGEMENT OF LITERATURE, ETC.

Wisdom, and knowledge, as well as virtue, diffused generally among the body of the people, being necessary for the preservation of their rights and liberties; and as these depend on spreading the opportunities and advantages of education in the various parts of the country, and among the different orders of the

people, it shall be the duty of legislatures and magistrates, in all future periods of this commonwealth, to cherish the interests of literature and the sciences, and all seminaries of them; especially the university at Cambridge, public schools and grammar schools in the towns; to encourage private societies and public institutions, rewards and immunities, for the promotion of agriculture, arts, sciences, commerce, trades, manufactures, and a natural history of the country; to countenance and inculcate the principles of humanity and general benevolence, public and private charity, industry and frugality, honesty and punctuality in their dealings; sincerity, good humor, and all social affections, and generous sentiments among the people.

This Article, the "education clause," expresses the Commonwealth's interest in and commitment to ensuring an educated citizenry. The Supreme Judicial Court squarely addressed the meaning of the clause in *McDuffy v. Secretary of the Executive Office of Education* (1993). That case involved a challenge to the educational funding system in the Commonwealth: the plaintiffs claimed the funding system was insufficient, and thus, was a violation of the education clause. The court ultimately concluded the education clause "imposes a mandatory duty on the 'legislatures and magistrates' to provide an adequate education to the young people of the State." *Id.* This duty is dynamic and will "evolve together with society." *Id.*

The Supreme Judicial Court addressed the education clause again in *Doe v. Superintendent of Schools of Worcester* (1995). In that case, the court held that, while the Commonwealth has a duty to educate its children and students have a right to an education, education is not a fundamental right. *Id.* Therefore, any denial of education by the state need only survive rational basis scrutiny, not the heavier burden imposed by a strict scrutiny analysis. *Id.* The court retreated from *McDuffy* still further in *Hancock v. Commissioner of Education* (2005). In *Hancock*, the plaintiffs challenged the extent to which the Commonwealth had fulfilled its obligation to provide an adequate education to its public school students. A plurality of the court affirmed that the Massachusetts Constitution obligates the Commonwealth to provide an adequate education, but concluded that the state had met its burden—the Legislature had responded to the *McDuffy* decision and, over the years, appropriated many millions of dollars toward addressing public education in Massachusetts. The government, the plurality reasoned, had not ignored its constitutional obligation.

CHAPTER VI. OATHS AND SUBSCRIPTIONS; INCOMPATIBILITY OF AND EXCLUSION FROM OFFICES; PECUNIARY QUALIFICATIONS; COMMISSIONS; WRITS; CONFIRMATION OF LAWS; HABEAS CORPUS; THE ENACTING STYLE; CONTINUANCE OF OFFICERS; PROVISION FOR FUTURE REVISAL OF THE CONSTITUTION, ETC.

ARTICLE I. Oaths, Declarations, Affirmations

[Any person chosen governor, lieutenant governor, councillor, senator or representative, and accepting the trust, shall before he proceed to execute the duties of his place or office, make and subscribe the following declaration, viz.—

"I, A.B., do declare, that I believe the Christian religion, and have a firm persuasion of its truth; and that I am seised and possessed, in my own right, of the property required by the constitution as one qualification for the office or place to which I am elected."

And the governor, lieutenant governor, and councillors shall make and subscribe the said declaration, in the presence of the two houses of assembly; and the senators and representatives first elected under this constitution, before the president and five of the council of the former constitution, and forever afterwards before the governor and council for the time being.]

And every person chosen to either of the places or offices aforesaid, as also any person appointed or commissioned to any judicial, executive, military, or other office under the government, shall, before he enters on the discharge of the business of his place or office, take and subscribe the following declaration, and oaths or affirmations, viz.—

["I, A.B., do truly and sincerely acknowledge, profess, testify and declare, that the Commonwealth of Massachusetts is, and of right ought to be, a free, sovereign and independent state; and I do swear, that I will bear true faith and allegiance to the said commonwealth, and that I will defend the same against traitorous conspiracies and all hostile attempts whatsoever: and that I do renounce and abjure all allegiance, subjection and obedience to the king, queen, or government of Great Britain, (as the case may be) and every other foreign power whatsoever: and that no foreign prince, person, prelate, state or potentate, hath, or ought to have, any jurisdiction, superiority, preëminence, authority, dispensing or other power, in any matter, civil, ecclesiastical or spiritual, within this commonwealth, except the authority and power which is or may be vested by their constituents in the congress of the United States: and I do further testify and declare, that no man or body of men hath or can have any right to absolve or discharge me from the obligation of this oath, declaration, or affirmation; and that I do make this acknowledgment, profession, testimony, declaration, denial, renunciation and abjuration, heartily and truly, according to the common meaning and acceptation of the foregoing words, without any equivocation, mental evasion, or secret reservation whatsoever—So help me, GOD."]

"I, A.B., do solemnly swear and affirm, that I will faithfully and impartially discharge and perform all the duties incumbent on me as ______: according to the best of my abilities and understanding, agreeably, to the rules and regulations of the constitution, and the laws of this commonwealth—So help me, GOD."

Provided always, that when any person chosen or appointed as aforesaid, shall be of the denomination of the people called Quakers, and shall decline

taking the said oath[s], he shall make his affirmation in the foregoing form, and subscribe the same, omitting the words ["I do swear," "and abjure," "oath or," "and abjuration" in the first oath; and in the second oath, the words] "swear and," and [in each of them] the words "So help me, God;" subjoining instead thereof, "This I do under the pains and penalties of perjury."

And the said oaths or affirmations shall be taken and subscribed by the governor, lieutenant governor, and councillors, before the president of the senate, in the presence of the two houses of assembly; and by the senators and representatives first elected under this constitution, before the president and five of the council of the former constitution; and forever afterwards before the governor and council for the time being: and by the residue of the officers aforesaid, before such persons and in such manner as from time to time shall be prescribed by the legislature.

This Article establishes the oaths that are required before taking office in the Commonwealth. The current form of the oath is prescribed by Amendment VI, ratified in 1821. The oath now reads:

> "I, A.B., do solemnly swear, that I will bear true faith and allegiance to the Commonwealth of Massachusetts, and will support the constitution thereof. So help me God."

A modified form of the oath is authorized for Quakers. Amendment VII, also ratified in 1821, states that the Governor, Lieutenant Governor, Councillors, Senators, and Representatives are required to take the oath of office and the oath prescribed by Amendment VI; no other oath is required to qualify them to perform their duties of office.

Though an oath is required before taking office, it is possible that an inadvertent error in administering an oath will not prevent an individual from taking office. See *Commonwealth v. Di Stasio* (1937). For example, the Supreme Judicial Court determined that a Superior Court judge was properly sitting on the bench despite an error in administering the oath to the Governor who appointed him. *Id.* The Court held that the "[t]he authority of the trial judge was recognized by the public as having been acquired under the forms of law and as being apparently valid[,]" as he had been a sitting judge for over a year. *Id.*

ARTICLE II. Plurality of Offices; Incompatible Offices; Disqualification for Office by Reason of Bribery of Corruption

No governor, lieutenant governor, or judge of the supreme judicial court, shall hold any other office or place, under the authority of this commonwealth, except such as by this constitution they are admitted to hold saving that the judges of the said court may hold the offices of justices of the peace through the state; nor shall they hold any other place or office, or receive any pension or salary from any other state or government or power whatever.

No person shall be capable of holding or exercising at the same time, within this state more than one of the following offices, viz.—judge of probate—sheriff—register of probate—or register of deeds—and never more than any two offices which are to be held by appointment of the governor, or the governor and council, or the senate, or the house of representatives, or by the election of the people of the state at large, or of the people of any county, military offices and the offices of justices of the peace excepted, shall be held by one person.

No person holding the office of judge of the supreme judicial court—secretary—attorney-general—solicitor-general—treasurer or receiver-general—judge of probate—[commissary-general—president, professor, or instructor of Harvard College]—sheriff—clerk of the house of representatives—register of probate—register of deeds—clerk of the supreme judicial court—clerk of the inferior court of common pleas—or officer of the customs, including in this description naval officers—shall at the same time have a seat in the senate or house of representatives; but their being chosen or appointed to, and accepting the same, shall operate as a resignation of their seat in the senate or house of representatives; and the place so vacated shall be filled up.

And the same rule shall take place in case any judge of the said supreme judicial court, or judge of probate, shall accept a seat in council; or any councillor shall accept of either of those offices or places.

And no person shall ever be admitted to hold a seat in the legislature, or any office of trust or importance under the government of this commonwealth, who shall, in the due course of law, have been convicted of bribery or corruption in obtaining an election or appointment.

This Article prevents certain state governmental officials from holding more than one "place or office"; it does not apply to city or town officials. *Wood v. Board of Election Com'rs of Cambridge* (1929). From time to time, the courts have been called upon to determine whether two appointed or elected positions are conflicting under this Article with differing outcomes. For example, the Supreme Judicial Court has held that a Superior Court judge may continue to sit on the Superior Court while serving on a local draft board at the appointment of the President of the United States without violating this Article. *Opinion of the Justices* (1940). Similarly, the Governor may hold a position on a committee charged with organizing a commemorative celebration without violating this Article. *Opinion of the Justices* (1958). On the other hand, the Governor may not maintain a membership in the Federal Defense Advisory Counsel. *Opinion of the Justices* (1955). In the event a government official, subject to this Article, accepts a conflicting office, "the acceptance of the second office is in law an implied resignation of the first, whenever it may be resigned by the mere act of the incumbent, without the assent or concurrence of a superior authority." *Commonwealth v. Hawkes* (1878).

ARTICLE III. Computation of the Value of Money; Property Qualifications for Office

[In all cases where sums of money are mentioned in this constitution, the value thereof shall be computed in silver at six shillings and eight pence per ounce: and it shall be in the power of the legislature, from time to time, to increase such qualifications, as to property, of the persons to be elected to offices, as the circumstances of the commonwealth shall require.]

In 1840, through the ratification of the Amendment XIII, the property qualification for certain offices was eliminated. The computation of the value of property is therefore no longer relevant.

ARTICLE IV. Form and Execution of Commissions

All commissions shall be in the name of the Commonwealth of Massachusetts, signed by the governor and attested by the secretary or his deputy, and have the great seal of the commonwealth affixed thereto.

This Article requires that the Governor sign commissions for all appointments stating that the individual took the requisite oath. Those commissions must be delivered to and attested by the Secretary of State or the Deputy Secretary.

ARTICLE V. Form and Execution of Writs

All writs issuing out of the clerk's office in any of the courts of law, shall be in the name of the Commonwealth of Massachusetts: they shall be under the seal of the court from whence they issue: they shall bear test of the first justice of the court to which they shall be returnable, who is not a party, and be signed by the clerk of such court.

"[A writ] is the foundation of [an] action and is the process by which the defendant is brought into court." *Union Savings Bank of Boston v. Cameron* (1946). Once a writ is issued and delivered to an officer with the intent that it be served upon the defendant, the action is commenced. *Id.* Because the writ is crucial to the commencement of an action, it must conform to the requirements of law. Specifically, the writ must be signed by the Chief Justice of the court from which it issues and it must bear the seal of that court. In addition, the writ must be signed by the clerk of the court. Irregularities in the form of the writ or in its service upon the defendant are fatal to the action if properly raised by the defendant. *Simonds v. Parker and Kittridge v. Bancroft* (1840). To successfully challenge the form or the service of a writ, the defendant must raise his or her objections before pleading to the merits. *Carpenter v. Aldrich* (1841).

ARTICLE VI. Continuation of Former Laws

All the laws which have heretofore been adopted, used and approved in the Province, Colony or State of Massachusetts Bay, and usually practiced on in the

courts of law, shall still remain and be in full force, until altered or repealed by the legislature; such parts only excepted as are repugnant to the rights and liberties contained in this constitution.

The original settlers brought with them various English laws and statutes. *Commonwealth v. Lopes* (1945). Those laws and statutes and others enacted prior to the American Revolution were in force at the time the Massachusetts Constitution was adopted. This Article preserves those early laws and statutes as part of the law of the Commonwealth until such time as the Legislature alters or repeals any of them. *Hannigan v. New Gamma-Delta Chapter of Kappa Sigma Fraternity, Inc.* (1975). "Unless there is a violation of a constitutional guarantee, [under this Article] the Legislature may modify or abrogate common law practices[.]" *New Bedford Standard-Times Publishing Company v. Clerk of the Third District Court of Bristol* (1979).

ARTICLE VII. Habeas Corpus

The privilege and benefit of the writ of habeas corpus shall be enjoyed in this commonwealth in the most free, easy, cheap, expeditious and ample manner; and shall not be suspended by the legislature, except upon the most urgent and pressing occasions, and for a limited time not exceeding twelve months.

This Article guarantees the availability of writs of habeas corpus in the Commonwealth. The purpose of habeas corpus, often referred to as "The Great Writ," is to provide relief against unlawful imprisonment, and is available where one has been deprived of liberty without due process of law. *Sheriff of Suffolk County v. Pires* (2002). There are two significant limitations on the use of a writ of habeas corpus. The first is that it "it cannot be employed as a substitute for ordinary appellate procedure." *Crowell v. Commonwealth* (1967). The second limitation results from the intent of the writ—the "immediate delivery of the party deprived of personal liberty." *Wyeth v. Richardson* (1857). Consequently, such a writ may only be granted when it will result in the petitioner's immediate release from custody. *Stokes v. Superintendent* (1983). There are several types of challenges that, in general, are not appropriate for a writ of habeas corpus, including such issues as insufficiency of evidence at a state court proceeding, the admission of evidence when no objection was made, and the revocation of a bail order.

ARTICLE VIII. Style of Enacting Clause of Acts, Statutes, and Laws

The enacting style, in making and passing all acts, statutes and laws, shall be—"Be it enacted by the Senate and House of Representatives in General Court assembled, and by the authority of the same."

Before a bill becomes a law, there must be action on the part of both the Senate and the House of Representatives, and the bill must also be approved by the Governor. *Opinion of the Justices* (1938). The ultimate process in passing a bill may vary depending on the type of bill or the type of law the bill will become; for example, Amendment LXIII addresses the process for passing appropriation statutes.

ARTICLE IX. Continuation of Former Officers in Office
To the end there may be no failure of justice, or danger arise to the commonwealth from a change of the form of government—all officers, civil and military, holding commissions under the government and people of Massachusetts Bay in New England, and all other officers of the said government and people, at the time this constitution shall take effect, shall have, hold, use, exercise and enjoy, all the powers and authority to them granted or committed, until other persons shall be appointed in their stead: and all courts of law shall proceed in the execution of the business of their respective departments; and all the executive and legislative officers, bodies and powers shall continue in full force, in the enjoyment and exercise of all their trusts, employments and authority; until the general court and the supreme and executive officers under this constitution are designated and invested with their respective trusts, powers and authority.

This Article ensured there was no disruption to the government when the constitution took effect. It states that anyone holding an office would remain in office with the same powers until a successor was appointed.

ARTICLE X. Revision of Constitution
[In order the more effectually to adhere to the principles of the constitution, and to correct those violations which by any means may be made therein, as well as to form such alterations as from experience shall be found necessary—the general court which shall be in the year of our Lord one thousand seven hundred and ninety-five, shall issue precepts to the selectmen of the several towns, and to the assessors of the unincorporated plantations, directing them to convene the qualified voters of their respective towns and plantations, for the purpose of collecting their sentiments on the necessity or expediency of revising the constitution, in order to amendments.

And if it shall appear by the returns made, that two thirds of the qualified voters throughout the state, who shall assemble and vote in consequence of the said precepts, are in favor of such revision or amendment, the general court shall issue precepts, or direct them to be issued from the secretary's office to the several towns to elect delegates to meet in convention for the purpose aforesaid.

The said delegates to be chosen in the same manner and proportion as their representatives in the second branch of the legislature are by this constitution to be chosen.]

In 1821, this Article was superseded by Amendment IX, which was later annulled and superseded by Amendment XLVIII. The drafters of the constitution recognized that future amendments to the document were inevitable. This Article, therefore, set out the original procedure for making such amendments. At this writing, the constitution is amended in accordance with Amendment XLVIII. As of this writing, the constitution has been amended 120 times.

ARTICLE XI. Preservation and Publication of Constitution

This form of government shall be enrolled on parchment and deposited in the secretary's office, and be a part of the laws of the land—and printed copies thereof shall be prefixed to the book containing the laws of this commonwealth, in all future editions of the said laws.

From time to time is has been important to reorganize the constitution in order to remove all "sections, articles, clauses and words which by the lapse of time, or by repeal, or annulment, or otherwise have ceased to be in force." *Opinion of the Justices* (1920). Such reorganization is not a violation of this article. The newly reorganized document is viewed as if it were the same document originally adopted in 1780.

Articles of Amendment

ARTICLE I. Bills and Resolves Not Approved Within Certain Time Limits
If any bill or resolve shall be objected to, and not approved by the governor, and if the general court shall adjourn within ten days after the same shall have been laid before the governor for his approbation, and thereby prevent his returning it with his objections, as provided by the constitution, such bill or resolve shall not become a law, nor have force as such.

Amendment I was ratified in 1821. It was amended by Amendment XC, § 2, inserting "ten days" where the original had "five days" as part of Amendment XC's extension of the Governor's veto period. This Amendment essentially prevents the Legislature from subverting a gubernatorial veto by providing the Governor with the equivalent of a "pocket veto," the ability to veto a measure by simply not signing it, but only when the Legislature has adjourned prematurely. This rule is functionally identical to Article I, § 7, cl. 2 of the U.S. Constitution, which requires that a bill not returned to Congress within the allotted time become law, unless Congress has made such return impossible by adjourning. *Pocket Veto Case* (1929); *Wright v. United States* (1938).

ARTICLE II. Chartering Cities and Establishing Municipal Governments
SECTION 1. *Right of Local Self-Government.*—It is the intention of this article to reaffirm the customary and traditional liberties of the people with respect to the conduct of their local government, and to grant and confirm to the people

of every city and town the right of self-government in local matters, subject to the provisions of this article and to such standards and requirements as the general court may establish by law in accordance with the provisions of this article.

SECTION 2. Local Power to Adopt, Revise or Amend Charters.—Any city or town shall have the power to adopt or revise a charter or to amend its existing charter through the procedures set forth in sections three and four. The provisions of any adopted or revised charter or any charter amendment shall not be inconsistent with the constitution or any laws enacted by the general court in conformity with the powers reserved to the general court by section eight.

No town of fewer than twelve thousand inhabitants shall adopt a city form of government, and no town of fewer than six thousand inhabitants shall adopt a form of government providing for a town meeting limited to such inhabitants of the town as may be elected to meet, deliberate, act and vote in the exercise of the corporate powers of the town.

SECTION 3. Procedure for Adoption or Revision of a Charter by a City or Town.—Every city and town shall have the power to adopt or revise a charter in the following manner: A petition for the adoption or revision of a charter shall be signed by at least fifteen per cent of the number of legal voters residing in such city or town at the preceding state election. Whenever such a petition is filed with the board of registrars of voters of any city or town, the board shall within ten days of its receipt determine the sufficiency and validity of the signatures and certify the results to the city council of the city or board of selectmen of the town, as the case may be. As used in this section, the phrase "board of registrars of voters" shall include any local authority of different designation which performs the duties of such registrars, and the phrase "city council of the city or board of selectmen of the town" shall include local authorities of different designation performing the duties of such council or board. Objections to the sufficiency and validity of the signatures on any such petition as certified by the board of registrars of voters shall be made in the same manner as provided by law for objections to nominations for city or town offices, as the case may be.

Within thirty days of receipt of certification of the board of registrars of voters that a petition contains sufficient valid signatures, the city council of the city or board of selectmen of the town shall by order provide for submitting to the voters of the city or town the question of adopting or revising a charter, and for the nomination and election of a charter commission.

If the city or town has not previously adopted a charter pursuant to this section, the question submitted to the voters shall be: "Shall a commission be elected to frame a charter for (name of city or town)?" If the city or town has previously adopted a charter pursuant to this section, the question submitted to the voters shall be: "Shall a commission be elected to revise the charter of (name of city or town)?"

The charter commission shall consist of nine voters of the city or town, who shall be elected at large without party or political designation at the city or town

election next held at least sixty days after the order of the city council of the city or board of selectmen of the town. The names of candidates for such commission shall be listed alphabetically on the ballot used at such election. Each voter may vote for nine candidates.

The vote on the question submitted and the election of the charter commission shall take place at the same time. If the vote on the question submitted is in the affirmative, the nine candidates receiving the highest number of votes shall be declared elected.

Within eighteen months after the election of the members of the charter commission, said commission shall submit the charter or revised charter to the city council of the city or the board of selectmen of the town, and such council or board shall provide for publication of the charter and for its submission to the voters of the city or town at the next city or town election held at least two months after such submission by the charter commission. If the charter or revised charter is approved by a majority of the voters of the city or town voting thereon, it shall become effective upon the date fixed in the charter.

SECTION 4. Procedure for Amendment of a Charter by a City or Town.—Every city and town shall have the power to amend its charter in the following manner: The legislative body of a city or town may, by a two-thirds vote, propose amendments to the charter of the city or town; provided, that (1) amendments of a city charter may be proposed only with the concurrence of the mayor in every city that has a mayor, and (2) any change in a charter relating in any way to the composition, mode of election or appointment, or terms of office of the legislative body, the mayor or city manager or the board of selectmen or town manager shall be made only by the procedure of charter revision set forth in section three.

All proposed charter amendments shall be published and submitted for approval in the same manner as provided for adoption or revision of a charter.

SECTION 5. Recording of Charters and Charter Amendments.—Duplicate certificates shall be prepared setting forth any charter that has been adopted or revised and any charter amendments approved, and shall be signed by the city or town clerk. One such certificate shall be deposited in the office of the secretary of the commonwealth and the other shall be recorded in the records of the city or town and deposited among its archives. All courts may take judicial notice of charters and charter amendments of cities and towns.

SECTION 6. Governmental Powers of Cities and Towns.—Any city or town may, by the adoption, amendment, or repeal of local ordinances or by-laws, exercise any power or function which the general court has power to confer upon it, which is not inconsistent with the constitution or laws enacted by the general court in conformity with powers reserved to the general court by section eight, and which is not denied, either expressly or by clear implication, to the city or town by its charter. This section shall apply to every city and town, whether or not it has adopted a charter pursuant to section three.

SECTION 7. Limitations on Local Powers.—Nothing in this article shall be deemed to grant to any city or town the power to (1) regulate elections other than those prescribed by sections three and four; (2) to levy, assess and collect taxes; (3) to borrow money or pledge the credit of the city or town; (4) to dispose of park land; (5) to enact private or civil law governing civil relationships except as an incident to an exercise of an independent municipal power; or (6) to define and provide for the punishment of a felony or to impose imprisonment as a punishment for any violation of law; provided, however, that the foregoing enumerated powers may be granted by the general court in conformity with the constitution and with the powers reserved to the general court by section eight; nor shall the provisions of this article be deemed to diminish the powers of the judicial department of the commonwealth.

SECTION 8. Powers of the General Court.—The general court shall have the power to act in relation to cities and towns, but only by general laws which apply alike to all cities, or to all towns, or to all cities and towns, or to a class of not fewer than two, and by special laws enacted (1) on petition filed or approved by the voters of a city or town, or the mayor and city council, or other legislative body, of a city, or the town meeting of a town, with respect to a law relating to that city or town; (2) by a two-thirds vote of each branch of the general court following a recommendation by the governor; (3) to erect and constitute metropolitan or regional entities, embracing any two or more cities or towns or cities and towns, or established with other than existing city or town boundaries, for any general or special public purpose or purposes, and to grant to these entities such powers, privileges and immunities as the general court shall deem necessary or expedient for the regulation and government thereof; or (4) solely for the incorporation or dissolution of cities or towns as corporate entities, alteration of city or town boundaries, and merger or consolidation of cities and towns, or any of these matters.

Subject to the foregoing requirements, the general court may provide optional plans of city or town organization and government under which an optional plan may be adopted or abandoned by majority vote of the voters of the city or town voting thereon at a city or town election; provided, that no town of fewer than twelve thousand inhabitants may be authorized to adopt a city form of government, and no town of fewer than six thousand inhabitants may be authorized to adopt a form of town government providing for a town meeting limited to such inhabitants of the town as may be elected to meet, deliberate, act and vote in the exercise of the corporate powers of the town.

This section shall apply to every city and town whether or not it has adopted a charter pursuant to section three.

SECTION 9. Existing Special Laws.—All special laws relating to individual cities or towns shall remain in effect and have the force of an existing city or town charter, but shall be subject to amendment or repeal through the adoption, revision or amendment of a charter by a city or town in accordance with the

provisions of sections three and four and shall be subject to amendment or repeal by laws enacted by the general court in conformity with the powers reserved to the general court by section eight.

This Amendment was ratified in 1821. It was amended by Amendment LXX, ratified in 1926. It was further amended by Amendment LXXXIX, ratified in 1966. Finally, it was amended as reflected above, by Amendment CXIII, ratified in 1978. The courts often refer to this Amendment as "Article Eighty-Nine," or the "Home Rule Amendment." Amendment CXIII, ratified in 1978, made the minor change of substituting "eighteen months" for "ten months" in the first sentence. The original Amendment authorized the Legislature to establish city or other municipal governments to replace town meeting government in towns with 12,000 inhabitants or more, so long as it was with the consent, and upon the application of, a majority of the town's inhabitants. It provided also that the Legislature had the power to annul all the by-laws of such a city government. Amendment LXX added a paragraph providing an intermediate option, allowing the Legislature to establish a representative form of town government with a selectmen meeting in towns with populations of 6,000 or more, provided again that the Legislature did so with the consent, and upon application of, a majority of the inhabitants.

In 1966, Amendment LXXXIX gave to municipalities the power to charter themselves as either cities or towns with selectperson boards instead of requiring them to petition the Legislature to establish such governmental structures. Municipalities are not bound by a uniform pattern of executive and administrative functions; each charter may be unique. There is a "great diversity of substance and of detail among the charters of the several cities." *Paquette v. City of Fall River* (1932); *Pirrone v. City of Boston* (1973).

The form of home rule granted under the amendment allows a municipality to act without intervening legislative action, and has been referred to as "self-executing," which is, according to the Supreme Judicial Court, "the strongest type of home rule." *Bloom v. Worcester* (1973) (quotation omitted).

Right of Local Self-Government

Section One establishes the "basic general policy." *In re Answer of the Justices*, 356 Mass. 769, 771, 250 N.E.2d 450, 452 (1969). The right of local self-governance is subject to the other provisions of article LXXXIX and "such standards . . . as the general court may establish. . . in accordance with art. 89." *Opinion of the Justices* (1969) (quotation omitted). Sections Six through Eight define and limit the powers specifically granted to cities and towns by Section One. Prior to the ratification of Amendment LXXXIX, cities and towns possessed only those powers explicitly granted them by the Legislature, including the power to enact local legislation, and towns possessed no inherent right to self-government.

See *Paddock v. Town of Brookline* (1964). Following the ratification of Amendment LXXXIX in 1966, cities and towns were free to adopt, amend, or revise their charters in accordance with the substantive and procedural requirements of the remaining section of the article. *Opinion of the Justices* (1969). The power to grant a city charter, however, remained with the Legislature. *Sullivan v. Lawson* (1929).

Importantly, the Home Rule Amendment does not prevent the Legislature from exercising "extensive authority" over cities and towns. *Powers v. Sec. of Admin.* (1992). The Supreme Judicial Court has expressly and repeatedly interpreted the amendment as not imposing any expansive limitation on the Legislature. For instance, when a conflict of authority arises between the elected government of a municipality and an authority appointed pursuant to a legislative act, "[Section One] require[s] that the elected government give way." *Powers,* 412 Mass. at 126. Further, the Legislature has the power to decide which of its existing laws apply to a municipality, just as it has the power to enact new laws upon petition of a municipality's residents. *Opinion of the Justices* (1975). In addition, the Legislature has the authority under the Amendment to create standard forms of municipal government that could be voluntarily adopted. *Id.* The court has nonetheless acknowledged the Amendment's significance as an expression of the intent "to reaffirm the customary and traditional liberties" of self-governance. *Opinion of the Justices* (1982). In amending Amendment II, the Home Rule Amendment (Amendment LXXXIX) gave cities and towns municipal powers they did not previously possess. Cities and towns are now free to exercise any function the Legislature confers on them, so long as that function is not denied by their own charter, reserved to the state, or inconsistent with the constitution or Massachusetts General Laws. *Bd. of Appeals of Hanover v. Hous. Appeals Comm.* (1973).

Governmental Powers of Cities and Towns

The court has held the Amendment's grant of power to municipalities is limited by the requirement that any exercise of that power not be "inconsistent with the constitution or laws enacted by the general court." *Bloom v. Worcester* (1973). Action by a municipality is presumed to be valid. *Connors v. City of Boston* (1999). The critical issue is the meaning of "inconsistent." If the Legislature has not "expressly forbidden the adoption of local ordinances and by-laws on a subject," and the "State legislative purpose can be achieved in the face of a local ordinance or by-law on the same subject," then such ordinance or by-law is not inconsistent. *Bloom.* Accordingly, the first step in determining whether an ordinance or by-law is consistent with a general law is "ascertaining [whether the] legislative intent" of the law was to "preclude local action." *Id.* The second step is to determine whether, absent discernible legislative intent to preclude local action, in "any circumstances . . . legislative purpose . . . [would be] frustrated." *Id.* The delegation of responsibility for certain regulation by the General Court to an administrative agency may constitute preemption of a local ordinance.

Though the Amendment is silent on municipal executive orders, such an order might also be inconsistent with or repugnant to state legislation and invalid under Amendment II. In *Connors v. City of Boston* (1999), the mayor had issued an executive order extending group health insurance benefits to the domestic partners of city employees and their dependents. The Supreme Judicial Court held the executive order repugnant to specific statutory language prohibiting the extension of coverage to anyone other than those persons described in the statute. *Id.*; see Mass. Gen. Laws ch. 32B, §§ 1–2. In *Bloom*, on the other hand, the Supreme Judicial Court held that a Worcester ordinance establishing a municipal human rights committee not inconsistent with any of the statutes at issue. The court found no legislative intent in Mass. Gen. Law chs. 151B or 151C, the statutes that created the Massachusetts Commission Against Discrimination (MCAD), to preclude such municipal action. *Bloom.* The court also held the ordinance consistent with the MCAD's authority to create local agencies to investigate discrimination. *Id.*

Limitations on Local Powers

The Amendment imposes limits upon the broad powers granted cities and towns under section six. For instance, this section prohibits a municipality from levying taxes, though municipalities may still assess fees. Mass. Const., amend. LXXXIX, § 7. Fees are distinguished from taxes by three characteristics: (1) a fee is charged in exchange for a particular service that benefits the party paying the fee; (2) a fee is paid by choice; and, (3) a fee is not collected to raise general revenue but is specifically intended to compensate the governmental entity providing the service (usually placed in an earmarked fund rather than a general fund). *Emerson College v. Boston* (1984). In *Commonwealth v. Caldwell* (1987), the Appeals Court held that a slip fee charged to vessels moored in Beverly waters was, in fact, a fee since it paid for services the harbormaster provided to those moored in the waters, was voluntary, and were not collected to raise revenue generally but "directly compensated Beverly, at least in part, for the cost of providing the harbormaster's services." *Id.*

The fifth clause of section seven, which denies cities and towns the power "to enact private or civil law governing civil relationships except as an incident to an exercise of an independent municipal power," is perhaps the most ambiguous of the section's restrictions. See *Marshall House, Inc. v. Rent Rev. & Grievance Bd.* (1970). The clause does not prohibit the enactment of laws that may affect some aspects of civil relationships, only those that directly govern the legal basis of those relationships. The language in this Amendment "strike[s] a balance by enabling home rule units to enact private law only as an incident to the exercise of some independent municipal power." *Marshal House, Inc. v. Rent Review & Grievance Bd. of Brookline* (1970). A city's independent municipal powers would include the city's "police powers," which include the power to regulate traffic, maintain a clean water supply, and operating the sewer system. *Id.*; see *Bannerman v. City of Fall River* (1984).

Powers of the General Court

When the Legislature does act to enlarge or reduce the powers of the towns and cities, section eight requires that it do so either by (1) general laws which apply to at least two such cities and towns, or (2) special laws enacted pursuant to the procedures specified in section eight. This authority has been strictly construed by the courts. *Opinion of the Justices* (1982). A "general law" is one that deals with state, regional, or general concerns. *Opinion of the Justices* (1982). A "general law" described in section eight can involve granting power to an administrative agency. See *Worchester v. Dep't. of Pub. Utils.* (1984). General laws include even those that have a special effect on one or more individual cities or towns. *Opinion of the Justices* (1970). The court distinguishes between the application and impact of a law in determining whether a law is "special." *Edwards v. Boston* (1990).

A law that applies to a specific site in a specific city or town is valid under this amendment when it deals with a matter of state, regional, or general concern. *Clean Harbors of Braintree, Inc. v. Bd. of Health of Braintree*, 415 Mass. 876, 877, 881–82 (1993). Special laws single out a town or city for special treatment. *Edwards v. Boston* (1990). These laws cannot be enacted unless one of the four procedures in section eight is followed. See, e.g., *Opinion of the Justices* (1969). Once a special law is enacted it cannot thereafter be unilaterally rescinded by a municipality but it is subject to change through subsequent action by the Legislature. *Nugent v. Wellesley* (1980). A special law may prohibit further related amendments. See *Opinion of the Justices* (1969). The Legislature has the power to "create, change, and destroy municipal corporations"; for example, the General Court and Governor have been authorized to dissolve fire districts, appoint a police board, and order a city to pay a Civil War veteran. In each of the above cases, the special act by the Legislature was for the public good. *Paddock v. Town of Brookline* (1964). At this writing, municipalities may amend and revise special legislation enacted after November 8, 1966, pursuant to clauses one or two of section eight, unless specifically forbidden by legislation. See Mass. Gen. Laws ch. 43B, § 19.

ARTICLE III. Qualifications of Voters

Every citizen of eighteen years of age and upwards, excepting persons who are incarcerated in a correctional facility due to a felony conviction, and under guardianship and persons temporarily or permanently disqualified by law

because of corrupt practices in respect to elections who shall have resided within the town or district in which he may claim a right to vote, six calendar months next preceding any election of governor, lieutenant governor, senators or representatives, shall have a right to vote in such election of governor, lieutenant governor, senators and representatives; and no other person shall be entitled to vote in such election.

This Amendment was ratified in 1821. The Massachusetts Constitution is concerned only with final elections, generally speaking, and does not refer to primaries and nominations. *Opinion of the Justices* (1971). Initially, Amendment III broadened the suffrage for Governor, Lieutenant Governor, Senators, and Representatives beyond that provided for in the original constitution. It reduced the property requirements to not being a "pauper" and to having paid any State or County tax (if not exempt from such tax). Early on, "pauper" was narrowly defined as a "person[] receiving aid and assistance from the public, under the provisions made by law for the support and maintenance of the poor." *Opinion of the Justices* (1832).

This provision has been frequently amended. Its history is largely the history of the extension of suffrage in the Commonwealth. Amendment XXVIII, ratified in 1881, excused certain veterans of the requirement that they not be a "pauper" and, if a pauper, from paying a poll tax. Amendment XXXI, ratified in 1890, amended Amendment XXVIII by replacing "pauper" with "receiving or having received aid from any city or town." Amendment XXXII, ratified in 1891, dropped the requirement of having paid taxes. Amendment XL, ratified in 1912, added the provision disqualifying "persons temporarily or permanently disqualified by law because of corrupt practices in respect to elections." Amendment LXVIII, ratified in 1924, extended the suffrage to women by striking the qualifying word "male" in the original amendment. Amendment XCIII, ratified in 1970, removed the original one-year durational residence requirement. Amendment XCIV, ratified in 1970, reduced the voting age from twenty-one to nineteen. Amendment XCV, ratified in 1972, struck the eligibility requirement that one not be a "pauper." Amendment C, ratified in 1974, reduced the voting age to eighteen. Finally, Amendment CXX, ratified in 2000, denied incarcerated felons the franchise. The disenfranchisement of incarcerated felons has been upheld as constitutional; states have broad powers in qualifying voters, and the denial of one's right to vote is not necessarily punishment. *King v. City of Boston* (2004).

The original article of Amendment extended suffrage to some who were not qualified under the original constitution, but it and all subsequent amendments have also provided, in the last line, that "no other person shall be entitled to vote in such election." This language means that the Legislature cannot be more generous than the constitution in extending suffrage—which was possible under the original language.

ARTICLE IV. Notaries Public

Notaries public shall be appointed by the governor in the same manner as judicial officers are appointed, and shall hold their offices during seven years, unless sooner removed by the governor with the consent of the council, upon the address of both houses of the legislature.

This Amendment was ratified in 1821. It had originally provided procedures for filling vacancies in the offices of Secretary and Treasurer, but these provisions were removed by Amendment XVII, ratified in 1855. Amendment XXXVII, ratified in 1907, provides that notaries public (as well as justices of the peace) may be removed by the Governor and Council alone. Amendment LIII, ratified in 1918, eliminated the last two clauses of the original amendment, which dealt with removal of military officials in general and the appointment of a Commissary-General in particular. Amendment LVII, ratified in 1918, added language making women eligible to be notary publics. Amendment LXIX, ratified in 1924, added the language providing for re-registration of women under their new names—presumably after marriage.

The first part of the original amendment essentially equates the office of Notary Public with that of Justice of the Peace. Amendment XXXVII, ratified in 1907, continues this linkage, by providing that both officers can be removed by the Governor and Council without need for address of both houses of the Legislature. As amended by Amendment LVII, ratified in 1918, it became the first act of "women's liberation" in the constitution by explicitly opening that office to women. Prior to this amendment, the court had used an originalist interpretation in denying women the office; the common practice when the original amendment was adopted was to appoint only men to the judiciary, and notaries were analogous to judges. *Opinion of the Justices* (1896).

ARTICLE VI. Oath of Office

Instead of the oath of allegiance prescribed by the constitution, the following oath shall be taken and subscribed by every person chosen or appointed to any office, civil or military under the government of this commonwealth, before he shall enter on the duties of his office, to wit;

"I, A.B., do solemnly swear, that I will bear true faith and allegiance to the Commonwealth of Massachusetts, and will support the constitution thereof. So help me GOD."

Provided, That when any person shall be of the denomination called Quakers, and shall decline taking said oath, he shall make his affirmation in the foregoing form, omitting the word "swear" and inserting instead thereof the word "affirm;" and omitting the words "So help me GOD," and subjoining, instead thereof, the words "This I do under the pains and penalties of perjury."

This Amendment was ratified in 1821. This is a companion to Amendment VII. It amends the original constitution, Part II, c. VI, art. I, by eliminating several key oaths which had been required of all public officers.

ARTICLE VII. Tests Abolished

No oath, declaration or subscription, excepting the oath prescribed in the preceding article and the oath of office, shall be required of the governor, lieutenant governor, councillors, senators or representatives, to qualify them to perform the duties of their respective offices.

This Amendment was ratified in 1821. This is a companion to Amendment VI. It amends the original constitution, Part II, c. VI, art. I, by removing several oaths that had been required of the Governor, Lieutenant Governor, Councillors, Senators, and Representatives.

ARTICLE VIII. Incompatibility of Offices

No judge of any court of this commonwealth (except the court of sessions) and no person holding any office under the authority of the United States (postmasters excepted) shall, at the same time, hold the office of governor, lieutenant governor, or councillor, or have a seat in the senate or house of representatives of this commonwealth; and no judge of any court in this commonwealth (except the court of sessions) nor the attorney-general, solicitor-general, county attorney, clerk of any court, sheriff, treasurer and receiver-general, register of probate, nor register of deeds, shall continue to hold his said office after being elected a member of the Congress of the United States, and accepting that trust; but the acceptance of such trust by any of the officers aforesaid shall be deemed and taken to be a resignation of his said office; and judges of the courts of common pleas shall hold no other office under the government of this commonwealth, the office of justice of the peace and militia offices excepted.

This Amendment was ratified in 1821. This supplements Part II, c. VI, art. II of the original constitution in making the holding of certain offices at the same time incompatible.

An officer or office-holder is properly understood as one whose duties are public in nature and who wields some portion of the sovereign authority of the state. *Attorney Gen. v. Tillinghast* (1909). An officer may be distinguished from an employee whose duties are merely clerical, or who acts solely as an agent, although an officer may be subordinate to another officer. A critical issue is whether the position is a continuing one created and governed by statute or by private contract. *Id.* This Amendment does not apply to town or city offices. *Wood v. Bd. of Election Comm'rs* (1929). Federal appointments of individuals to local positions, even upon recommendation by the Governor, do not necessarily fall within category of "office under the government of the commonwealth." *Opinion of the Justices* (1940).

ARTICLE X. Commencement of the Political Year

The political year shall begin on the first Wednesday of January instead of the last Wednesday of May, and the general court shall assemble every year on the said first Wednesday of January, and shall proceed at that session to make all

the elections, and do all the other acts which are by the constitution required to be made and done at the session which has heretofore commenced on the last Wednesday of May. And the general court shall be dissolved on the day next preceding the first Wednesday of January, without any proclamation or other act of the governor. But nothing herein contained shall prevent the general court from assembling at such other times as they shall judge necessary, or when called together by the governor.

All the other provisions of the constitution, respecting the elections and proceedings of the members of the general court, or of any other officers or persons whatever, that have reference to the last Wednesday of May, as the commencement of the political year, shall be so far altered as to have like reference to the first Wednesday of January.

This article shall go into operation on the first day of October next following the day when the same shall be duly ratified and adopted as an amendment of the constitution.

All the provisions of the existing constitution inconsistent with the provisions herein contained are hereby wholly annulled.

This Amendment, ratified in 1831, changed the timing of the political year. It has been amended several times, by Amendment XV, ratified in 1855; Amendment LXIV, ratified in 1918; Amendment LXXII, ratified in 1938; Amendment LXXV, ratified in 1944; Amendment LXXX, ratified in 1950; and Amendment LXXXII, ratified in 1964. Amendment XV superseded X in part, removing the section providing for meeting times for the Governor and other named officers. Amendment LXXII provided for the General Court to meet biennially, but the amendment was annulled by LXXV and any provisions affected by LXXII were restored. Amendments LXXX, and LXXXII are discussed with LXIV below.

ARTICLE XII. Apportionment of Representatives, Etc.

[In order to provide for a representation of the citizens of this commonwealth, founded upon the principles of equality a census of the ratable polls, in each city, town and district of the commonwealth, on the first day of May, shall be taken and returned into the secretary's office, in such manner as the legislature shall provide, within the month of May, in the year of our Lord one thousand eight hundred and thirty-seven, and in every tenth year thereafter, in the month of May, in manner aforesaid, and each town or city having three hundred ratable polls at the last preceding decennial census of polls may elect one representative, and for every four hundred and fifty ratable polls in addition to the first three hundred, one representative more.

Any town having less than three hundred ratable polls shall be represented thus; the whole number of ratable polls, at the last preceding decennial census of polls, shall be multiplied by ten, and the product divided by three hundred, and such town may elect one representative as many years within ten years, as three hundred is contained in the product aforesaid.

Any city or town having ratable polls enough to elect one or more representatives, with any number of polls beyond the necessary number, may be represented as to that surplus number by multiplying such surplus number by ten and dividing the product by four hundred and fifty; and such city or town may elect one additional representative as many years within the ten years as four hundred and fifty is contained in the product aforesaid.

Any two or more of the several towns and districts may, by consent of a majority of the legal voters present at a legal meeting in each of said towns and districts respectively called for that purpose, and held previous to the first day of July in the year in which the decennial census of polls shall be taken, form themselves into a representative district, to continue until the next decennial census of polls, for the election of a representative or representatives, and such district shall have all the rights, in regard to representation, which would belong to a town containing the same number of ratable polls.

The governor and council shall ascertain and determine within the months of July and August, in the year of our Lord one thousand eight hundred and thirty-seven, according to the foregoing principles, the number of representatives, which each city, town and representative district is entitled to elect, and the number of years within the period of ten years then next ensuing, that each city, town and representative district may elect an additional representative, and where any town has not a sufficient number of polls to elect a representative each year then how many years within the ten years, such town may elect a representative, and the same shall be done once in ten years thereafter by the governor and council, and the number of ratable polls in each decennial census of polls, shall determine the number of representatives, which each city, town and representative district may elect as aforesaid, and when the number of representatives to be elected by each city, town or representative district is ascertained and determined as aforesaid, the governor shall cause the same to be published forthwith for the information of the people and that number shall remain fixed and unalterable for the period of ten years. All the provisions of the existing constitution inconsistent with the provisions herein contained, are hereby wholly annulled.]

This provision was ratified in 1836. The whole of this provision is placed in brackets to reflect the fact that, though never explicitly amended or annulled, it has been entirely superseded by later amendment (Amendment XIII [1840]) in a long series in which each later amendment entirely superseded those before it. See Amendments XXI (1857), LXXI (1930), XCII (1970), CI (1974), and CXVII (1990). Amendment XII itself supersedes without explicitly amending those provisions of the original constitution that addressed the number of representatives and the proportional distribution of Representatives around the state. See Part II, c. I, sec. 3, art. II.

This provision makes the first in a variety of changes to the House of Representatives. Part II, c. I, sec. 3, art. II provided that towns would have one Representative in the Legislature for 150 ratable polls and an additional Representative for each 225 ratable polls. It also grandfathered-in existing towns with fewer than 150 ratable polls by giving them one Representative. Prior to the Amendment, the constitution did not explicitly provide for the representation of persons not living in towns. This Amendment clarifies that persons living in cities and districts are also to be counted and included. Further, it establishes a decennial census for the first time for the purpose of making sure that distributions of Representatives are maintained equitably. Towns below the minimum and towns and cities with fractional population surpluses are given proportional fractional representation through a complicated formula and the option of capturing additional seats for fractional populations by combining for that purpose. The number of representatives was decreased, apparently having become a serious problem. With the Amendment, there was to be one Representative for the first 300 ratable polls, and one for each additional 450. The amendment also established procedures for increasing the openness and fairness of representation decision-making.

ARTICLE XIII. Basis of Representation, Etc.

[A census of the inhabitants of each city and town, on the first day of May, shall be taken, and returned into the secretary's office, on or before the last day of June, of the year one thousand eight hundred and forty, and of every tenth year thereafter, which census shall determine the apportionment of senators and representatives for the term of ten years. The several senatorial districts now existing shall be permanent. The senate shall consist of forty members: and in the year one thousand eight hundred and forty, and every tenth year thereafter, the governor and council shall assign the number of senators to be chosen in each district, according to the number of inhabitants in the same. But, in all cases, at least one senator shall be assigned to each district. The members of the house of representatives shall be apportioned in the following manner: Every town or city containing twelve hundred inhabitants, may elect one representative; and two thousand four hundred inhabitants shall be the mean increasing number which shall entitle it to an additional representative. Every town containing less than twelve hundred inhabitants, shall be entitled to elect a representative as many times, within ten years, as the number one hundred and sixty is contained in the number of the inhabitants of said town. Such towns may also elect one representative for the year in which the valuation of estates within the commonwealth shall be settled. Any two or more of the several towns may, by consent of a majority of the legal voters present at a legal meeting, in each of said towns respectively, called for that purpose, and held before the first day of August, in the year one thousand eight hundred and forty, and every tenth year thereafter, form themselves into a representative district, to continue for the term of ten years; and such district shall have all the rights in regard to representation, which would belong to a town containing the same number

of inhabitants. The number of inhabitants which shall entitle a town to elect one representative, and the mean increasing number, which shall entitle a town or city to elect more than one, and also the number by which the population of towns, not entitled to a representative every year, is to be divided, shall be increased respectively, by one tenth of the numbers above mentioned, whenever the population of the commonwealth shall have increased to seven hundred and seventy thousand, and for every additional increase of seventy thousand inhabitants, the same addition of one tenth shall be made, respectively, to the said numbers above mentioned. In the year of each decennial census, the governor and council shall, before the first day of September, apportion the number of representatives which each city, town, and representative district is entitled to elect, and ascertain how many years within ten years, any town may elect a representative, which is not entitled to elect one every year; and the governor shall cause the same to be published forthwith. Nine councillors shall be annually chosen from among the people at large, on the first Wednesday of January, or as soon thereafter as may be, by the joint ballot of the senators and representatives assembled in one room, who shall, as soon as may be, in like manner, fill up any vacancies that may happen in the council, by death, resignation or otherwise. No person shall be elected a councillor, who has not been an inhabitant of this commonwealth for the term of five years immediately preceding his election; and not more than one councillor shall be chosen from any one senatorial district in the commonwealth.]

No possession of a freehold or of any other estate shall be required as a qualification for holding a seat in either branch of the general court, or in the executive council.

All but the last paragraph of this provision, ratified in 1840, is placed in brackets to reflect the fact that, although never explicitly amended or annulled, it has been entirely superseded by later amendment (Amendment XXI [1857]) in a long series in which each later amendment entirely superseded those before it. See Amendments LXXI, ratified in 1930; XCII, ratified in 1970; CI, ratified in 1974; and CXVII, ratified in 1990. Amendment XIII itself supersedes without explicitly amending the provisions of Amendment XII and those provisions of the original constitution which deal with the number of Senators and the proportional distribution of them around the state. See Part II, c. I, sec. II, art. I. The last paragraph, which has never been amended, supersedes the provisions of the original constitution which had imposed property requirements for holding the offices of Senator and Representative. See Part II, c. I, sec. II, art. V and Part II, c. I, sec. III, art. III.

This Amendment makes the second in a variety of changes to representation in the House of Representatives and the first in a variety of changes to representation in the Senate and the Governor's Council. Representation under this amendment was to be determined by number of inhabitants rather than "ratable polls." Changes to the means of determining number of Representatives were also made, and the amendment provided for an increase in representation proportions as the population of the state increased, in an effort to keep the number of Representatives constant. Pursuant to this amendment, the number of Senators for the first time is to be determined based on number of inhabitants, rather than on property. The Amendment also froze the number of senatorial districts existing at the time. Under this Amendment, Councillors were to be elected from the people at large instead of from among the Senators and then from the people at large only if not enough Senators were willing to abandon their Senate seats for the Council. See Part II, c. II, sec. III, art. II. Such reluctance was common.

ARTICLE XIV. Election to Be by Plurality of Votes

In all elections of civil officers by the people of this commonwealth, whose election is provided for by the constitution, the person having the highest number of votes shall be deemed and declared to be elected.

This article of Amendment was ratified in 1855. It provides for plurality election only for those persons whose elections are "provided for by the constitution." The court has not applied the requirement to municipal elections, insofar as such elections are provided for by statute or charter, even though under constitutional authority. See *Opinion of the Justices* (1975).

ARTICLE XV. Time of Annual Elections

The meeting for the choice of governor, lieutenant-governor, senators and representatives, shall be held on the Tuesday next after the first Monday in November, [annually]; but in case of a failure to elect representatives on that day, a second meeting shall be holden for that purpose on the fourth Monday of the same month of November.

Ratified in 1855, this amendment changed the date for electing the mentioned officers. In addition, the amendment makes the date of the election of Representatives the same as that of the others—unless the election of Representatives cannot be managed in the same day. It also for the first time speaks of the Representatives as being elected at a "meeting" for that purpose.

Previously, the Governor, Lieutenant Governor, and Senators were elected at a town meeting held the first Monday in April to accommodate a political year that began on the last Wednesday in May. See Part II, c. I, sec. II, art. II (Senators); Part II, c. II, sec. I, art. III (Governor); Part II, c. II, sec. II, art. I (Lieutenant Governor). Representatives were elected in May, at least ten days before the last Wednesday in May. See Part II, c. I, sec. III, art. V. The word "annually" is bracketed to reflect the fact that the term of office of each of the mentioned officers was changed to two years by Article of Amendment 64, ratified in 1918, and the term of office of the Governor and Lieutenant. Governor was changed to four years by Article of Amendment 82, ratified in 1964.

ARTICLE XVI. Councillors, Etc.

Eight councillors shall be [annually] chosen by the inhabitants of this commonwealth, qualified to vote for governor. The election of councillors shall be determined by the same rule that is required in the election of governor. The legislature, at its first session after this amendment shall have been adopted, and at its first session after the next state census shall have been taken, and at its first session after each decennial state census thereafterwards, shall divide the commonwealth into eight districts of contiguous territory, each containing a number of inhabitants as nearly equal as practicable, without dividing any town or ward of a city, and each entitled to elect one councillor: provided, however, that if, at any time, the constitution shall provide for the division of the commonwealth into forty senatorial districts, then the legislature shall so arrange the councillor districts that each district shall consist of five contiguous senatorial districts, as they shall be, from time to time, established by the legislature. No person shall be eligible to the office of councillor who has not been an inhabitant of the commonwealth for the term of five years immediately preceding his election. The day and manner of the election, the return of the votes, and the declaration of the said elections, shall be the same as are required in the election of governor. [Whenever there shall be a failure to elect the full number of councillors, the vacancies shall be filled in the same manner as is required for filling vacancies in the senate; and vacancies occasioned by death, removal from the state, or otherwise, shall be filled in like manner, as soon as may be after such vacancies shall have happened.] And that there may be no delay in the organization of the government on the first Wednesday of January, the governor, with at least five councillors for the time being, shall, as soon as may be, examine the returned copies of the records for the election of governor, lieutenant-governor, and councillors; and ten days before the said first Wednesday in January he shall issue his summons to such persons as appear to be chosen, to attend on that day to be qualified accordingly; and the secretary shall lay the returns before the senate and house of representatives on the said first Wednesday in January, to be by them examined; and in case of the election of either of said officers, the choice shall be by them declared and published; but in case there shall be no election of either of said officers, the legislature shall proceed to fill such vacancies in the manner provided in the constitution for the choice of such officers.

Ratified in 1855, this amendment changes the number of Councillors to eight and provides for their direct election rather than their election by the Legislature, as provided for in Part II, c. II, sec. III, art. II and Amend. Art. XIII. Brackets around the provision regarding the filling of vacancies in the Council reflect the changes wrought in that process by Article of Amendment XXV, ratified in 1860. Pursuant to Amendment LXIV (and its own later amendments), Councillors are now elected biennially, rather than annually.

The amendment states that each councillor district shall be "entitled to elect one councilor." The amendment does not require that a Councillor so elected be a resident or inhabitant of that district. *Bigney v. Sec. of Commonwealth* (1938). The only residency requirement imposed by Article XVI is contained in those words stating that one is eligible to be a Councillor only if he or she has resided in the Commonwealth for at least five years. *Connolly v. Sec. of Commonwealth* (1989).

ARTICLE XVII. Election of Secretary, Treasurer, and Receiver General
The secretary, treasurer and receiver-general, auditor, and attorney-general, shall be chosen [annually,] on the day in November prescribed for the choice of governor; and each person then chosen as such, duly qualified in other respects, shall hold his office for the term of [one year] from the third Wednesday in January next thereafter, and until another is chosen and qualified in his stead. The qualification of the voters, the manner of the election, the return of the votes, and the declaration of the election, shall be such as are required in the election of governor. In case of a failure to elect either of said officers on the day in November aforesaid, or in case of the decease, in the meantime, of the person elected as such, such officer shall be chosen on or before the third Wednesday in January next thereafter, from the people at large, by joint ballot of the senators and representatives, in one room; and in case the office of secretary, or treasurer and receiver-general, or auditor, or attorney-general, shall become vacant, from any cause, during an annual or special session of the general court, such vacancy shall in like manner be filled by choice from the people at large; but if such vacancy shall occur at any other time, it shall be supplied by the governor by appointment, with the advice and consent of the council. The person so chosen or appointed, duly qualified in other respects, shall hold his office until his successor is chosen and duly qualified in his stead. In case any person chosen or appointed to either of the offices aforesaid, shall neglect, for the space of ten days after he could otherwise enter upon his duties, to qualify himself in all respects to enter the discharge of such duties, the office to which he has been elected or appointed shall be deemed vacant. No person shall be eligible to either of said offices unless he shall have been an inhabitant of this commonwealth five years next preceding his election or appointment.

Ratified in 1855, this Amendment provided for the popular election of these officers. Previously, the offices of Secretary, Treasurer, and Receiver General had been appointed by the Legislature, while the Attorney General had been appointed by the Governor and Council. Prior to this amendment, the constitution had not included a provision for an office of "auditor." *Mass. Bay Transp. Auth. v. Auditor of Commonwealth* (2000). The bracketed provisions reflect the change of term of the offices to two years effected by Article of Amendment LXIV, ratified in 1918, and the change of term of office to four years effected by Article of Amendment LXXXII, ratified in 1964.

ARTICLE XVIII. Public Support of Religious Institutions

SECTION 1. No law shall be passed prohibiting the free exercise of religion.

SECTION 2. No grant, appropriation or use of public money or property or loan of credit shall be made or authorized by the commonwealth or any political subdivision thereof for the purpose of founding, maintaining or aiding any infirmary, hospital, institution, primary or secondary school, or charitable or religious undertaking which is not publicly owned and under the exclusive control, order and supervision of public officers or public agents authorized by the commonwealth or federal authority or both, except that appropriations may be made for the maintenance and support of the Soldiers' Home in Massachusetts and for free public libraries in any city or town, and to carry out legal obligations, if any, already entered into; and no such grant, appropriation or use of public money or property or loan of public credit shall be made or authorized for the purpose of founding, maintaining or aiding any church, religious denomination or society. Nothing herein contained shall be construed to prevent the commonwealth from making grants-in-aid to private higher educational institutions or to students or parents or guardians of students attending such institutions.

SECTION 3. Nothing herein contained shall be construed to prevent the commonwealth, or any political division thereof, from paying to privately controlled hospitals, infirmaries, or institutions for the deaf, dumb or blind not more than the ordinary and reasonable compensation for care or support actually rendered or furnished by such hospitals, infirmaries or institutions to such persons as may be in whole or in part unable to support or care for themselves.

SECTION 4. Nothing herein contained shall be construed to deprive any inmate of a publicly controlled reformatory, penal or charitable institution of the opportunity of religious exercises therein of his own faith; but no inmate of such institution shall be compelled to attend religious services or receive religious instruction against his will, or, if a minor, without the consent of his parent or guardian.

SECTION 5. This amendment shall not take effect until the October first next succeeding its ratification and adoption by the people.

The Amendment was originally ratified in 1855. The current version reflects Amendment XLVI, ratified in 1917, which replaced the original entirely. *Town of Milton v. Att'y Gen.*, 314 Mass. 234, 239 (1943). Amendment CIII, ratified in 1974, replaced section two of Amend. Art. XLVI with the section two included here.

Free Exercise of Religion

The Supreme Judicial Court employs a balancing test when analyzing claims alleging an unconstitutional burden of the free exercise of religion. *The Soc'y of Jesus of New England v. Commonwealth* (2004). If a court finds that the state action complained of burdens the free exercise of religion, the state must demonstrate an "interest sufficiently compelling to justify that burden." *Id.* For a court to find that a state action burdens the free exercise of religion the party must demonstrate "a sincerely held religious belief" and show that such belief "conflicts with" the state action at issue. *Id.* If the claimant satisfies these elements, the Commonwealth must show that the action challenged "pursues an unusually important governmental goal, and that . . . an exemption would substantially hinder the fulfillment of the goal." *Id.*

The test used is identical to that adopted by the U.S. Supreme Court in *Wisconsin v. Yoder* (1972). The Supreme Court adopted a new, less stringent test in *Employment Div., Dep't of Human Resources of Or. v. Smith* (1990). The Supreme Judicial Court has rejected the Smith test. *Attorney Gen. v. Desilets* (1994). If a claim is brought under both the Massachusetts and U.S. Constitutions, the court will conduct an analysis under Amendment XVIII, § 1 before analyzing the issue under the First Amendment. *Id.* In applying the balancing test, the Supreme Judicial Court examines the interest stated and the demonstrated burden "in a concrete, pragmatic, and fact-specific way." *Soc'y of Jesus of New England v. Commonwealth* (2004).

Prohibition Against Aid to Private Institutions

The purpose of the prohibition against aid to private institutions is to "prevent direct assistance to private or sectarian charitable institutions and to preclude expenditure of public funds or appropriations for them." *Opinion of the Justices* (1968). The language of the "anti-aid" section of the Massachusetts amendment is more specific and restrictive than the First Amendment's Establishment Clause. *Opinion of the Justices* (1987). In 1970, the Supreme Judicial Court addressed a bill which provided that nonpublic elementary and secondary schools would be reimbursed by the Commonwealth for the reasonable cost of providing secular education. *Opinion of the Justices* (1970). The court held that the bill, if enacted, would violate Amendment XLVI, § 2, because action under the bill would count as "aiding" a nonpublic school or school inculcating a denominational doctrine. *Id.* Explicitly restricting state aid to nonreligious nonpublic schools would not save the statute. *Opinion of the Justices* (1970).

Amendment CIII, ratified in 1974, eliminated special reference to religious institutions, stating: "any school or institution of learning, whether under public control or otherwise, wherein any denominational doctrine is inculcated." Amendment CIII also added an exception to section two of Amendment XLVI to make grants available to private institutions of higher education or to students or parents or guardians of students attending such institutions. See *Commonwealth v. Sch. Comm. of Springfield* (1981).

Though statutes examined under the Anti-Aid Amendment enjoy a presumption of validity, the Supreme Judicial Court has adopted a three-part inquiry to test the constitutionality of payments by the Commonwealth to schools: "(1) [W]hether the purpose of the challenged statute is to aid private schools; (2) whether the statute does in fact substantially aid such schools; and (3) whether the statute avoids the political and economic abuses which prompted the passage of art. 46." *Sch. Comm. of Springfield.* These three criteria represent not precise limits, but rather guidelines to an appropriate analysis. *Id.*

The inquiry under the first part is whether public funds have been used for the purpose of "'founding, maintaining, or aiding' private schools." *Id.* A court will first look to explicit legislative purposes and legislative goals explicitly stated in the same piece of legislation. *Id.* The inquiry then moves to the payment made to the institution not only in its form, but also to its substance "to detect 'any technique of circumvention.'" *Id.* The second prong asks whether aid constitutes a substantial, if not major portion of the total expense of a school. The third prong requires resort to the history and purpose of section two. *Id.* The 1917 constitutional convention "was concerned about aid to sectarian institutions, and, more generally, with halting the politically divisive and financially wasteful practice of direct aid to private schools and institutions." *Id.* Section two of this amendment will not interfere with the performances of obligations under a contract already entered into.

ARTICLE XIX. Election of Sheriffs, Registers of Probate, and Clerks of Court

The legislature shall prescribe, by general law, for the election of sheriffs, registers of probate, and clerks of the courts, by the people of the several counties, and that district-attorneys shall be chosen by the people of the several districts, for such term of office as the legislature shall prescribe.

This Amendment was ratified in 1855. Article of Amendment XXXVI, ratified in 1894, removed a reference in the original to "commissioners of insolvency." Amendment XIX does not affect the powers of the Attorney General. *Commonwealth v. Kozlowsky* (1921). It also does not apply to clerks of district courts. *Commonwealth v. Mather* (1876). Nor does it affect the offices mentioned in the text other than by the manner of their election. *Attorney Gen. v. Pelletier* (1922). The General Court has the power to control these offices in any manner other than the manner of the officer's election. *Id.* This amendment does not, however, proscribe the legislative enactment of term limits for the applicable offices. *Opinion of the Justices* (1982).

ARTICLE XX. Qualifications of Person Eligible for Office

No person shall [have the right to vote, or] be eligible to office under the constitution of this commonwealth, who shall not be able to read the constitution in the English language, and write his name: —provided, however, that the provisions of this amendment shall not apply to any person prevented by a physical disability from complying with its requisitions, nor to any person who now has the right to vote, nor to any persons who shall be sixty years of age or upwards at the time this amendment shall take effect.

Amendment XX, ratified in 1857, provides that persons may not vote in elections if they cannot read the constitution in the English language and write their names. Amendment XXIII, ratified in 1859 and annulled in 1863 by Amendment XXVI, provided that all foreign-born persons be disabled from voting until having resided in the United States two years after they had been naturalized as an American citizen. The language in the first line is bracketed to reflect the fact that it violates the Federal Voting Rights Act, see *Katzenbach v. Morgan* (1966); *South Carolina v. Katzenbach* (1966).

ARTICLE XXIV. Vacancies in the Senate

Any vacancy in the senate shall be filled by election by the people of the unrepresented district, upon the order of a majority of senators elected.

This amendment, ratified in 1860, supersedes the provisions of Part II, c. I, sec. II, art. IV of the original constitution. It is another in the series of nineteenth-century amendments increasing elective power over public offices. Part II, c. I, sec. II, art. IV had provided that vacancies be filled by the Legislature. It is not clear whether the Amendment means that the Senators have the power still, if they so desire, to resort to the old method of filling vacancies, or whether they can refuse to fill a vacancy if they choose not to. The Supreme Judicial Court has ruled that the Senate need not wait until an impending vacancy occurs to prepare to fill that vacancy, so long as there is no overlap between successor and predecessor. *Wyler v. Sec'y of the Commonwealth* (2004).

ARTICLE XXV. Vacancies in the Council

In case of a vacancy in the council, from a failure of election or other cause, the senate and house of representatives shall, by concurrent vote, choose some eligible person from the people of the district wherein such vacancy occurs, to fill that office. If such vacancy shall happen when the legislature is not in session, the governor, with the advice and consent of the council, may fill the same by appointment of some eligible person.

This Amendment, ratified in 1860, supersedes the provisions of Article of Amendment XIII and Part II, c. II, sec. III, art. II. This Amendment makes clear that the Legislature has the power under Amendment XIII to select another

Councillor from among the people at large, places certain restrictions on the process, and, for the first time, gives the Governor and Council the power to make an interim appointment. The Supreme Judicial Court has noted that nothing in the constitution prevents the election of a Councillor who is not a resident of the electing district. *Bigney v. Sec'y of Commonwealth* (1938). Amendment XXV, however, is a reflection of the view that, when the Senate or House or Representatives fills such a vacancy, the Councillor should be a resident of the councillor district where the vacancy occurs. *Id.*

ARTICLE XXVIII. No Disqualification of Veterans From Voting

No person having served in the army or navy of the United States in time of war, and having been honorably discharged from such service, if otherwise qualified to vote, shall be disqualified therefor on account of receiving or having received aid from any city or town, or because of the non-payment of a poll tax.

Ratified in 1881, this provision originally superseded the provisions of Amendment III by relieving the described veterans of the voting requirement that they not be paupers and, if they were paupers, from any voting requirement that they paid a poll tax. Amendment XXXI, ratified in 1890, replaced the language "being a pauper" with the language "receiving or having received aid from any city or town" and struck out the language "if a pauper" which had appeared between the words "or" and "because" in the last clause. The original Amendment was an effort to reward persons who had served in wartime, especially the Civil War. Amendment XXXI presumably was passed to remove the stain of calling the veterans affected "paupers" and to remove the necessity for any veterans to pay a poll tax, whether "paupers" or not.

ARTICLE XXIX. Voting Precincts in Towns

The general court shall have full power and authority to provide for the inhabitants of the towns in this commonwealth more than one place of public meeting within the limits of each town for the election of officers under the constitution, and to prescribe the manner of calling, holding and conducting such meetings. All the provisions of the existing constitution inconsistent with the provisions herein contained are hereby annulled.

This provision was ratified in 1885, and it has not been amended. It is another of the nineteenth-century provisions liberalizing voting. Previously, all references to voting in the constitution were to votes at a town meeting held for that purpose. This provision empowers the Legislature to make voting more convenient by arranging for it to be done at numerous polling places located in the town or city. Prior to this Amendment, the Massachusetts Constitution recognized only a town as a voting unit. *Opinion of the Justices* (1918).

The Amendment was required to allow the division of towns into voting precincts. *Id.* This amendment does not prohibit the General Court from authorizing a town to hold town meetings outside of the town limits for deliberative purpose or any purpose other than for purposes of elections. *Opinion of the Justices* (1971).

ARTICLE XXX. Voter Qualifications

No person, otherwise qualified to vote in elections for governor, lieutenant-governor, senators, and representatives, shall, by reason of a change of residence within the commonwealth, be disqualified from voting for said officers in the city or town from which he has removed his residence, until the expiration of six calendar months from the time of such removal.

This provision was ratified in 1890, and has not been amended. This is another in the string of amendments liberalizing the election process. This provision ensures that no person becomes disfranchised as a result of moving from one location to another within the commonwealth.

ARTICLE XXXIII. Legislative Quorum

A majority of the members of each branch of the general court shall constitute a quorum for the transaction of business, but a less number may adjourn from day to day, and compel the attendance of absent members. All the provisions of the existing constitution inconsistent with the provisions herein contained are hereby annulled.

Ratified in 1891, this Amendment has not been amended. It annuls as inconsistent with it the provisions of Part II, c. I, sec. II, art. IX (quorum in the Senate), Amendment XXII, ratified in 1857 (quorum in the Senate), Part II, c. I, sec. III, art. IX (quorum in the House), and Amendment XXXIII, ratified in 1857 (quorum in the House). This provision increases the number of Senators and Representatives who must be present to make a quorum to 21 and 121, respectively, but, at the same time, gives the branches of the Legislature the power to adjourn in the absence of a quorum and compel absent members to attend. Overriding a gubernatorial veto requires only a two-thirds vote of the members present rather than a two-thirds vote of the entire membership. *Kay Jewelry Co. v. Bd. of Registration*, 305 Mass. 581, 586–89 (1940).

ARTICLE XXXVII. Removal of Justices of the Peace and Notaries Public

The governor, with the consent of the council, may remove justices of the peace and notaries public.

Ratified in 1907, this provision has not been amended. It implicitly amends Part II, c. III, arts. I and III of the original constitution. More important, it implicitly amends Amendment IV, ratified in 1821, which provided that notaries public could be removed by the Governor and Council, but only upon the address of both houses of the Legislature. Prior to this Amendment, it would have seemed justices of the peace served as commissioned officers holding seven-year terms that could be cut short only by death, resignation, or impeachment—or, depending upon how one reads Part II, c. III, art. I, they were also subject to removal by the Governor and Council "upon the address of both Houses of the Legislature." This Amendment simplifies and expedites the process for removing justices of the peace during their terms of office, eliminating the requirement originally found in Amendment IV that the Governor and Council first address the Legislature before removing a justice of the peace or notary.

ARTICLE XXXVIII. Voting Machines

Voting machines or other mechanical devices for voting may be used at all elections under such regulations as may be prescribed by law: provided, however, that the right of secret voting shall be preserved.

Ratified in 1911, this provision has not been amended. This is the first mention of secret voting in the constitution (see Amendment LXI) and the only constitutional protection of an interest in having one's voting choice be confidential, though earlier legislation provided for the secret ballot.

ARTICLE XLI. Taxation of Wild or Forest Lands

Full power and authority are hereby given and granted to the general court to prescribe for wild or forest lands retained in a natural state for the preservation of wildlife and other natural resources and lands for recreational uses, such methods of taxation as will develop and conserve the forest resources, wildlife and other natural resources and the environmental benefits of recreational lands within the commonwealth.

The original version of this Amendment was ratified in 1912. Amendment CX annulled and replaced XLI with the text included here. This is one of a series of amendments (beginning with Amendment XXXIX) empowering the Legislature to deal with specific public problems in light of concerns that there might otherwise be "internal" or "external" constitutional limitations upon its power to do so. This provision seems designed to prevent both sorts of problems. Without the provision, there might have been a claim, for example, that the Legislature lacked the power (an "internal" limit) to deal with preservation of forest lands because such legislation was not for the "common good." See Part II, c. I, sec. I, art. IV. More obviously, this provision seems designed to get around limits on the taxing power. Without the provision, the Legislature might have run into problems giving such lands a low assessed value as recreational lands instead of farms, residential areas, commercial areas, etc., given that Part II, c. I, § I, art. IV requires that all taxes be assessed in a fashion which is "equal," "proportional," and "reasonable."

Of course, to allow the Legislature to employ "such methods of taxation" does not necessarily mean that those methods do not also have to meet the requirements of Part II, c. I, sec. I, art. IV. The Supreme Judicial Court requires explicit constitutional language granting immunity from such "external" restrictions, and may interpret such language narrowly. See, e.g., *Commonwealth v. Colon-Cruz* (1984) (court, narrowly defining "prohibit," held amendment restraining court from construing the constitution as prohibiting the death penalty did not make death penalty statutes immune from other portions of the Declaration of Rights).

ARTICLE XLIII. Takings

The general court shall have power to authorize the commonwealth to take land and to hold, improve, sub-divide, build upon and sell the same, for the purpose of relieving congestion of population and providing homes for citizens: provided, however, that this amendment shall not be deemed to authorize the sale of such land or buildings at less than the cost thereof.

Ratified in 1915, this Amendment has not been amended. This is one of a series of amendments empowering the Legislature to deal with specific public problems in light of concerns that there might otherwise be "internal" or "external" constitutional limitations upon its power to do so. Besides making clear that the taking and holding of land is within the police power of the Commonwealth and not prohibited by principles of substantive due process, this Amendment authorizes the Legislature to provide for the taking of property by eminent domain without running afoul of Part I, art. X. The Supreme Judicial Court has recognized the power of eminent domain, embodied in this amendment, to be "one of the highest attributes of sovereignty," and statutes enacted under this power are entitled to compliance. *McAuliffe & Burke Co. v. Boston Hous. Auth.* (1956). Though the taking of particular property is typically done by state agencies pursuing appropriate goals, a taking may be legislated directly by the General Court. *Lutheran Serv. Ass'n v. Metro. Dist. Com'n* (1986). The power to appropriate private property under this Amendment may also be delegated by statute to cities or towns. *Burnham v. Mayor & Alderman of Beverly* (1941).

ARTICLE XLIV. Income Tax

Full power and authority are hereby given and granted to the general court to impose and levy a tax on income in the manner hereinafter provided. Such tax may be at different rates upon income derived from different classes of property, but shall be levied at a uniform rate throughout the commonwealth upon incomes derived from the same class of property. The general court may tax income not derived from property at a lower rate than income derived from property, and may grant reasonable exemptions and abatements. Any class of property the income from which is taxed under the provisions of this article

may be exempted from the imposition and levying of proportional and reasonable assessments, rates and taxes as at present authorized by the constitution. This article shall not be construed to limit the power of the general court to impose and levy reasonable duties and excises.

Ratified in 1915, this provision has not been amended. Article XLIV confers upon the General Court the power to impose and levy an income tax. *In re Vautier* (1960). This Amendment may have been seen as necessary to bring the Legislature out from under the restrictions of Part II, c. I, sec. I, art. IV, regarding the "proportionality," "equality," and "reasonableness" of tax legislation. *Duffy v. Burrill* (1919). Even if the Legislature had the power to tax income, it was not clear whether it could do so in a form that taxed income at different rates depending upon the kind of property that produced the income, whether income derived came from property at all, and whether the Legislature could allow reasonable exemptions and abatements.

The Massachusetts income tax is not a graduated tax like the federal system, but rather is a system of separate income taxes determined by the class of property from which income is derived. *Wolcott v. State Tax Comm'n* (1960). Income derived from the same class of property must be taxed at a uniform rate. *Comm'r of Revenue v. Lonstein* (1989). Distinctions between classes of property must be based on "actual underlying differences." *Id.* As long as some qualitative distinction exists, the court may uphold the classification. See *Filios v. Comm'r of Revenue* (1993) (holding distinction between contributory and noncontributory retirement system was actual underlying difference).

The state has the general power to tax income. *Ingraham v. State Tax Comm'n* (1975); *First Nat. Bank v. Comm'r of Corp. & Tax.* (1932) ("There can be no doubt that income is a proper subject for taxation."). The "income" that may be taxed is broad in scope and should be an actual gain—an actual increase in wealth and not "paper" income. *Bill DeLecua Enters., Inc. v. Commissioner of Revenue* (2000). This comprehensive scope of the income tax includes income received by a resident from out-of-state property on the basis that residents receive many benefits from their state of residence and should contribute to the support of the state, regardless of the source of income. *Ingraham.* Though a state may not impose a property tax on real estate located outside of its borders, Amendment XLIV does allow the taxation of income earned from real estate located outside of Massachusetts. See *Senior v. Braden* (1935); *Ingraham.*

Importantly, nothing in the Amendment authorizes the classification of the owners of property or of taxpayers for the same purposes. *Opinion of the Justices* (1929). A graduated rate structure that taxes based on classifications of owners of property is prohibited by Article XLIV. *Id.*; see also *Opinion of the Justices* (1981) (holding tax based on flat percentage of Federal tax would violate uniformity requirement of Article XLIV). At the same time, the General Court may legislatively create exemptions that have the effect of taxing Massachusetts citizens based upon their ability to pay. *Opinion of the Justices* (1982) (holding "uniform rate" requirement is not absolute because Article XLIV permits "reasonable exemptions and abatements").

In 1986, for example, the Supreme Judicial Court considered the constitutionality of an act that increased the number of exemptions and broadened the categories from 10 in 1982 to 184 in 1986. *Mass. Taxpayers Found., Inc. v. Sec'y of Admin.* (1986). The exemptions created by the act also had the effect of decreasing at a different rate for high-rate taxpayers. *Id.* The act was unconstitutional because it was a set of "intricately conceived exemptions, which unabashedly intended to apportion tax relief among the taxpayers based on their ability to pay." *Id.* "More," the court said, was "required to demonstrate that the balance between uniformity and reasonableness has been achieved than a mere mechanistic application of economic indices." *Id.*

Statutory exemptions may be phrased in terms of owners of property and yet still be constitutional if the essential distinction of the exemption is "one of the nature of the business and incidents which characterize the property employed therein." *Barnes v. State Tax Comm'n* (1973). While the General Court may legislate reasonable exemptions they may not create nonproportional tax credits. *Opinion of the Justices* (1968). Article XLIV also prohibits the taxation of fictional gain, but does not serve to eliminate transactional inequities from the tax system. *Bill DeLuca Enters., Inc. v. Comm'r of Revenue* (2000).

ARTICLE XLV. Absentee Voting

The general court shall have power to provide by law for voting, in the choice of any officer to be elected or upon any question submitted at an election, by qualified voters of the commonwealth who, at the time of such an election, are absent from the city or town of which they are inhabitants or are unable by reason of physical disability to cast their votes in person at the polling places or who hold religious beliefs in conflict with the act of voting on the day on which such an election is to be held.

The original Amendment XLV was ratified in 1918. It authorized the Legislature only to provide for absentee voting for the election of officers and upon questions when the voter involved was absent from the city or town of which he or she was an inhabitant on the day of election. Amendment LXXVI, ratified in 1944, annulled the original Amendment XLV and replaced it with one that essentially added the provision authorizing absentee voting laws for those unable to vote by reason of physical disability. It also reorganized the language of the amendment to make it a bit clearer. Amendment CV, ratified in 1976, annulled Amendment XLV as so amended, and replaced it with the language above, which merely added the final provision authorizing absentee voting laws for those whose religious beliefs forbid them to vote on a particular election day.

ARTICLE XLVII. Distribution of Necessaries in Emergencies

The maintenance and distribution at reasonable rates, during time of war, public exigency, emergency or distress, of a sufficient supply of food and other common necessaries of life and the providing of shelter, are public functions, and the commonwealth and the cities and towns therein may take and may provide the same for their inhabitants in such manner as the general court shall determine.

Ratified in 1918, this provision has not been amended. In this Amendment, the language of "public function" is used for at least the purpose of meeting the requirements of "public use" in Part I, art. X, concerning condemnation of property—the language speaks, among other things, of the power to "take" during the emergency conditions described. Otherwise, the purpose of the amendment seems to be to make clear that this is to be among the "police powers" in Part II, c. I, sec. I, art. IV, and not prohibited by the substantive due process strictures of Part I, art. XII. In 1935, the Supreme Judicial Court rejected a statute creating a corporation to be operated by a board of directors appointed by the Governor that would maintain funds for the insurance of real estate values and banks and other lending institutions. *Opinion of the Justices* (1935). The purposes of insuring real estate values and the money lending business, according to the court, were not public functions under the meaning of Article XLVII. *Id.* In 1947, on the other hand, the Supreme Judicial Court held that a bill authorizing the Commonwealth to raise and expend money to house World War II veterans and their families was a public function within the meaning of Article XLVII. *Opinion of the Justices* (1947).

ARTICLE XLVIII. Initiative and Referendum

I. DEFINITION.

Legislative power shall continue to be vested in the general court; but the people reserve to themselves the popular initiative, which is the power of a specified number of voters to submit constitutional amendments and laws to the people for approval or rejection; and the popular referendum, which is the power of a specified number of voters to submit laws, enacted by the general court, to the people for their ratification or rejection.

THE INITIATIVE

II. INITIATIVE PETITIONS.

SECTION 1. *Contents.*—An initiative petition shall set forth the full text of the constitutional amendment or law, hereinafter designated as the measure, which is proposed by the petition.

SECTION 2. *Excluded Matters.*—No measure that relates to religion, religious practices or religious institutions; or to the appointment, qualification, tenure, removal, recall or compensation of judges; or to the reversal of a judicial decision; or to the powers, creation or abolition of courts; or the operation of which is restricted to a particular town, city or other political division or to particular districts or localities of the commonwealth; or that makes a specific

appropriation of money from the treasury of the commonwealth, shall be proposed by an initiative petition; but if a law approved by the people is not repealed, the general court shall raise by taxation or otherwise and shall appropriate such money as may be necessary to carry such law into effect.

Neither the eighteenth amendment of the constitution, as approved and ratified to take effect on the first day of October in the year nineteen hundred and eighteen, nor this provision for its protection, shall be the subject of an initiative amendment.

No proposition inconsistent with any one of the following rights of the individual, as at present declared in the declaration of rights, shall be the subject of an initiative or referendum petition: The right to receive compensation for private property appropriated to public use; the right of access to and protection in courts of justice; the right of trial by jury; protection from unreasonable search, unreasonable bail and the law martial; freedom of the press; freedom of speech; freedom of elections; and the right of peaceable assembly.

No part of the constitution specifically excluding any matter from the operation of the popular initiative and referendum shall be the subject of an initiative petition; nor shall this section be the subject of such a petition.

The limitations on the legislative power of the general court in the constitution shall extend to the legislative power of the people as exercised hereunder.

SECTION 3. *Mode of Originating.*—Such petition shall first be signed by ten qualified voters of the commonwealth and shall be submitted to the attorney-general not later than the first Wednesday of the August before the assembling of the general court into which it is to be introduced, and if he shall certify that the measure and the title thereof are in proper form for submission to the people, and that the measure is not, either affirmatively or negatively, substantially the same as any measure which has been qualified for submission or submitted to the people at either of the two preceding biennial state elections, and that it contains only subjects not excluded from the popular initiative and which are related or which are mutually dependent, it may then be filed with the secretary of the commonwealth. The secretary of the commonwealth shall provide blanks for the use of subsequent signers, and shall print at the top of each blank a fair, concise summary, as determined by the attorney-general, of the proposed measure as such summary will appear on the ballot together with the names and residences of the first ten signers. All initiative petitions, with the first ten signatures attached, shall be filed with the secretary of the commonwealth not earlier than the first Wednesday of the September before the assembling of the general court into which they are to be introduced, and the remainder of the required signatures shall be filed not later than the first Wednesday of the following December.

SECTION 4. *Transmission to the General Court.*—If an initiative petition, signed by the required number of qualified voters, has been filed as aforesaid, the secretary of the commonwealth shall, upon the assembling of the general court, transmit it to the clerk of the house of representatives, and the proposed measure shall then be deemed to be introduced and pending.

III. LEGISLATIVE ACTION. GENERAL PROVISIONS.

SECTION 1. *Reference to Committee.*—If a measure is introduced into the general court by initiative petition, it shall be referred to a committee thereof, and the petitioners and all parties in interest shall be heard, and the measure shall be considered and reported upon to the general court with the committee's recommendations, and the reasons therefor, in writing. Majority and minority reports shall be signed by the members of said committee.

SECTION 2. *Legislative Substitutes.*—The general court may, by resolution passed by yea and nay vote, either by the two houses separately, or in the case of a constitutional amendment by a majority of those voting thereon in joint session in each of two years as hereinafter provided, submit to the people a substitute for any measure introduced by initiative petition, such substitute to be designated on the ballot as the legislative substitute for such an initiative measure and to be grouped with it as an alternative therefor.

IV. LEGISLATIVE ACTION ON PROPOSED CONSTITUTIONAL AMENDMENTS.

SECTION 1. *Definition.*—A proposal for amendment to the constitution introduced into the general court by initiative petition shall be designated an initiative amendment, and an amendment introduced by a member of either house shall be designated a legislative substitute or a legislative amendment.

SECTION 2. *Joint Session.*—If a proposal for a specific amendment of the constitution is introduced into the general court by initiative petition signed in the aggregate by not less than such number of voters as will equal three per cent of the entire vote cast for governor at the preceding biennial state election, or if in case of a proposal for amendment introduced into the general court by a member of either house, consideration thereof in joint session is called for by vote of either house, such proposal shall, not later than the second Wednesday in May, be laid before a joint session of the two houses, at which the president of the senate shall preside; and if the two houses fail to agree upon a time for holding any joint session hereby required, or fail to continue the same from time to time until final action has been taken upon all amendments pending, the governor shall call such joint session or continuance thereof.

SECTION 3. *Amendment of Proposed Amendments.*—A proposal for an amendment to the constitution introduced by initiative petition shall be voted upon in the form in which it was introduced, unless such amendment is amended by vote of three-fourths of the members voting thereon in joint session, which vote shall be taken by call of the yeas and nays if called for by any member.

SECTION 4. *Legislative Action.*—Final legislative action in the joint session upon any amendment shall be taken only by call of the yeas and nays, which shall be entered upon the journals of the two houses; and an unfavorable vote at any stage preceding final action shall be verified by call of the yeas and nays, to be entered in like manner. At such joint session a legislative amendment receiving the affirmative votes of a majority of all the members elected, or an initiative amendment receiving the affirmative votes of not less than one-fourth of all the members elected, shall be referred to the next general court.

SECTION 5. *Submission to the People.*—If in the next general court a legislative amendment shall again be agreed to in joint session by a majority of all the members elected, or if an initiative amendment or a legislative substitute shall again receive the affirmative votes of at least one-fourth of all the members elected, such fact shall be certified by the clerk of such joint session to the secretary of the commonwealth, who shall submit the amendment to the people at the next state election. Such amendment shall become part of the constitution if approved, in the case of a legislative amendment, by a majority of the voters voting thereon, or if approved, in the case of an initiative amendment or a legislative substitute, by voters equal in number to at least thirty per cent of the total number of ballots cast at such state election and also by a majority of the voters voting on such amendment.

V. LEGISLATIVE ACTION ON PROPOSED LAWS.

SECTION 1. *Legislative Procedure.*—If an initiative petition for a law is introduced into the general court, signed in the aggregate by not less than such number of voters as will equal three per cent of the entire vote cast for governor at the preceding biennial state election, a vote shall be taken by yeas and nays in both houses before the first Wednesday of May upon the enactment of such law in the form in which it stands in such petition. If the general court fails to enact such law before the first Wednesday of May, and if such petition is completed by filing with the secretary of the commonwealth, not earlier than the first Wednesday of the following June nor later than the first Wednesday of the following July, a number of signatures of qualified voters equal in number to not less than one half of one per cent of the entire vote cast for governor at the preceding biennial state election, in addition to those signing such initiative petition, which signatures must have been obtained after the first Wednesday of May aforesaid, then the secretary of the commonwealth shall submit such proposed law to the people at the next state election. If it shall be approved by voters equal in number to at least thirty per cent of the total number of ballots cast at such state election and also by a majority of the voters voting on such law, it shall become law, and shall take effect in thirty days after such state election or at such time after such election as may be provided in such law.

SECTION 2. *Amendment by Petitioners.*—If the general court fails to pass a proposed law before the first Wednesday of May, a majority of the first ten signers

of the initiative petition therefor shall have the right, subject to certification by the attorney-general filed as hereinafter provided, to amend the measure which is the subject of such petition. An amendment so made shall not invalidate any signature attached to the petition. If the measure so amended, signed by a majority of the first ten signers, is filed with the secretary of the commonwealth before the first Wednesday of the following June, together with a certificate signed by the attorney-general to the effect that the amendment made by such proposers is in his opinion perfecting in its nature and does not materially change the substance of the measure, and if such petition is completed by filing with the secretary of the commonwealth, not earlier than the first Wednesday of the following June nor later than the first Wednesday of the following July, a number of signatures of qualified voters equal in number to not less than one half of one per cent of the entire vote cast for governor at the preceding biennial state election in addition to those signing such initiative petition, which signatures must have been obtained after the first Wednesday of May aforesaid, then the secretary of the commonwealth shall submit the measure to the people in its amended form.

VI. CONFLICTING AND ALTERNATIVE MEASURES.
If in any judicial proceeding, provisions of constitutional amendments or of laws approved by the people at the same election are held to be in conflict, then the provisions contained in the measure that received the largest number of affirmative votes at such election shall govern.

A constitutional amendment approved at any election shall govern any law approved at the same election.

The general court, by resolution passed as hereinbefore set forth, may provide for grouping and designating upon the ballot as conflicting measures or as alternative measures, only one of which is to be adopted, any two or more proposed constitutional amendments or laws which have been or may be passed or qualified for submission to the people at any one election: provided, that a proposed constitutional amendment and a proposed law shall not be so grouped, and that the ballot shall afford an opportunity to the voter to vote for each of the measures or for only one of the measures, as may be provided in said resolution, or against each of the measures so grouped as conflicting or as alternative. In case more than one of the measures so grouped shall receive the vote required for its approval as herein provided, only that one for which the largest affirmative vote was cast shall be deemed to be approved.

THE REFERENDUM

I. WHEN STATUTES SHALL TAKE EFFECT.
No law passed by the general court shall take effect earlier than ninety days after it has become a law, excepting laws declared to be emergency laws and laws which may not be made the subject of a referendum petition, as herein provided.

II. EMERGENCY MEASURES.

A law declared to be an emergency law shall contain a preamble setting forth the facts constituting the emergency, and shall contain the statement that such law is necessary for the immediate preservation of the public peace, health, safety or convenience. A separate vote, which shall be recorded, shall be taken on the preamble, and unless the preamble is adopted by two-thirds of the members of each House voting thereon, the law shall not be an emergency law. Upon the request of two members of the Senate or of five members of the House of Representatives, the vote on the preamble in such branch shall be taken by call of the yeas and nays. But if the governor, at any time before the election at which it is to be submitted to the people on referendum, files with the secretary of the commonwealth a statement declaring that in his opinion the immediate preservation of the public peace, health, safety or convenience requires that such law should take effect forthwith and that it is an emergency law and setting forth the facts constituting the emergency, then such law, if not previously suspended as hereinafter provided, shall take effect without suspension, or if such law has been so suspended such suspension shall thereupon terminate and such law shall thereupon take effect: but no grant of any franchise or amendment thereof, or renewal or extension thereof for more than one year shall be declared to be an emergency law.

III. REFERENDUM PETITIONS.

SECTION 1. *Contents.*—A referendum petition may ask for a referendum to the people upon any law enacted by the general court which is not herein expressly excluded.

SECTION 2. *Excluded Matters.*—No law that relates to religion, religious practices or religious institutions; or to the appointment, qualification, tenure, removal or compensation of judges; or to the powers, creation or abolition of courts; or the operation of which is restricted to a particular town, city or other political division or to particular districts or localities of the commonwealth; or that appropriates money for the current or ordinary expenses of the commonwealth or for any of its departments, boards, commissions or institutions shall be the subject of a referendum petition.

SECTION 3. *Mode of Petitioning for the Suspension of a Law and a Referendum thereon.*—A petition asking for a referendum on a law, and requesting that the operation of such law be suspended, shall first be signed by ten qualified voters and shall then be filed with the secretary of the commonwealth not later than thirty days after the law that is the subject of the petition has become law. The secretary of the commonwealth shall provide blanks for the use of subsequent signers, and shall print at the top of each blank a fair, concise summary of the proposed law as such summary will appear on the ballot together with the names and residences of the first ten signers. If such petition is completed by filing with the secretary of the commonwealth not later

than ninety days after the law which is the subject of the petition has become law a number of signatures of qualified voters equal in number to not less than two per cent of the entire vote cast for governor at the preceding biennial state election, then the operation of such law shall be suspended, and the secretary of the commonwealth shall submit such law to the people at the next state election, if sixty days intervene between the date when such petition is filed with the secretary of the commonwealth and the date for holding such state election; if sixty days do not so intervene, then such law shall be submitted to the people at the next following state election, unless in the meantime it shall have been repealed; and if it shall be approved by a majority of the qualified voters voting thereon, such law shall, subject to the provisions of the constitution, take effect in thirty days after such election, or at such time after such election as may be provided in such law; if not so approved such law shall be null and void; but no such law shall be held to be disapproved if the negative vote is less than thirty per cent of the total number of ballots cast at such state election.

SECTION 4. *Petitions for Referendum on an Emergency Law or a Law the Suspension of which is not asked for.*—A referendum petition may ask for the repeal of an emergency law or of a law which takes effect because the referendum petition does not contain a request for suspension, as aforesaid. Such petition shall first be signed by ten qualified voters of the commonwealth, and shall then be filed with the secretary of the commonwealth not later than thirty days after the law which is the subject of the petition has become law. The secretary of the commonwealth shall provide blanks for the use of subsequent signers, and shall print at the top of each blank a fair, concise summary of the proposed law as such summary will appear on the ballot together with the names and residences of the first ten signers. If such petition filed as aforesaid is completed by filing with the secretary of the commonwealth not later than ninety days after the law which is the subject of the petition has become law a number of signatures of qualified voters equal in number to not less than one and one half per cent of the entire vote cast for governor at the preceding biennial state election protesting against such law and asking for a referendum thereon, then the secretary of the commonwealth shall submit such law to the people at the next state election, if sixty days intervene between the date when such petition is filed with the secretary of the commonwealth and the date for holding such state election. If sixty days do not so intervene, then it shall be submitted to the people at the next following state election, unless in the meantime it shall have been repealed; and if it shall not be approved by a majority of the qualified voters voting thereon, it shall, at the expiration of thirty days after such election, be thereby repealed; but no such law shall be held to be disapproved if the negative vote is less than thirty per cent of the total number of ballots cast at such state election.

GENERAL PROVISIONS

I. IDENTIFICATION AND CERTIFICATION OF SIGNATURES.
Provision shall be made by law for the proper identification and certification of signatures to the petitions hereinbefore referred to, and for penalties for signing any such petition, or refusing to sign it, for money or other valuable consideration, and for the forgery of signatures thereto. Pending the passage of such legislation all provisions of law relating to the identification and certification of signatures to petitions for the nomination of candidates for state offices or to penalties for the forgery of such signatures shall apply to the signatures to the petitions herein referred to. The general court may provide by law that no co-partnership or corporation shall undertake for hire or reward to circulate petitions, may require individuals who circulate petitions for hire or reward to be licensed, and may make other reasonable regulations to prevent abuses arising from the circulation of petitions for hire or reward.

II. LIMITATION ON SIGNATURES.
Not more than one-fourth of the certified signatures on any petition shall be those of registered voters of any one county.

III. FORM OF BALLOT.
A fair, concise summary, as determined by the attorney general, subject to such provision as may be made by law, of each proposed amendment to the constitution, and each law submitted to the people, shall be printed on the ballot, and the secretary of the commonwealth shall give each question a number and cause such question, except as otherwise authorized herein, to be printed on the ballot in the following form:—

In the case of an amendment to the constitution:

Do you approve of the adoption of an amendment to the constitution summarized below, (here state, in distinctive type, whether approved or disapproved by the General Court, and by what vote thereon)?

YES: ____________ NO: ____________

(Set forth summary here)

In the case of a law:

Do you approve the law summarized below:

YES: ____________ NO: ____________

(Set forth summary here)

IV. INFORMATION FOR VOTERS.
The secretary of the commonwealth shall cause to be printed and sent to each person eligible to vote in the commonwealth or to each residence of

one or more persons eligible to vote in the commonwealth the full text of every measure to be submitted to the people, together with a copy of the legislative committee's majority and minority reports, if there be such, with the names of the majority and minority members thereon, a statement of the votes of the general court on the measure, and a fair, concise summary of the measure as such summary will appear on the ballot; and shall, in such manner as may be provided by law, cause to be prepared and sent other information and arguments for and against the measure.

V. THE VETO POWER OF THE GOVERNOR.
The veto power of the governor shall not extend to measures approved by the people.

VI. THE GENERAL COURT'S POWER OF REPEAL.
Subject to the veto power of the governor and to the right of referendum by petition as herein provided, the general court may amend or repeal a law approved by the people.

VII. AMENDMENT DECLARED TO BE SELF-EXECUTING.
This article of amendment to the constitution is self-executing, but legislation not inconsistent with anything herein contained may be enacted to facilitate the operation of its provisions.

VIII. ARTICLES IX AND XLII OF THE AMENDMENTS OF THE CONSTITUTION ANNULLED.
Article IX and Article XLII of the amendments of the constitution are hereby annulled.

A product of the 1917–18 convention and ratified in 1918, the original Amendment XLVIII added initiative and referendum procedure to the constitution. In so doing, it explicitly annulled and superseded Amendment XLII, ratified in 1913, which had taken the first steps toward a referendum process in the Commonwealth, by giving to the Legislature the power to refer legislation to the people for a referendum at the next general election. Because the original amendment addressed not only legislation but the constitutional amendment process, it also replaced Article of Amendment IX, ratified in 1821, regarding the process for amending the constitution thereafter.

Amendment XLVIII has itself been amended several times. Amendment LXVII, ratified in 1922, changed the language of the original section two having to do with emergency measures. Rather than requiring a roll call vote in every instance, it provided that emergencies might be declared without a roll call unless two members of the Senate or five members of the House of Representatives requested it. Amendment LXXIV, ratified in 1944, changed the cut-off for precluding questions that had recently been defeated from three years to any that had been considered at either of the two preceding biennial elections. Amendment LXXXI, ratified in 1950, changed the signature requirements for placing a matter on the ballot or sending a matter to the Legislature from the absolute numbers which had been specified to a percentage of the popular vote cast for Governor in the preceding election. It also altered some deadlines. Amendment CVIII, ratified in 1978, made only a minor change—requiring that the Secretary of State mail information on measures to appear on the ballot to all residences with one or more "eligible voters" rather than only to "registered voters."

The Initiative

An initiative measure must propose a law, rather that simply present an announcement of public opinion. See *Paisner v. Att'y Gen.* (1983). The lawmaking power of the electorate through an initiative is equal to that of the Legislature. *Opinion of the Justices* (1996). Laws made by way of initiative must comport with the state constitution to the same extent as laws made by the Legislature. *Commonwealth v. Higgins* (1931); *Sears v. Treasurer & Receiver Gen.* (1951).

This Amendment also places some limits on the subject matter of measures proposed by initiative petition, though not the subject matter of measures proposed by legislators. *Opinion of the Justices* (1982). The Amendment excludes measures "that make[] a specific appropriation of money from the treasury of the commonwealth." *Tax Equity Alliance v. Comm'r of Revenue* (1987). But under the Amendment, the Legislature must raise by taxation or otherwise appropriate money necessary to carry out the laws enacted by way of initiative, unless the Legislature acts to repeal the law. *Bates v. Dir. of the Office of Campaign & Political Fin.* (2002). Further, the specific exclusion of appropriations does not prohibit the making of laws by way of initiative that will subsequently require the raising and appropriation of funds; neither does it require specific language in laws made by way of initiative to the effect that they are subject to appropriation. *Id.* For an initiative measure to be effective, the process must be in strict compliance with this Amendment; a constitutional error in the initiative process may not be disregarded despite a significant popular vote percentage in favor of the measure. *Massachusetts Teachers Ass'n v. Sec'y of Commonwealth.*

Any ten registered voters can begin the initiative process. The full text of a measure must be put before the original ten voters who sign it. *Capezzuto v. State Ballot Law Comm'n* (1990). Those voters file their proposed legislation or amendment with the Attorney General. A petition may contain more than one subject, but the constitution requires that those subjects be related. *Mass. Teachers Assoc.* The test for relatedness is quite broad: If "one can identify a common purpose to which each subject of an initiative petition can reasonably be said to be germane, the relatedness test is met." *Id.* After the voters file their proposed legislation or amendment, the Attorney General determines whether or not it is an appropriate subject for the initiative under the terms of the amendment—whether the initiative is a law or constitutional amendment—and he or she decides whether to certify the petition. See, e.g., *Paisner v. Attorney Gen.* (1983). If certified, the Secretary of State supplies the voters with printed forms for collecting signatures amounting to 3 percent of those voting in the last gubernatorial election. The Secretary attaches a fair and concise summary, prepared by the Attorney General, of the proposed matter that is the subject matter of a petition. *Barnes v. Sec. of Commonwealth* (1965). The Attorney General's judgment as to what is to be included in a summary is granted a certain amount of deference by Massachusetts courts. *Mazzone v. Attorney Gen.* (2000). It is the summary, rather than the title of the measure placed on the petition, that informs voters of the contents of proposed law. *Nigro v. Attorney Gen.* (1988).

The measure next goes to the Legislature. If a proposal for amendment has been introduced to the General Court by initiative petition and the two Houses fail to agree on a time for holding a joint session, then the Governor is obligated to call such joint session or continuance thereof so that the proposal may be introduced before the second Wednesday in May of the year in which the proposal was introduced. *Opinion of the Justices* (1956). If a joint session fails to act on a proposed amendment, the only remedy is to direct the Governor to call a joint session or continuance of a joint session. *League of Women Voters v. Sec. of Commonwealth* (1997). The provision in the Amendment for "final legislative action" means action according to established legislative procedure, as modified by the constitutional requirements of the Amendment. *Opinion of the Justices* (1935). The words of this section do not preclude the joint session from making rules to regulate the procedure touching matters to be considered. *Id.* The Amendment requires the affirmative vote of at least one-fourth of the members of both Houses of two successive General Courts before a proposed amendment can be submitted to the people. *Opinion of the Justices* (1935). For legislative amendments made to initiative measures, this Amendment requires a majority (instead of one-fourth) of the members of the Legislature to approve the amendment. *Opinion of the Justices* (1982).

The second General Court that must vote on a proposed amendment need not be the next General Court after the first that voted on the proposed amendment. *Id.* The amendment only requires two successive General Courts to vote on a proposed amendment before it may be submitted to the people. *Id.* The one-fourth vote requirement is intended to be a "legislative minority check" to assure that initiative amendments submitted to the people have a reasonable amount of public support. *Opinion of the Justices* (1982). In considering the proposed initiative measure, the General Court bears the burden of determining the constitutionality of the measure before voting. *Opinion of the Justices* (1941).

If the measure is a proposed law and it fails in the Legislature as submitted, it can still be placed on the next ballot if additional signatures are obtained amounting to 0.5 percent of those voting in the last gubernatorial election. If it is a proposed constitutional amendment, it can pass only if it is voted for by two consecutive sessions of the Legislature as provided for. Voters are unable to avoid this provision by a signature campaign, but fewer votes are required in the Legislature to pass an initiative amendment on to the voters—one-fourth rather than a majority. In each case, the vote at the election in which the measure appears on the ballot must be by a majority of those voting on the question and, in the case of an initiative amendment or legislative substitute (rather than a legislatively proposed amendment), by at least 30 percent of those voting at the election.

Laws passed through this process are not subject to veto by the Governor. Alternatively, any law passed through this process is subject to repeal by the Legislature. The Governor, however, may veto laws proposed by the initiative process, yet ultimately enacted by the General Court. *Opinion of the Justices* (1976). Further, the Legislature has the power to propose its own substitutes which will then appear on the ballot with any initiative law or amendment as a substitute for it. The Legislature's proposed substitute must offer a true alternative, rather than a second approach that departs from the initiative's basic purpose. See *Buckley v. Sec'y of Commonwealth* (1976). If, in the instance of an initiative measure and a legislative substitute, both were to receive the required majority of the vote, the version that receives the largest number of votes prevails. *Id.*

The Amendment also excludes matters dealing with "the powers, creation or abolition of courts," but does not preclude the enactment by way of initiative of a measure that would subsidiarily increase, diminish, or change the work of the courts. *Cohen v. Attorney Gen.* (1968). In 1968, the Supreme Judicial Court considered an initiative amendment for the purpose of reducing the House from 240 to 160 members and for a decennial division of the Commonwealth into senatorial and representative districts. *Id.* The role of the courts in this initiative measure was the proposed duty of the Chief Justice of the Superior Court to name the chairman and appoint a commission to divide the Commonwealth in the representative and senatorial districts. The court held that the law would not violate the exclusion because it would only increase the work of the courts in a subsidiary and incidental way. *Id.*

That part of the Amendment that states that "[t]he limitations on the legislative power of the general court in the constitution shall extend to the legislative power of the people as exercised hereunder," prohibits the enactment by way of initiative of laws that would change the qualifications for public office as prescribed by the constitution. *League of Women Voters v. Sec. of the Commonwealth* (1997). In 1997, the Supreme Judicial Court considered the constitutionality of an approved initiative limiting the number of consecutive terms for which a public officer may be listed on the ballot for the same public office and eliminating the pay and privileges of public officers if reelected after serving a number of consecutive terms specified in the law. *Id.* Because the Legislature may not change the qualifications for elected office, and those limitations extend to the legislative power of the people, the approved initiative was unconstitutional. *Id.*

The Referendum

All laws, except emergency measures, are suspended from operation for ninety days so that the people can raise the question of whether they should come into effect by the referendum process. *Opinion of the Justices* (1975). Within thirty days after enactment, ten voters may file with the Secretary of State a petition for a referendum. That petition can request that the law be suspended until the election. To place the referendum on the ballot, signatures in the amount of 1.5 percent of the vote at the last gubernatorial election are required within ninety days of enactment. If it is also to be suspended, then 2 percent is required. If it has been declared an emergency measure by the Legislature, it cannot be so suspended. Even after suspension, the Governor can end the suspension by declaring it an emergency measure. *Opinion of the Justices* (1975). The vote at the election must be a majority in favor of the law—or the law will not take effect—so long as the number of persons voting against the law constitutes at least 30 percent of all persons voting.

An emergency preamble to a law enacted by the General Court indicates the law is an emergency law within the meaning of this section, and therefore that it may become effective prior to the expiration of the ninety-day limit. See *Coyle v. Swanson* (1962). Necessities of public health, safety, and convenience may be asserted to justify the declaration of an emergency. *Prescott v. Sec. of Commonwealth* (1938). Both the Legislature and the Governor have wide discretion in declaring the existence of an emergency. *Id.* The Governor may take action—by filing with the Secretary of State a statement of emergency under the Amendment only after a law has been passed. *Opinion of the Justices* (1975).

The matters excluded from the referendum that relate to appropriations made by the General Court fall into two categories: laws which appropriate money for the current or ordinary expenses of the Commonwealth; and laws which appropriate money for any of the departments, boards, commissions, or institutions of the Commonwealth. *Yont v. Sec. of Commonwealth* (1931). The exclusion of religious matters from referenda was to avoid the consequences of statewide discussion of such matters. *Collins v. Sec. of Commonwealth* (1990).

ARTICLE XLIX. Conservation of Natural Resources

The people shall have the right to clean air and water, freedom from excessive and unnecessary noise, and the natural, scenic, historic, and esthetic qualities of their environment; and the protection of the people in their right to the conservation, development and utilization of the agricultural, mineral, forest, water, air and other natural resources is hereby declared to be a public purpose.

The general court shall have the power to enact legislation necessary or expedient to protect such rights.

In the furtherance of the foregoing powers, the general court shall have the power to provide for the taking, upon payment of just compensation therefor, or for the acquisition by purchase or otherwise, of lands and easements or such other interests therein as may be deemed necessary to accomplish these purposes.

Lands and easements taken or acquired for such purposes shall not be used for other purposes or otherwise disposed of except by laws enacted by a two thirds vote, taken by yeas and nays, of each branch of the general court.

Ratified in 1918, the original Amendment was completely changed by Article of Amendment XCVII, ratified in 1972. As originally written, the Amendment was in the form and tradition of the other amendments extending the police power and the condemnation power; it spoke explicitly of "conservation, development, and utilization of the agricultural, mineral, forest, water and other natural resources of the commonwealth" as "public uses" and explicitly required the paying of just compensation for takings. As amended in 1972, the provision is more explicit in announcing rights in the people to a clean environment. It declares protection of the people in those rights as a "public purpose," as well as an express grant of authority to the Legislature to enact laws to further these ends. The fourth paragraph limits the Legislature's authority under this provision. The two-thirds vote requirement is only applicable when the "lands" or "easements" were "taken or acquired" for the purposes stated in the Amendment: "[T]he protection of the people in their right to the conservation, development and utilization of the agricultural, mineral, forest, water, air and other natural resources. . . ."

ARTICLE L. Regulation of Advertising on Public Ways

Advertising on public ways, in public places and on private property within public view may be regulated and restricted by law.

Ratified in 1918, this Amendment has not been amended. This provision appears to confirm that the regulation of certain kinds of advertising may be undertaken for the common good within the police power, without violating Part I, Art. VII (common good limit) or Part I, Art. XII (due process). In 1935, in *General Outdoor Advertising Co. v. Department of Public Works*, the Supreme Judicial Court stated that the primary purpose of the amendment of Article L was to set aside *Commonwealth v. Boston Advertising Company* (1905), which defined the limits of legislative power over advertising on privately owned land in public view.

Article L empowers the legislature to regulate and restrict advertising on private property. *Strazzalla v. Bldg. Inspector of Wellesley* (1970). The Legislature may delegate this power to municipalities. *Id.* The power under Article L to regulate and restrict also includes the power to prohibit. *John Donnelly & Sons, Inc. v. Outdoor Adver. Bd.* (1975). Article L does not authorize the General Court to legislate, or municipalities to regulate, advertising on private property that is not in public view. *Opinion of the Justices* (1919).

ARTICLE LI. Preservation of Ancient Landmarks

The preservation and maintenance of ancient landmarks and other property of historical or antiquarian interest is a public use, and the commonwealth and the cities and towns therein may, upon payment of just compensation, take such property or any interest therein under such regulations as the general court may prescribe.

Ratified in 1918, this provision has not been amended. This provision established that certain governmental operations are a "public use" in the language of Part I, art. X, so that eminent domain can be used so long as just compensation is paid. This power may be delegated to cities and towns. *Burnham v. Beverly* (1941).

ARTICLE LII. Legislative Recess

The general court, by concurrent vote of the two houses, may take a recess or recesses amounting to not more than thirty days.

Ratified in 1918, the original Amendment was amended by Amendment CII, ratified in 1974. This provision originally permitted the Legislature to recess for thirty days or fewer on concurrent vote of both Houses so long as the recess did not extend beyond the sixtieth day of their first assembling. Amendment CII dropped the last part of this provision. The original constitution seemed to provide no power to recess the Legislature. Part II, c. I, sec. I, art. I, speaks of "dissolving"; Part II, c. I, sec. II, art. VI and Part II, c. I, sec. III, art. VIII, speak of "adjourning"; and Part II, c. II, sec. I, art. V, speaks of the Governor taking a number of actions, none of which includes "recessing" the Legislature.

ARTICLE LVI. Return by Governor of Bills and Resolves

The governor, within ten days after any bill or resolve shall have been laid before him, shall have the right to return it to the branch of the general court in which it originated with a recommendation that any amendment or amendments specified by him be made therein;

Such bill or resolve shall thereupon be before the general court and subject to amendment and re-enactment. If such bill or resolve is re-enacted in any form it shall again be laid before the governor for his action, but he shall have no right to return the same a second time with a recommendation to amend.

Ratified in 1918, the original amendment was amended by Section 3 of Amendment XC, ratified in 1968, to provide ten days, rather than five, in which the Governor may take action regarding legislation that has been passed by both Houses of the General Court. The Amendment supplements the procedures for exercise of the Governor's veto in Part II, c. I, sec. I, art. II, and in other amendments that have supplemented those procedures, such as Amendment I, ratified in 1821. Time runs from when the Governor receives the bill and the date of receipt is excluded from the computation of days. *Opinion of the Justices* (1935). Sundays and holidays are excluded from the computation. *Id.* Amendment LVI as amended does not empower the Governor to approve only part of a bill; that office only has the power to suggest amendments with the return of the entire bill. *Opinion of the Justices* (1936).

The Governor's duty under Amendment LVI is a personal one and cannot be delegated. *Tuttle v. Boston* (1913). In 1913, while the five-day limit was still in effect, the Supreme Judicial Court was asked whether a pension statute was passed and became a law or was vetoed by the Governor. *Id.* The court held that a veto message left on the desk of the clerk after the close of business but before the end of the constitutionally effective day was not exercised by the Governor of the constitutional right described in Amendment LVI. *Id.*

ARTICLE LIX. Revocation and Amendment of Charters, Franchises, or Acts of Incorporation

Every charter, franchise or act of incorporation shall forever remain subject to revocation and amendment.

Ratified in 1918, this provision has not been amended. Interpreting this provision in 1927, the Supreme Judicial Court held that a bill extending the lease of the Boston Elevated Railway to the Commonwealth was not unconstitutional under Amendment LIX. *Opinion of the Justices* (1927). The extension, according to the court, did not represent a charter, franchise, or act of incorporation, but a contract as to public business between the Commonwealth and a public service corporation. *Id.* This Amendment does not apply to a public corporation operated for purely public purposes. *Opinion of the Justices* (1956) (Massachusetts Port Authority a public corporations created for a public purpose).

ARTICLE LX. Building Zones in Towns and Cities

The general court shall have power to limit buildings according to their use or construction to specified districts of cities and towns.

Ratified in 1918, this provision has not been amended. This Amendment makes no reference to compensation clause "public uses" and cites no specific concern with taxation limits; rather, it appears a raw extension of "police power" to deal with zoning issues. Importantly, zoning power is not constitutionally dependent on Article LX. *Commonwealth v. Sostilio* (1966). The power to zone falls under the police power, and, "[a]ll contracts between individuals, and even charters granted by the State, are subject to the exercise of [the police] power." *Brett v. Bldg. Comm'n of Brookline* (1924). As to buildings, however, the power of the General Court, is made Supreme by Amendment LX. *Bennett v. Bd. of Appeal* (1929). The General Court may delegate this power to cities and towns, and it follows that the power to grant zoning deviations may also be delegated. *Opinion of the Justices* (1960).

ARTICLE LXI. Compulsory Voting at Elections

The general court shall have authority to provide for compulsory voting at elections, but the right of secret voting shall be preserved.

Ratified in 1918, this provision has not been amended. It is not clear what in the constitution would have prevented the Legislature from enacting such legislation. Perhaps there were general fears about charges that the right to vote includes the right not to vote. This provision confirms the existence of an interest in secret voting. See Amendment XXXVIII.

ARTICLE LXII. Commonwealth's Credit; Borrowing Money for Certain Purposes

SECTION 1. The commonwealth may give, loan or pledge its credit only by a vote, taken by the yeas and nays, of two-thirds of each house of the General Court present and voting thereon. The credit of the commonwealth shall not in any manner be given or loaned to or in aid of any individual, or of any private association, or of any corporation which is privately owned and managed.

SECTION 2. The commonwealth may borrow money to repel invasion, suppress insurrection, defend the commonwealth, or to assist the United States in case of war, and may also borrow money in anticipation of receipts from taxes or other sources, such loan to be paid out of the revenue of the year in which it is created.

SECTION 3. In addition to the loans which may be contracted as before provided, the commonwealth may borrow money only by a vote, taken by the yeas and nays, of two-thirds of each house of the general court present and voting thereon. The governor shall recommend to the general court the term for which any loan shall be contracted.

SECTION 4. Borrowed money shall not be expended for any other purpose than that for which it was borrowed or for the reduction or discharge of the principal of the loan.

Ratified in 1918, this provision was amended in 1964 by Amendment LXXXIV. At the time this Amendment was ratified, Massachusetts was one of four states having no constitutional restrictions on the contracting of debts or loans by the state. *Ayer v. Comm'r of Admin.* (1960). The Commonwealth also had the second-highest debt of any state in the union. *Id.* The purpose of the Article is to restrict the ability of the legislature to contract debts or loans. *Id.*

Litigation over this provision has concerned entities, private or public, charged with the obligation to expend money toward some purpose. The funds for the expenditures are typically raised by the issuance of bonds guaranteed by the Commonwealth. Public money cannot be lent or applied to the aid of private entities. *Opinion of the Justices* (1927). Thus, when an agency of the Commonwealth entered into a rental contract with a private entity and the contract included an indemnification clause, the indemnification clause was "arguably a pledge of the credit of the Commonwealth in aid of a private individual or corporation" and the state agency would not be bound by it. *Lovering v. Beaudette* (1991).

The Commonwealth can guarantee bonds for public purposes, whether achieved through a public or private entity. See *Opinion of the Justices* (1996). Any private benefit deriving from a project funded by the Commonwealth must be incidental to the primary public purpose. *Opinion of the Justices* (1977). The Commonwealth however, may not guarantee bonds for a private purpose through a public entity. *Opinion of the Justices* (1935). A state-operated bank, formed for the purpose of insuring privately owned entities and for discounting certain mortgage obligations, could not lend funds to private individuals or entities. *Id.* Nonetheless, the court found that a law regarding public management of a railway and allowing loans by the Commonwealth was not unconstitutional. *Opinion of the Justices* (1927). "The Commonwealth cannot do through a public agency as the proposed corporation that which it is forbidden to do directly"—that is, to lend funds directly to private parties for private purposes. *Opinion of the Justices* (1935). Determining whether an entity is public requires analysis of multiple factors, such as whether the entity holds property in its own name; whether the entity can issue bonds in its own name (and not in the name of the Commonwealth); and whether it is an agent of the Commonwealth. *Opinion of the Justices* (1956). Some entities, like municipal corporations, bear resemblance to both a public and private entity; municipal corporations, however, are considered private entities.

Amendment LXII restricts the ability of the legislature to contract debts or loans by forcing state assistance to public service corporations on a "'pay-as-you-go' basis, not involving any absolute or contingent debt obligation on the part of the Commonwealth." *Opinion of the Justices* (1958). Nonetheless, borrowing by "a public authority which has a substantive existence independent of the Commonwealth does not constitute borrowing by the Commonwealth." *Opinion of the Justices* (1968).

Amendment LXII does not prohibit the Commonwealth from issuing and selling bonds and expending the funds raised from those sales to purchase public benefits from private corporations. *Opinion of the Justices* (1996). In 1996, the Supreme Judicial Court addressed the constitutionality of a bill that would authorize the state Treasurer to, with the approval of the Governor, issue and sell bonds, and would authorize the use of the money raised from the sale of the bonds to modify the clearances over rail lines to improve rail capacity and access over certain freight railways in the Commonwealth. *Id.* The improvement of the capacity of freight railways was a benefit to private railway companies. See *id.* The court held constitutional those portions of the bill that would involve borrowing by the Commonwealth to confer a private benefit on railway companies because they "would authorize only the quid pro quo purchase of the benefits for a purpose that is presumably public." *Id.*

This Amendment empowers the Commonwealth to borrow in anticipation from receipts from taxes or other sources when the loan is to be paid out of the revenue of the year in which it is created. Borrowing not in anticipation of receipts is simply borrowing and is covered by section three of the Amendment, which requires a two-thirds vote by the yeas and nays. See *Singleton v. Treasurer & Receiver Gen.* (1960) (because the statute did not provide for borrowing in anticipation of receipts, the borrowing fell under section three and required a two-thirds vote by the yeas and nays).

ARTICLE LXIII. Collection of Revenue

SECTION 1. *Collection of Revenue.*—All money received on account of the commonwealth from any source whatsoever shall be paid into the treasury thereof.

SECTION 2. *The Budget.*—Within three weeks after the convening of the general court the governor shall recommend to the general court a budget which shall contain a statement of all proposed expenditures of the commonwealth for the fiscal year, including those already authorized by law, and of all taxes, revenues, loans and other means by which such expenditures shall be defrayed. In the first year of the term of office of a governor who has not served in the preceding year said governor shall recommend such budget within eight weeks after the convening of the general court. The budget shall be arranged in such form as the general court may by law prescribe, or, in default thereof, as the governor shall determine. For the purpose of preparing his budget, the governor shall have power to require any board, commission, officer or department to furnish him with any information which he may deem necessary.

SECTION 3. *The General Appropriation Bill.*—All appropriations based upon the budget to be paid from taxes or revenues shall be incorporated in a single bill which shall be called the general appropriation bill. The general court may increase, decrease, add or omit items in the budget. The general court may provide for its salaries, mileage, and expenses and for necessary expenditures in anticipation of appropriations, but before final action on the general appropriation bill it shall not enact any other appropriation bill except on recommendation of the governor. The governor may at any time recommend to the general court supplementary budgets which shall be subject to the same procedure as the original budget.

SECTION 4. *Special Appropriation Bills.*—After final action on the general appropriation bill or on recommendation of the governor, special appropriation bills may be enacted. Such bills shall provide the specific means for defraying the appropriations therein contained.

SECTION 5. *Submission to the Governor.*—The governor may disapprove or reduce items or parts of items in any bill appropriating money. So much of such bill as he approves shall upon his signing the same become law. As to each item disapproved or reduced, he shall transmit to the house in which the bill originated his reason for such disapproval or reduction, and the procedure shall then be the same as in the case of a bill disapproved as a whole. In case he shall fail so to transmit his reasons for such disapproval or reduction within ten days after the bill shall have been presented to him, such items shall have the force of law unless the general court by adjournment shall prevent such transmission, in which case they shall not be law.

Ratified in 1918, this provision has been amended most recently by Amendment CVII, ratified in 1978. Amendment LXIII sets up a system of appropriation and was intended to centralize the Commonwealth's financial affairs and put their control in the hands of the General Court. *Opinion of the Justices* (1978); *Opinion of the Justices* (1956).

A law violates Amendment LXII if its collected revenues are not paid into the state treasury and, if so, the funds held in trust were not distributed according to legislative direction. Further, money received by the Commonwealth from fines and license and permit fees is money received on account of the Commonwealth within the meaning of Amendment LXII. *Manchester v. Dept. of Envtl. Quality Eng'g* (1980); *Opinion of the Justices* (1956). Money not subject to the protections or laws governing public funds is not money received on account of the Commonwealth. *Horton v. Attorney Gen.* (1930). Doubt or dispute as to the legality of the exaction of funds does not preclude an agent of the Commonwealth from paying the funds into the treasury thereof. *Oakley Country Club v. Long* (1949). Under this Amendment, one department of government cannot transfer part of the funds appropriated to it by the Legislature to another, because such a transfer would undermine the Legislature's constitutional power to manage the financial affairs of the Commonwealth. See *Baker v. Commonwealth* (1942).

Section two of Amendment LXII grants the Governor the power and confers upon him the duty to recommend appropriations to the General Court by submission of an annual budget within three weeks of the convening of the General Court. See *Opinion of the Justices* (1999). "Revenue" here refers not only to taxes but to income not included in taxes, such as fines and fees from licenses and permits, and other sources of government income recognized as such from time immemorial. *Opinion of the Justices* (1956). Under section three of Amendment LXII, the General Court has the power to attach conditions to the expenditure of money appropriated by it. *Opinion of the Justices* (1936). As well, the Legislature may insert items into an appropriation bill to the same extent the Governor may, under this Amendment, omit the same items. *Opinion of the Justices* (1981).

In respect to both sections three and four of Amendment LXII, the words "final action" refer to the "final step" in the process by which a bill becomes a law.

Opinion of the Justices (1936). Unless a bill is returned by the Governor to the House of Representatives with his objections or unless he fails to return the bill within the appropriate time, "final action" is the approval of the bill by the Governor. *Id.* The words "enact" and "enacted" refer only to legislative action. *Id.* Section four requires that special appropriation bills be enacted only after final action has been taken on the general appropriation bill for that period.

Section five of Amendment LXII grants the Governor the power to not sign, and thereby veto, an appropriation bill. *Alliance, AFSCME/SEIU v. Sec'y of Admin.* (1992). This section confers upon the Governor a qualified veto power, enabling that office to reduce a sum of money appropriated or disapprove the appropriation all together, but not to otherwise change the terms of the appropriation. *Opinion of the Justices* (1936). Specifically, this section does not empower the Governor to remove restrictions upon the use of an item appropriated. *Id.* As noted above, the Governor's power to omit items in an appropriation bill is coextensive with the Legislature's power to insert them. *Opinion of the Justices* (1981). The purpose here was to give the executive a central role in the budgetary process and to provide a veto power beyond that conferred upon the Governor by Part II, c. 1, Sec. 1, Art. II. *Id.* at 823–24.

In *Barnes v. Secretary of Administration,* the Governor exercised his power under Amendment LXII to reduce by over $20 million the funds appropriated for the Emergency Assistance program, which provides rent, mortgage, and utility arrearage benefits to eligible persons at risk of becoming homeless, temporary shelter, other emergency benefits for eligible homeless persons. *Barnes v. Sec'y of Admin.* (1992). The court concluded the Governor may reduce the amount appropriated for any item in an appropriation bill. See *id.* The courts are reluctant to examine the motives of the Governor. *Id.*

The Governor may disapprove certain restrictive words and phrases pertaining to six items in a general appropriation bill. *Opinion of the Justices* (1981). Though the appropriating power is the Legislature's, if that body were able to compel the Governor to either accept general legislation or risk forfeiture of appropriations, then the balance of powers struck by this Amendment and, indeed, the fundamental principles of separation of powers, would be undermined. *Id.* The Governor may disapprove of certain language defining the items of appropriation in a bill laid before him by the General Court, when the disapproval does not direct the manner in which the funds are to be used or impose restrictions or conditions upon the expenditure of them; in that case, disapproval amounts to the disapproval of separable legislation, a permissible action under Amendment LXII. *Id.* At the same time, disapproval by the Governor of provisions reflecting the intent to allocate appropriations for particular programs is invalid. See *id.* While the Governor is free to reduce or disapprove each item, he cannot disapprove legislative restrictions alone. *Id.* Further, the Governor may not disapprove language when that action has the effect of enlarging the amount of funds appropriated for other purposes specified. See *Opinion of the Justices*

(1994). When the Governor's disapproval is ineffective, the item, as written by the Legislature, becomes effective upon its signing. *Id.*

ARTICLE LXIV. Election of State Officers

SECTION 1. The governor, lieutenant-governor, secretary, treasurer and receiver-general, attorney-general, and auditor shall be elected quadrennially and councillors, senators and representatives shall be elected biennially. The terms of the governor and lieutenant-governor shall begin at noon on the Thursday next following the first Wednesday in January succeeding their election and shall end at noon on the Thursday next following the first Wednesday in January in the fifth year following their election. If the governor elect shall have died before the qualification of the lieutenant-governor elect, the lieutenant-governor elect upon qualification shall become governor. If both the governor elect and the lieutenant-governor elect shall have died both said offices shall be deemed to be vacant and the provisions of Article LV of the Amendments to the Constitution shall apply. The terms of the secretary, treasurer and receiver-general, attorney-general, and auditor shall begin with the third Wednesday in January succeeding their election and shall extend to the third Wednesday in January in the fifth year following their election and until their successors are chosen and qualified. The terms of the councillors shall begin at noon on the Thursday next following the first Wednesday in January succeeding their election and shall end at noon on the Thursday next following the first Wednesday in January in the third year following their election. The terms of senators and representatives shall begin with the first Wednesday in January succeeding their election and shall extend to the first Wednesday in January in the third year following their election and until their successors are chosen and qualified.

SECTION 2. The General Court shall assemble every year on the first Wednesday in January.

SECTION 3. The first election to which this article shall apply shall be held on the Tuesday next after the first Monday in November in the year nineteen hundred and sixty-six, and thereafter elections for the choice of a governor, lieutenant-governor, secretary, treasurer and receiver-general, attorney-general, and auditor shall be held quadrennially on the Tuesday next after the first Monday in November and elections for the choice of councillors, senators and representatives shall be held biennially on the Tuesday next after the first Monday in November.

Ratified in 1918, this provision has been amended several times. It originally provided for biennial elections for the officers listed. Amendment LXXX, ratified in 1950, replaced the original section one with a version in which the times of the beginning and ending of the offices were changed and added the provisions in the third and fourth sentences providing for the deaths of the Governor- and Lieutenant Governor–elect. Article of Amendment LXXXII, ratified in 1964, provided for quadrennial election of all the officers mentioned in section one, except for the Councillors, Senators, and Representatives, who continue to be elected biennially.

The original amended Part II, c. IV, art. II, by providing that no person could serve as Treasurer and Receiver General for more than three successive terms. Part II, c. IV, art. II's limit was "more than five years successively." Having become a biennially elected position, the amendment increased the limit to six years to make it sensible. All limits on the post were abolished by Article of Amendment LXXXII, ratified in 1964, when it dropped section two from the replacement language it mandated for Article of Amendment LXIV. The current section two was section three in the original, but is otherwise unchanged. There was a period, however, when it was changed implicitly by Amendment LXXII, ratified in 1937. That amendment provided that the General Court would assemble on the first Wednesday in January *biennially*. But that amendment was annulled by Amendment LXXV, ratified in 1944, and all provisions inconsistent with it were reinstated.

ARTICLE LXV. Members of the Legislature Not to Be Appointed to Certain Offices

No person elected to the general court shall during the term for which he was elected be appointed to any office created or the emoluments whereof are increased during such term, nor receive additional salary or compensation for service upon any recess committee or commission except a committee appointed to examine a general revision of the statutes of the commonwealth when submitted to the general court for adoption.

Ratified in 1918, this provision has not been amended. Amendment LXV has been interpreted as prohibiting a person elected to the General Court from serving in another office at the same time. The Supreme Judicial Court had occasion to interpret the Amendment's breadth in a 1964 case in which the Governor and the Council asked the court whether a member of the Legislature could serve as registrar of motor vehicles when the latter position's salary had been increased during the term for which he had been elected to the Legislature. See *Opinion of the Justices* (1964). The court concluded that the appointment violated Amendment LXV. *Id.*

ARTICLE LXIX. Women May Hold Public Office

SECTION 1. No person shall be deemed to be ineligible to hold state, county or municipal office by reason of sex.

SECTION 2. Article IV of the articles of amendment of the constitution of the commonwealth, as amended by Article LVII of said amendments, is hereby

further amended by striking out the words "Change of name shall render the commission void, but shall not prevent reappointment under the new name", and inserting in place thereof the following words: —Upon the change of name of any woman, she shall re-register under her new name and shall pay such fee therefor as shall be established by the general court.

Ratified in 1924, this Amendment was part of a package with Amendment LXVIII, ratified at the same time, which modified Amendment III to extend to women the right to vote. Amendment LXIX removed gender qualifications from all public offices and provided that a change of surname by a woman would not void her notary commission, and would further only require her to re-register under her new name. In so doing, this Amendment explicitly changed the language of Amendment IV, ratified in 1821, as amended by Amendment LVII, ratified in 1918, the latter providing that women were eligible to be notaries public.

Note that no provision in the original constitution, apart from the exclusive use of male pronouns, disabled women from running for office. The Supreme Judicial Court, however, had inferred such a restriction, based upon the continuing historical practice of excluding women from public offices. *Opinion of the Justices* (1896). The court later recognized, following ratification of the Nineteenth Amendment to the U.S. Constitution, that such "unbroken usage" could no longer justify gender restrictions. *Opinion of the Justices* (1922).

ARTICLE LXXVIII. Use of Revenue from Operation of Motor Vehicles

Article LXXVIII. No revenue from fees, duties, excises or license taxes relating to registration, operation or use of vehicles on public highways, or to fuels used for propelling such vehicles, shall be expended for other than cost of administration of laws providing for such revenue, making of refunds and adjustments in relation thereto, payment of highway obligations, or cost of construction, reconstruction, maintenance and repair of public highways and bridges and of the enforcement of state traffic laws; and such revenue shall be expended by the commonwealth or its counties, cities and towns for said highway purposes only and in such manner as the general court may direct; provided, that this amendment shall not apply to revenue from any excise tax imposed in lieu of local property taxes for the privilege of registering such vehicles.

This Amendment was ratified in 1948 and annulled by Amendment CIV in 1974, which provided the text as it now stands. The Amendment concerns the expenditure of highway revenue for mass transportation purposes. As the Supreme Judicial Court has explained, this provision "requires only that art. 78 revenues be expended for certain transportation-related purposes." *Mitchell v. Sec'y of Admin.* (1992). The Amendment gives the Legislature broad power to determine how this goal shall be met, so long, "in any given fiscal year, expenditures for art. 78 purposes at least equal revenue received from art. 78 sources." *Id.*

ARTICLE LXXXIII. Public Office Succession in Emergencies
The general court shall have full power and authority to provide for prompt and temporary succession to the powers and duties of public offices, of whatever nature and whether filled by election or appointment, the incumbents of which may become unavailable for carrying on the powers and duties of such offices in periods of emergency resulting from disaster caused by enemy attack, and to adopt such other measures as may be necessary and proper for insuring continuity of the government of the commonwealth and the governments of its political subdivisions.

Ratified in 1964, this provision has not been amended. Amendment LXXXIII grants the Legislature the power to provide for continuity of government in times of emergency. "Emergency" is defined as "disaster," specifically a disaster resulting from an enemy attack.

ARTICLE LXXXVI. Election of Governor and Lieutenant Governor from Same Party
Names of candidates of political parties for the offices of governor and lieutenant-governor shall be grouped on the official ballot for use at state elections according to the parties they represent, and the voter may cast a single vote for any such group, which shall count as a vote for each candidate in such group, but may not cast a vote for only one of the candidates in such group.

Ratified in 1966, this provision has not been amended. This Amendment authorizes the joint election of Governor and Lieutenant Governor. *Opinion of the Justices* (1975). Voters may not case a vote for only one of the candidates in such a pairing. The provision does not concern the procedures that govern primary elections. See *id.*

ARTICLE LXXXVII. Executive Department Reorganization Plan
SECTION 1. For the purpose of transferring, abolishing, consolidating or co-ordinating the whole or any part of any agency, or the functions thereof, within the exec-utive department of the government of the commonwealth, or for the purpose of authorizing any officer of any agency within the executive department of the government of the commonwealth to delegate any of his functions, the governor may prepare one or more reorganization plans, each bearing an identifying number and may present such plan or plans to the general court, together with a message in explanation thereof.

SECTION 2. (a) Every such reorganization plan shall be referred to an appropriate committee, to be determined by the Clerks of the Senate and the House of Representatives, with the approval of the President and Speaker, which committee shall not later than thirty days after the date of the Governor's presentation of said plan hold a public hearing thereon and shall not later than ten days after such hearing report that it approves or disapproves such plan and

such reorganization plan shall have the force of law upon expiration of the sixty calendar days next following its presentation by the governor to the general court, unless disapproved by a majority vote of the members of either of the two branches of the general court present and voting, the general court not having been prorogued within such sixty days.

(b) After its presentation by the governor to the general court, no such reorganization plan shall be subject to amendment by the general court before expiration of such sixty days.

(c) Any such reorganization plan may provide for its taking effect on any date after expiration of such sixty days and every such reorganization plan shall comply with such conditions as the general court may from time to time prescribe by statute regarding the civil service status, seniority, retirement and other rights of any employee to be affected by such plan.

SECTION 3. Article LXVI of the Amendments to the Constitution is hereby annulled.

This Amendment was ratified in 1966 and has not been amended. The Amendment concerns the procedure that the Governor must follow should he or she choose to transfer, abolish, consolidate, or coordinate the functions of any executive agency, or authorize an officer to delegate certain functions. The Governor must prepare a plan, with an explanation, to the General Court for its approval or disapproval within the time limits established by the Amendment. The Legislature may amend the plan within sixty days.

ARTICLE LXXXVIII. Industrial Development of Towns and Cities

The industrial development of towns and cities is a public function and the commonwealth and the cities and towns therein may provide for the same in such manner as the general court may determine.

Ratified in 1966, this Amendment has not been amended. The purpose of the Amendment is "to foster the expansion of the economy" by providing a role for the government in stimulating industrial development. *Opinion of the Justices* (1977). In light of the purpose of the Amendment, the Supreme Judicial Court has reasoned that the words "industrial development," though undefined, include nonmanufacturing enterprises; it may apply to "activities which are not confined to the process of fabricating new products from raw materials." *Id.*

ARTICLE XCI. Disability of the Governor

Whenever the governor transmits to the president of the senate and the speaker of the house his written declaration that he is unable to discharge the powers and duties of his office, the office of governor shall be deemed to be vacant within the meaning of this Constitution.

Whenever the chief justice and a majority of the associate justices of the supreme judicial court, or such other body as the general court may by law provide, transmit to the president of the senate and the speaker of the house their written declaration that the governor is unable to discharge the powers and duties of his office, the office of governor shall be deemed to be vacant within the meaning of this Constitution.

Thereafter, in either of the above cases, whenever the governor transmits to the president of the senate and the speaker of the house his written declaration that no inability exists such vacancy shall be deemed to have terminated four days thereafter and the governor shall resume the powers and duties of his office unless the chief justice and a majority of the associate justices of the supreme judicial court, or such other body as the general court may by law provide, transmit within said four days to the president of the senate and the speaker of the house their written declaration that the governor is unable to discharge the powers and duties of his office. Thereupon the general court shall decide the issue, assembling within forty-eight hours for that purpose if not in session. If the general court within twenty-one days after receipt of the latter written declaration, or, if the general court is not in session, within twenty-one days after the general court is required to assemble, determine by a vote, taken by yeas and nays, of two thirds of each house present and voting thereon, that the governor is unable to discharge the powers and duties of his office, the office of governor shall continue to be deemed to be vacant; otherwise such vacancy shall be deemed to have terminated and the governor shall resume the powers and duties of his office.

The above provisions shall be applicable to the lieutenant governor when the lieutenant governor in case of a vacancy is performing all the duties incumbent upon the governor as provided in this Constitution.

If a vacancy in the office of governor, as described in this Article, continues for six months and if such six-month period expires more than five months prior to a biennial state election other than an election for governor, there shall be an election of governor at such biennial state election for the balance of the unexpired four-year term.

Ratified in 1968, this Amendment has not been amended. This Amendment concerns situations in which the Governor can no longer discharge the powers and duties of his office. Notice of such disability may be transmitted to the legislature by the Governor himself or herself, or by a majority of the Supreme Judicial Court, or by such other body as the Legislature determines. The Governor may declare that his or her disability no longer obtains; to the extent that declaration is challenged, the General Court must decide the issue. These provisions are also applicable to the Lieutenant Governor. The Amendment also establishes a procedure for electing a new Governor should the office remain vacant for six months.

ARTICLE XCVI. Authorization of Loans to Students Attending Institutions of Higher Learning

The general court shall have the power to authorize the commonwealth to make loans, on such terms as it may deem reasonable, to any residents of the commonwealth for tuition and board at any college, university or other institution of higher learning.

This Amendment was ratified in 1972 and has not been amended. The Amendment is a direct grant of power to the Legislature to allow the Commonwealth to make loans to students who are residents and attending any college, university, or other institution of higher learning.

ARTICLE XCIX. Assessment of Agricultural or Horticultural Lands

Full power and authority are hereby given and granted to the general court to prescribe, for the purpose of developing and conserving agricultural or horticultural lands, that such lands shall be valued, for the purpose of taxation, according to their agricultural or horticultural uses; provided, however, that no parcel of land which is less than five acres in area or which has not been actively devoted to agricultural or horticultural uses for the two years preceding the tax year shall be valued at less than fair market value under this article.

Ratified in 1972, this Amendment has not been amended. This Amendment grants the legislature the authority to set the valuation of agricultural and horticultural lands.

ARTICLE CI. Apportionment and Qualification of Representatives and Senators

SECTION 1. The federal census shall be the basis for determining the representative districts for the ten year period beginning with the first Wednesday in the third January following the taking of said census.

The house of representatives shall consist of one hundred and sixty members. The general court shall, at its first regular session after the year in which said census was taken, divide the commonwealth into one hundred and sixty representative districts of contiguous territory so that each representative will represent an equal number of inhabitants, as nearly as may be; and such districts shall be formed, as nearly as may be, without uniting two counties or parts of two or more counties, two towns or parts of two or more towns, two cities or parts of two or more cities, or a city and a town, or parts of cities and towns, into one district. Such districts shall also be so formed that no town containing less than twenty-five hundred inhabitants according to said census shall be divided. The general court may by law limit the time within which judicial proceedings may be instituted calling in question any such division. Every representative, for one year at least immediately preceding his election, shall have been an inhabitant of the district for which he is chosen

and shall cease to represent such district when he shall cease to be an inhabitant of the commonwealth. The manner of calling and conducting the elections for the choice of representatives, and of ascertaining their election, shall be prescribed by law.

SECTION 2. Said federal census shall likewise be the basis for determining the senatorial districts and also the councillor districts for the ten year period beginning with the first Wednesday in the third January following the taking of such census. The senate shall consist of forty members. The general court shall, at its first regular session after the year in which said census is taken, divide the commonwealth into forty districts of contiguous territory, each district to contain, as nearly as may be, an equal number of inhabitants according to said census; and such districts shall be formed, as nearly as may be, without uniting two counties, or parts of two or more counties, into one district. The general court may by law limit the time within which judicial proceedings may be instituted calling in question such division. Each district shall elect one senator, who shall have been an inhabitant of this commonwealth five years at least immediately preceding his election and at the time of his election shall be an inhabitant of the district for which he is chosen; and he shall cease to represent such senatorial district when he shall cease to be an inhabitant of the commonwealth. The manner of calling and conducting the elections for the choice of senators and councillors, and of ascertaining their election, shall be prescribed by law.

SECTION 3. Original jurisdiction is hereby vested in the supreme judicial court upon the petition of any voter of the commonwealth, filed with the clerk of the supreme judicial court for the commonwealth, for judicial relief relative to the establishment of house of representatives, councillor and senatorial districts.

SECTION 4. Article XCII of the Amendments to the Constitution is hereby annulled.

This Amendment continues the history of changes to representation in the House, Senate, and Council from Amendments XII and XIII. Amendments XII and XIII are included here because, though Amendment XII was completely superseded by later amendments and Amendment XIII was superseded in all but its last paragraph, none of the superseding amendments explicitly annulled or amended XII and XIII. (All of the amendments between Amendment XIII and Amendment CI, which dealt with the subject of representation in the House, Senate, and Council (Amendments XXI, ratified in 1857; XXII, ratified in 1857; LXXI, ratified in 1930; and CXII, ratified in 1970), were explicitly annulled and, therefore, do not appear here.) Amendment LXXI explicitly amended Amendments XXI and XXII. Amendment CXII explicitly superseded Amendment LXXI and annulled Amendments XXI and XXII. Amendment CI explicitly superseded and annulled Amendment CXII.

Amendment CI originally stipulated the taking of a state census. Section one was amended by Amendment CIX, ratified in 1978, to provide for a census according to the standards of the federal census. Amendment CXVII, ratified in 1990, replaced language which continued the mandate for the Commonwealth to take a state census on a decennial basis, with the first paragraphs of both section one and two, which appear here. The timing of when the federal census shall be utilized (the "first Wednesday in the third January") was added by Amendment CXIX in 2000.

In respect to both Houses of the General Court, the census basis for proportional representation was changed from "inhabitants" to "legal voters." This Amendment reduced the membership of the House of Representatives. The distribution of representatives is no longer among the municipalities (and such districts as they may join together to make), but instead is now among the counties and such districts into which they must be divided. One Senator is elected for each of forty senatorial districts, replacing the previous system that permitted more than one Senator from a district, depending upon population. For the first time, residency is a constitutional requirement for maintaining one's position as Senator; previously, residency was constitutionally required only to be elected. The districting established for the Senate serve for the Governor's Council as well.

Section three of this Amendment creates a direct route for relief to the Supreme Judicial Court for any person who is aggrieved by the establishment of Council, Senate, or House districts. The Supreme Judicial Court has declared that great deference will be given to any legislative redistricting plan, in part because "[i]t would be impossible for the Legislature to satisfy all of the requirements perfectly." *Mayor of Cambridge v. Sec. of the Commonwealth* (2002). The two general requirements of districting are territorial integrity and equal representation. *Id.* In the first part of the analysis, a redistricting plan may be in violation of these requirements when a plaintiff can show that equal representation can be maintained with fewer divisions of a given municipality, provided that such modifications do not force the further dividing of neighboring municipalities. *Id.* The second part requires "a plaintiff [to] demonstrate that the Legislature had no reasonable justification for selecting a redistricting plan that creates more divisions of cities, towns, or counties." *Id.*

ARTICLE CXI. Assignment or Admission to Public Schools

No student shall be assigned to or denied admittance to a public school on the basis of race, color, national origin or creed.

Ratified in 1978, this Amendment has not been amended. This Amendment "was designed to limit forced busing and to protect neighborhood schools." *Comfort v. Lynn School Committee* (2005). The only evil the Amendment was designed to prevent was forced busing; voluntary student transfer programs do not fall within the Amendment's reach. *Id.*

ARTICLE CXIV. Discrimination Against Handicapped Persons
No otherwise qualified handicapped individual shall, solely by reason of his handicap, be excluded from the participation in, denied the benefits of, or be subject to discrimination under any program or activity within the commonwealth.

Ratified in 1980, this Amendment has not been amended. For the purposes of this Amendment, a "handicapped" individual is one "who has a physical or mental impairment that substantially limits one or more major life activities." *Shedlock v. Dep't. of Correction* (2004). Actions to enforce Amendment CXIV rights may be brought under Mass. Gen. L. c. 93, § 103. The Supreme Judicial Court has held that "the effects of corrective devices should not be considered when assessing whether a plaintiff's ability to perform a major life activity" has been substantially impaired. *Id.* (quotation omitted). Further, deliberately requiring a person to endure unnecessary hardship to access a particular program or service, "when that hardship could be easily eliminated by a reasonable accommodation, can amount to a form of 'discrimination.'" *Id.* Finally, courts must apply the terms of Amendment CXIV in light of the circumstances. See *id.* (applying Amendment CXIV in prison context).

ARTICLE CXV. Imposition of Additional Costs on Municipalities
No law imposing additional costs upon two or more cities or towns by the regulation of the compensation, hours, status, conditions or benefits of municipal employment shall be effective in any city or town until such law is accepted by vote or by the appropriation of money for such purposes, in the case of a city, by the city council in accordance with its charter, and in the case of a town, by a town meeting or town council, unless such law has been enacted by a two-thirds vote of each house of the general court present and voting thereon, or unless the general court, at the same session in which such law is enacted, has provided for the assumption by the commonwealth of such additional cost.

Ratified in 1980, this Amendment has not been amended. Pursuant to this Amendment, the legislature may not impose additional costs upon two or more cities or towns by regulating the compensation, hours, status, conditions, or benefits of municipal employment unless the city or town (1) accepts the law; (2) the Commonwealth assumes the additional costs; or (3) the Legislature enacts the law by a two-thirds vote in each house. See *City of Cambridge v. Attorney Gen.* (1991). The Amendment accordingly "limits the Legislature's power to regulate the terms of municipal employment." *Id.* Importantly, the Supreme Judicial Court has not interpreted Amendment CXV to exempt a municipality from generally applicable laws that regulate private business and individual activities and result in indirect costs to cities and towns voluntarily engaging in those activities. *Id.*

ARTICLE CXVIII. Compensation of Members of the General Court
The base compensation as of January first, nineteen hundred and ninety-six, of members of the general court shall not be changed except as provided in this article. As of the first Wednesday in January of the year two thousand and one and every second year thereafter, such base compensation shall be increased or decreased at the same rate as increases or decreases in the median household income for the commonwealth for the preceding two year period, as ascertained by the governor.

Ratified in 1998, this Amendment has not been amended. This Amendment ties legislative pay raises to "the median household income for the commonwealth for the preceding two year period, as ascertained by the governor."

BIBLIOGRAPHICAL ESSAY

Because we are not formally trained historians, the parts of this book that address the history of the Massachusetts Constitution should be viewed simply as an overview of significant events in the development of the constitution and constitutional law in the Commonwealth. We relied extensively for guidance upon numerous secondary sources in preparing these sections, discovering that the historian Marc W. Kruman was correct when he observed that, "[f]or generations, historians of revolutionary state constitution making have been obsessed with the Massachusetts Constitution of 1780." Marc W. Kruman, *Between Liberty and Authority: State Constitution Making in Revolutionary America* (Chapel Hill: University of North Carolina Press, 1997), 15. The products of that obsession are well in evidence in the wealth of scholarship about the history of the Commonwealth of Massachusetts and its constitution. We make no claim to have exhausted these sources, with one exception: in discussing what the text means and how it applies, we have made every effort to rely, as any lawyer would, upon judicial decisions interpreting the various part of the Massachusetts Constitution.

To relate the legal history of the Commonwealth prior to the convention that resulted in the constitution of 1780, we relied upon many works that are rightly regarded as classics in the field. Again, this list is by no means exhaustive. For the historical background about political life in the colonies prior to the revolution and the efforts at self-government that followed, we consulted Gordon Wood, *The Creation of the American Republic, 1776–1787* (Chapel Hill: University of North Carolina Press, 1969), Ronald M. Peters, Jr., *The Massachusetts Constitution of 1780: A Social Compact* (Amherst: The University of Massachusetts Press, 1978), and Kruman, *Between Authority and Liberty*. Though these authors disagree in some of their interpretations of the events surrounding the framing of the Massachusetts Constitution and even the meaning of the text itself, as well as their conclusions about the motivations that animated state constitution makers in the revolutionary period, each provides valuable insights into the "Massachusetts moment" of 1779–1780. Also insightful is Willi Paul Adams's study, *The First American Constitutions: Republican Ideology and the Making of the State Constitutions in the Revolutionary Era* (Chapel Hill: University of North Carolina Press, 1980), in which Adams explores both the events surrounding the framing of the constitution of 1780 as well as the commitment of Massachusetts citizens at the time of the Revolution to the rule of law and to constitutionalism as an ordering principle. Other important works on colonial and revolutionary-era politics and government building in Massachusetts include George Lee Haskins, *Law and Authority in Early Massachusetts: A Study in Tradition and Design* (New York: Macmillan, 1960), and George Dargo, *Roots of the Republic: A New Perspective on Early American Constitutionalism* (New York: Praeger, 1974), which cover in great detail the constitutional precedents that existed in the Massachusetts Bay Colony.

The list of superlative short treatments of the constitution and its development through the turn of the twentieth century includes Louis A. Frothingham, *A Brief History of the Constitution and Government of Massachusetts* (Cambridge: Harvard University Press, 1916); and Samuel Eliot Morison, *A History of the Constitution of Massachusetts* (Boston: Wright & Potter, 1917). Other helpful short guides to the history of the Massachusetts Constitution include Robert J. Taylor's essay, "Construction of the Massachusetts Constitution," published in *Proceedings of the American Antiquarian Society* 90 (1980): 317; George C. Homans's essay, "John Adams and the Constitution of Massachusetts," published in *Proceedings of the American Philosophical Society* 125 (1981): 286; and "The Making and Growth of the Constitution," by Mary Newman and Robert Faulkner, published as the introductory essay to *The Constitution of the Commonwealth of Massachusetts* (Boston: Secretary of the Commonwealth, 2002), vii.

Much has been written in both the scholarly and popular literature about the primary author of the Massachusetts Constitution, John Adams, and few of the secondary sources listed below fail to mention Adams or the critical role he played in drafting the constitution of 1780. Among the more interesting works on Adams are Daniel R. Coquillette's "Radical Lawmakers in Colonial Massachusetts: The 'Countenance of Authoritie' and the 'Lawes and Libertyes,'" published in *The New England Quarterly* 67 (June 1994): 179; and Coquillette's essay, "Justinian in Braintree: John Adams, Civilian Learning, and Legal Elitism, 1758–1775," published in *Law in Colonial Massachusetts* 62 (1984): 359. David McCullough's popular biography *John Adams* (New York: Simon & Schuster, 2001) is a good and informative read; he also authored a short essay on Adams and education, *John Adams and the Good Life of the Mind* (Boston: Boston Athenæum, 2004), which is particularly instructive.

In discussing the history of the Supreme Judicial Court's role in shaping the constitutional principles of the Commonwealth, a number of books and law review articles proved helpful. Russell K. Osgood's comprehensively edited volume on the history of the court and its work, *The History of the Law in Massachusetts: The Supreme Judicial Court 1692–1992* (Boston: Supreme Judicial Court Historical Society, 1992), proved an indispensable resource. For a thorough review of the life and work of Lemuel Shaw, the classic text is Leonard W. Levy, *The Law of the Commonwealth and Chief Justice Shaw* (New York: Harper & Row, 1967); for a more concise study of Shaw's critical contributions to the development of law in Massachusetts and the still-young nation, see Leonard W. Levy, "America's Greatest Magistrate," in *Ranters Run Amok, and Other Adventures in the History of the Law* (Chicago: Ivan R. Dee, 2000), 217. For insight into judicial treatment of the issue of slavery by the Massachusetts courts following adoption of the constitution of 1780, we consulted John D. Cushing, "The Cushing Court and the Abolition of Slavery in Massachusetts: More Notes on the 'Quock Walker Case,'" published in *American Journal of Legal History* 5 (1961): 118; and Robert Cover, *Justice Accused: Antislavery and the Judicial Process* (New Haven: Yale University Press, 1975).

Our discussion of the various constitutional conventions and the history of amendments to the Massachusetts Constitution provides but a snapshot of the debates that surrounded all the various proposed changes to the foundational law of the Commonwealth. In addition to relying upon the various records of the convention proceedings, the reader who seeks more detailed discussions of these proceedings should review Morison, *A History of the Massachusetts Constitution,* and the authoritative work of Morris M. Goldings, "Massachusetts Amends: A Decade of State Constitutional Revision," published in *Harvard Journal on Legislation* 5 (1968): 373. As well, Sean Wilentz, in his magisterial work, *The Rise of American Democracy: Jefferson to Lincoln* (New York: Norton, 2005), devotes considerable space to the convention of 1821 and the central democratic debates of that meeting, while John Dinan provides a detailed look at the state constitutional conventions in *The American State Constitutional Tradition* (Lawrence: University of Kansas Press, 2006) and the convention of 1917–18 in particular in "Framing a 'People's Government': State-Constitution-Making in the Progressive Era," published in *Rutgers Law Journal* 30 (1999): 933.

What follows is a topical list of primary and secondary sources. This is very much a "lawyer's list," emphasizing those sources that offer legal analysis of and historical exegesis on the framing of the Massachusetts Constitution and the subsequent development of constitutional law in the Commonwealth.

THE CONSTITUTION OF 1780 AND MASSACHUSETTS CONSTITUTIONAL HISTORY

Primary Sources

Journal of the Convention for Framing a Constitution of Government for the State of Massachusetts Bay: From the Commencement of Their First Session, September 1, 1779, to the Close of Their Last Session, June 16, 1780 (Boston: Dutton & Wentworth, 1832).

The Report of a Constitution, or Form of Government for the Commonwealth of Massachusetts: Agreed Upon by the Committee—to be Laid Before the Convention of Delegates, Assembled at Cambridge, on the First Day of September, A.D. 1779 (Boston: Edes & Sons, 1779).

Oscar and Mary Handlin. *The Popular Sources of Political Authority: Documents on the Massachusetts Constitution of 1780* (Cambridge: Belknap Press of Harvard University, 1966).

Secondary Sources

Charles Francis Adams, ed. *The Works of John Adams* (Boston: Little, Brown, 1850–1856).

John Q. Adams. *The Social Compact, Exemplified in the Constitution of the Commonwealth of Massachusetts* (Providence: Knowles & Vose, 1842).

Willi Paul Adams. *The First American Constitutions: Republican Ideology and the Making of State Constitutions in the Revolutionary Era* (Chapel Hill: University of North Carolina Press, 1980).

Angelo T. Angelis. *Pregnant with Future Consequences: Political Culture in Revolutionary Massachusetts, 1774–1787* (Thesis (PhD), City University of New York, 2002).

Ellyn C. Ballou. "Prentiss Mellen, Maine's First Chief Justice: A Legal Biography." *Maine Law Review* 28 (1976): 317.

R. T. Baltimore. "The State Constitution Roots of the 'Separate but Equal' Doctrine: *Roberts v. City of Boston*." *Rutgers Law Journal* 17 (1986): 654.

S. B. Benjamin. "The Significance of the Massachusetts Constitution of 1780." *Temple Law Review* 70 (1997): 883.

Henry C. Black. "The Formation of the First State Constitutions." *Constitutional Review* 7 (1923): 22.

Matthew Charles Boesen. *From Charter to Constitution: Local Self-Government in Revolutionary Massachusetts, 1774–1780* (Thesis (Ph.D.), University of Virginia, 1998).

Robert J. Brink, et al. *Celebrating the 225th Anniversary of Massachusetts Constitution of 1780* (Boston: Social Law Library, 2005).

Robert E. Brown. "Democracy in Colonial Massachusetts." *New England Quarterly* 25 (1952): 291.

Alexander H. Bullock. "The Centennial of the Massachusetts Constitution." *Proceedings of the American Antiquarian Society* 1 (1882): 189.

Ellen M. Burrill. *A Monograph on the Charters and Constitution of Massachusetts* (Lynn: T. P. Nichols and Son, Co., 1932).

Fred Capone. "Board of Education v. School Committee of Quincy: When a Child in Massachusetts is Denied a Fundamental Education, the Massachusetts Constitution is Violated." *New England Law Review* 29 (1995): 311.

Alexander J. Cella. "The People of Massachusetts, a New Republic, and the Constitution of 1780: The Evolution of Principles of Popular Control of Political Authority." *Suffolk University Law Review* 14 (1980): 975.

Mary C. Clune. "Joseph Hawley's Criticism of the Constitution on Massachusetts." *Smith College Studies in History* 3 (1917): 5.

Patrick T. Conley and John P. Kaminski, eds. *The Constitution and the States: the Role of the Original Thirteen in the Framing and Adoption of the Federal Constitution* (Madison: Madison House, 1988).

Daniel R. Coquillette. "Radical Lawmakers in Colonial Massachusetts: The 'Countenance of Authoritie' and the 'Lawes and Libertyes.'" *The New England Quarterly* 67 (June 1994): 179.

_____. "Justinian in Braintree: John Adams, Civilian Learning, and Legal Elitism, 1758–1775." *Law in Colonial Massachusetts* 62 (1984): 359.

Robert Cover. *Justice Accused: Antislavery and the Judicial Process* (New Haven: Yale University Press, 1975).

John D. Cushing. "The Cushing Court and the Abolition of Slavery in Massachusetts: More Notes on the 'Quock Walker Case.'" *American Journal of Legal History* 5 (1961): 118.

Harry A. Cushing. "History of the Transition from Provincial to Commonwealth Government in Massachusetts." *Columbia Studies in History, Economics and Public Law* 7 (1896): 1.

Cornelius Dalton, et al. *Leading the Way: A History of the Massachusetts General Court, 1629-1980* (Boston: Office of Secretary of State, 1984).

George Dargo. *Roots of the Republic: A New Perspective on Early American Constitutionalism* (New York: Praeger, 1974).

______. "The Bicentennial of the United States Constitution: A View From the States." *Massachusetts Law Review*, Special Issue 72 (1987): 38.

Charles Henry J. Douglas. "The Financial History of Massachusetts from the Organization of the Massachusetts Bay Colony to the American Revolution." *Columbia Studies in History, Economics and Public Law* 1 (1892): 4.

Martin B. Duberman. "Friends Divided: Debate on the Massachusetts Constitution of 1853." *Mid-America* 45 (1963): 50.

David Hacket Fisher. "The Myth of the Essex Junto." *William and Mary Quarterly* 21 (1964): 195.

Christian G. Fritz. "Alternative Visions of American Constitutionalism: Popular Sovereignty and the Early American Constitutional Debate." *Hastings Constitutional Law Quarterly* 24 (1997): 287.

Louis A. Frothingham. *A Brief History of the Constitution and Government of Massachusetts with a Chapter on Legislative Procedure* (Boston: Houghton Mifflin, 1925).

D.M. Graham. "The Early State Constitutions." *Constitutional Review* 9 (1925): 222.

Frank W. Grinnell. "The Constitutional History of the Supreme Judicial Court of Massachusetts from the Revolution to 1813." *Massachusetts Law Quarterly* 2 (1917): 357.

_____. "A Forgotten Patriot: Jedediah Foster of Brookfield." *Proceedings of the Massachusetts Historical Society* 67 (1945): 128.

______. "Historical Note." *Massachusetts Law Quarterly* 27 (1942): 20.

______. "The Influence of Thomas Allen and the 'Berkshire Constitutionalists' on the Constitutional History of the United States." *American Bar Association Journal* 22 (1936): 168.

______. "John Winthrop and the Constitutional Thinking of John Adams." *Proceedings of the Massachusetts Historical Society* 63 (1930): 30.

______. "The Resolution of the Town of Concord on October 22, 1776, and Its Constitutional Significance." *Massachusetts Law Quarterly* 1 (1928): 60.

______. "A Study of the Contribution to the Massachusetts Constitution in 1779 of a Forgotten Patriot and Judge—Jedediah Foster of Brookfield in Worcester County." *Massachusetts Law Quarterly* 30 (1945): 28.

Michael G. Hall. "Origins in Massachusetts of the Constitutional Doctrine of Advice and Consent." *Proceedings of the Massachusetts Historical Society* 92 (1979): 3.

Theodore M. Hammett. "Revolutionary Ideology in Massachusetts: Thomas Allen's 'Vindication' of the Berkshire Constitutionalists, 1778." *William and Mary Quarterly* 33 (1976): 514.

Oscar and Mary Handlin. *Commonwealth: A Study of the Role of Government in the American Economy: Massachusetts, 1774–1861* (Cambridge: Belknap Press of Harvard University, 1969).

Albert Bushnell Hart, ed. *Commonwealth History of Massachusetts, Colony, Province and State* (New York: States History Co., 1927).

George Lee Haskins. *Law and Authority in Early Massachusetts: A Study in Tradition and Design* (New York: Macmillan, 1960).

George H. Haynes. *Representation and Suffrage in Massachusetts, 1620–1691* (Baltimore: Johns Hopkins University Press, 1894).

______. "The Conciliatory Proposition in the Massachusetts Constitution of 1788." *Proceedings of the American Antiquarian Society* 29 (1919): 294.

Edward F. Hennessey. "Massachusetts Roots of the Constitution of the United States." *Massachusetts Law Review* 72 (Fall 1987): 3.

______. "The Extraordinary Massachusetts Constitution of 1780." *Suffolk University Law Review* 14 (1980): 873.

George C. Homans. "John Adams and the Constitution of Massachusetts." *Proceedings of the American Philosophical Society* 125 (1981): 286.

Roderick L. Ireland. "How We Do It in Massachusetts: An Overview of How the Massachusetts Supreme Judicial Court Has Interpreted Its State Constitution to Address Contemporary Legal Issues." *Valparaiso University Law Review* 38 (2004): 405.

George M. Jarvis and Nicholas S. Racheotes. *The Massachusetts Constitution: A Citizen's Guide* (Newton Centre, MA: Government Research Publications, 1987).

Patrick J. Kelley. "Holmes' Early Constitutional Law Theory and Its Application in Takings Cases on the Massachusetts Supreme Judicial Court." *Southern Illinois University Law Journal* 18 (1994): 357.

Alfred H. Kelly, et al. *The American Constitution: Its Origins and Development* (New York: Norton, 1990).

David T. Konig. "The Theory and Practice of Constitutionalism in Pre-Revolutionary Massachusetts Bay: James Otis on the Writs of Assistance, 1761." *Dalhousie Law Journal* 8 (1984): 25.

Marc W. Kruman. *Between Liberty and Authority: State Constitution Making in Revolutionary America* (Chapel Hill: University of North Carolina Press, 1997).

James S. Leamon. *Revolution Downeast: The War for American Independence in Maine* (Amherst: University of Massachusetts Press, 1993).

Leonard W. Levy. *The Law of the Commonwealth and Chief Justice Shaw* (New York: Harper & Row, 1967).

_____. "America's Greatest Magistrate," in *Ranters Run Amok, and Other Adventures in the History of the Law* (Chicago: Ivan R. Dee, 2000).

Charles H. Lippy. "The 1780 Massachusetts Constitution: Religious Establishment or Civil Religion?" *Journal of Church and State* 20 (1978): 533.

Arthur Lord. "Some Objections Made to the State Constitution, 1780." *Proceedings of the Massachusetts Historical Society* 50 (1916): 54.

______. "The Massachusetts Constitution and the Constitutional Conventions." *Massachusetts Law Quarterly* 2 (1916): 1.

Donald S. Lutz. *The Origins of American Constitutionalism* (Baton Rouge: Louisiana State University Press, 1988).

______. *Popular Consent and Popular Control: Whig Political Theory in the Early State Constitutions* (Baton Rouge: Louisiana State Univ. Press, 1980).

Robert A. Marangola. "Independent State Constitutional Adjudication in Massachusetts: 1988–1998." *Albany Law Review* 61 (1998): 1625.

Paul D. Marsella. *Cases and Materials in Constitutional History* (Acton: Tapestry Press, 1999).

Massachusetts Bar Association. *Our Massachusetts Constitution: Its History and Purpose* (Boston: Massachusetts Bar Association, 1955).

Albert Mason. "A Short History of the Supreme Judicial Court of Massachusetts." *Massachusetts Law Quarterly* 2 (1916): 82.

Leo McAuliffe and Susan Z. Steinway. *Massachusetts: Annual State Bibliography* (Boston: Massachusetts State Library, 1985).

David McCullough. *John Adams and the Good Life of the Mind* (Boston: Boston Athenæum, 2004).

______. *John Adams* (New York: Simon & Schuster, 2001).

Andrew C. McLaughlin. *Foundations of American Constitutionalism* (New York: Fawcett, 1966).
______. "American History and American Democracy." *American Historical Review* 20 (1915): 255.
Jacob C. Meyer. *Church and State in Massachusetts from 1740 to 1833: A Chapter in the History of the Development of Individual Freedom* (New York: Russell & Russell, 1968).
Margret E. Monsell. "Stars in the Constellation of the Commonwealth: Massachusetts Towns and the Constitutional Right of Instruction." *New England Law Review* 29 (1995): 285.
William Morley. *The First State Constitutions* (Philadelphia: American Academy of Political and Social Science, 1893).
Samuel Eliot Morison. *A History of the Constitution of Massachusetts* (Boston: Wright & Potter, 1917).
______. "The Formation of the Constitution: An Address on the Occasion of the 175th Anniversary of the Constitution of October 25, 1955." *Massachusetts Law Quarterly* 40 (1955): 1.
______. "The Struggle over the Adoption of the Constitution of Massachusetts, 1780." *Proceedings of the Massachusetts Historical Society* 50 (1917): 353.
______. "The Vote of Massachusetts on Summoning a Constitutional Convention, 1776–1916." *Proceedings of the Massachusetts Historical Society* 50 (1917): 241.
Lee N. Newcomer. *The Embattled Farmers; A Massachusetts Countryside in the American Revolution* (New York: King's Crown Press, 1953).
Mary Newman and Robert Faulkner. "The Making of the Constitution," in *The Constitution of the Commonwealth of Massachusetts* (Boston: Office of the Secretary of State, 2002), vii.
Russell K. Osgood, ed. *The History of the Law in Massachusetts: The Supreme Judicial Court 1692–1992* (Boston: Supreme Judicial Court Historical Society, 1992).
Theophilus Parsons. *Memoir of Theophilus Parsons, Chief Justice of the Supreme Judicial Court of Massachusetts; with Notices of Some of His Contemporaries* (Boston: Ticknor & Fields, 1859).
Stephen E. Patterson. *Political Parties in Revolutionary Massachusetts* (Madison: University of Wisconsin, 1973).
Ronald M. Peters, Jr., et al. *The Massachusetts Constitution of 1780: A Social Compact* (Amherst: University of Massachusetts Press, 1978).
Paul C. Reardon. "The Massachusetts Constitution Marks a Milestone." *Publius* 12 (1982): 45.
John P. Reid. "In the Taught Tradition: The Meaning of Law in Massachusetts Bay Two-Hundred Years Ago." *Suffolk University Law Review* 14 (1980): 931.
William J. Reid and Herbert Regan. *Massachusetts: History and Government of the Bay State* (New York: Oxford Book Co., 1956).
Clinton Rossiter. *Seedtime of the Republic: The Origin of the American Tradition of Political Liberty* (New York: Harcourt, Brace, 1953).
Secretary of the Commonwealth. *Constitution of the Commonwealth and the Rearrangement Thereof* (Boston: Wright & Potter, 1920).
Robert A. Shanley. *The Problem of Simplifying the Massachusetts Constitution* (Amherst: Bureau of Govt. Research, University of Massachusetts, 1966).
Albert L. Sturm, et. al. *The Constitution of Massachusetts, A Critical Study: A Questionnaire* (Boston: Boston College Law School Library, 1953).
Robert J. Taylor. *Massachusetts, Colony to Commonwealth: Documents on the Formation of the Constitution 1775–1780* (Chapel Hill: University of North Carolina Press, 1961).
______. "Construction of the Massachusetts Constitution." *Proceedings of the American Antiquarian Society* 90 (1983): 317.

______. "Lawyer John Adams and the Massachusetts Constitution." *Boston Bar Journal* 24 (October 1980): 21.

______. *Western Massachusetts in the Revolution* (Providence: Brown University Press, 1954).

Emory Washburn. *Sketches of the Judicial History of Massachusetts: from 1630 to the Revolution in 1775* (Boston: Little, Brown, 1840).

William C. Webster. *Comparative Study of the State Constitutions of the American Revolution* (Philadelphia: American Academy of Political and Social Science, 1897).

Herbert P. Wilkins. "Non-Fliers in Philadelphia." *Massachusetts Law Review* 72 (1987): 7.

John Witte, Jr. "How to Govern A City on a Hill: The Early Puritan Contribution to American Constitutionalism." *Emory Law Journal* 39 (1990): 41.

Gordon S. Wood. *The Creation of the American Republic, 1776–1787* (Chapel Hill: University of North Carolina Press, 1969).

______. *The Radicalism of the American Revolution* (New York: Knopf, 1992).

______. *Revolutionary Characters: What Made the Founders Different* (New York: Penguin, 2006).

■ THE DECLARATION OF RIGHTS

Charles H. Baron. "The Supreme Judicial Court in Its Fourth Century: Meeting the Challenge of the 'New Constitutional Revolution.'" *Massachusetts Law Review* 77 (1992): 35.

Mary L. Bonauto. "*Goodridge* in Context." *Harvard Civil Rights-Civil Liberties Law Review* 40 (2005): 1.

Committee to Ratify the Massachusetts State Equal Rights Amendment. *Records of the Committee.* (Boston: 1975–1982).

Charles Deane. "Judge Lowell and the Massachusetts Declaration of Rights." *Proceedings of the Massachusetts Historical Society* 13 (1874): 299.

Lisa Donahue. "Confrontation in Massachusetts: What 'Face to Face' Really Means." *Suffolk Journal of Trial and Appellate Advocacy* 3 (1998): 37.

Elisha P. Douglass. *Rebels and Democrats: The Struggle for Equal Political Rights and Majority Rule During the American Revolution* (Chicago: Ivan R. Dee, 1989).

Dwight Duncan. "How Brown Is Goodridge?" *Boston University Public Interest Law Journal* 14 (2004): 27.

William C. Duncan. "*Goodridge* and the Rule of Law: Same-Sex Marriage in Massachusetts: The Meanings and Implications of *Goodridge v. Department of Public Health.*" *Boston University Public Interest Law Journal* 14 (2004): 42.

Lawrence Friedman. "Ordinary and Enhanced Rational Basis Review in the Massachusetts Supreme Judicial Court: A Preliminary Investigation," *Albany Law Review* 69 (2006): 415.

______. "The (Relative) Passivity of *Goodridge v. Department of Public Health.*" *Boston University Public Interest Law Journal* 14 (2004): 1.

Daniel W. Halston. "The Meaning of the Massachusetts 'Open Courts' Clause and Its Relevance to the Current Court Crisis." *Massachusetts Law Review* 88 (2004): 122.

Marjorie Heins. "Massachusetts Civil Rights Law." *Massachusetts Law Review* 76 (1991): 77.

Stephen P. Holbrook. "The Right to Bear Arms in the First State Bill of Rights: Pennsylvania, North Carolina, Vermont, and Massachusetts." *Vermont Law Review* 49 (1985): 255.

J. R. Pole. *The Pursuit of Equality in American History* (Berkley: University of California Press, 1993).

Charles P. Kindregan. "Same-Sex Marriage: The Cultural Wars and the Lessons of Legal History." *Family Law Quarterly* 38 (2004): 427.

Paul J. Liacos and Maureen McGee. "Where Does the Preservation of the Right to Justice Begin?" *Massachusetts Law Review* 81 (1996): 121.

Annie O'Connell. "'Legal Impediments to Marriage': Massachusetts' Marriage Evasion Statues, Same-Sex Marriage, and Privileges and Immunities Under the United States Constitution." *Brandeis Law Journal* 44 (2006): 509.

Alan Rogers. "'Success—At Long Last:' The Abolition of the Death Penalty in Massachusetts, 1928–1984." *Boston College Third World Law Journal* 22 (2002): 281.

______. "An Anchor to the Windward: The Right of the Accused to an Impartial Jury in Massachusetts Capital Cases." *Suffolk University Law Review* 33 (1999): 35.

Joseph W. Singer. "Same Sex Marriage, Full Faith and Credit, and the Evasion of Obligation." *Stanford Journal of Civil Rights and Civil Liberties* 1 (2005): 1.

David Skeels. "Due Process and the Massachusetts Constitution." *Massachusetts Law Review* 84 (1999): 76.

Craig J. Tiedemann. "Taking a Closer Look at Massachusetts Public School Expulsions: Proposing an Intermediate Standard of Judicial Review After *Doe v. Superintendent of Schools*." *New England Law Review* 31 (1997): 605.

Robert J. Taylor. "American Constitutions and the Right to Bear Arms." *Proceedings of the Massachusetts Historical Society* 95 (1983): 52.

Emory Washburn. "The Origin and Sources of Bill of Rights Declared in the Constitution of Massachusetts." *Proceedings of the Massachusetts Historical Society* 8 (1866): 294.

Rory Weiner. "Universal Health Insurance Under State Equal Protection." *Western New England Law Review* 23 (2002): 327.

Herbert P. Wilkins. "Judicial Treatment of the Massachusetts Declaration of Rights in Relation to Cognate Provisions of the United States Constitution." *Suffolk University Law Review* 14 (1980): 887.

Alexander Wohl. "New Life for Old Liberties—The Massachusetts Declaration of Rights: A State Constitutional Case Study." *New England Law Review* 25 (1990): 177.

Mark E. Wojcik. "The Wedding Bells Heard Around the World: Years from Now, Will We Wonder Why We Worried About Same Sex Marriage?" *Northern Illinois University Law Review* 24 (2004): 589.

THE FRAME OF GOVERNMENT

Wilbur Bowman Armstrong. *The Government in Massachusetts* (South Lancaster: College Press, 1939).

Charles Baron and Lawrence Friedman. "The Constitutional Jurisprudence of the Marshall Court: The First Half Decade." *Boston Bar Journal* 29 (March/April 2005): 10.

Richard Birdsall. "The Reverend Thomas Allen: Jeffersonian Calvinist." *New England Quarterly* 30 (1957): 147.

David Blumberg. "Influence of the Massachusetts Supreme Judicial Court on State High Court Decision Making 1982–1997: A Study in Horizontal Federalism." *Albany Law Review* 61 (1998): 1583.

Ellen E. Brennan. *Plural Office-Holding in Massachusetts, 1760-1780, Its Relation to the "Separation" of Departments of Government* (Chapel Hill: University of North Carolina Press, 1945).

Kenneth Bressler. "Rediscovering the Right to Instruct Legislators." *New England Law Review* 26 (1991): 355.

Robert E. Brown. *Middle-Class Democracy and the Revolution in Massachusetts, 1691–1780* (Ithaca: Cornell University Press, 1955).

Harry A. Cushing. *History of the Transition from Provincial to Commonwealth Government in Massachusetts* (New York: AMS Press, 1970).

John Fiske. *The Beginnings of New England: Or, The Puritan Theocracy in Its Relations to Civil and Religious Liberty* (Boston: Houghton, Mifflin, 1898).

Richard Fossey. "The Constitutional Duty to 'Cherish' Public Schools in Massachusetts: More than a Matter of Money." *Education Law Quarterly* 87 (1994): 699.

Ronald T. Gerwatowski. "Of Comity and Common Sense: The Need for Federal Courts to Certify Questions of Unsettled State Constitutional Law." *Massachusetts Law Review* 75 (1990): 3.

Carlos E. Gonzalez. "Representational Structures Through Which We the People Ratify Constitutions: The Troubling Original Understanding of the Constitutions' Ratification Clauses." *U.C. Davis Law Review* 38 (2005): 1373.

Alexander G. Gray and Thomas R. Kiley. "The Initiative and Referendum in Massachusetts." *New England Law Review* 26 (1991): 27.

Frank W. Grinnell. "The Government of Massachusetts Prior to the Federal Constitution." *Massachusetts Law Quarterly* 10 (1924): 175.

Van Beck Hall. *Politics Without Parties: Massachusetts, 1780-1791* (Pittsburgh: University of Pittsburgh Press, 1972).

Colleen B. McElhinney. "Historical Overview: Massachusetts Court Decisions Shaping Federal Constitutional Law." *Boston Bar Journal* 44 (Jan./Feb. 2000): 20.

Mark C. Miller. "Conflicts Between the Massachusetts Supreme Judicial Court and the Legislature: Campaign Finance Reform and Same-Sex Marriage." *Pierce Law Review* 4 (2006): 279.

Russell K. Osgood. "Early Versions and Practices of Separation of Powers: A Comment." *William and Mary Law Review* 30 (1989): 279.

Stephen E. Patterson. *Political Parties in Revolutionary Massachusetts* (Madison: University of Wisconsin Press, 1973).

Maura M. Pelham. Note, "Promulgating Preschool: What Constitutes a 'Policy Decision' Under Hancock v. Commissioner of Education." *New England Law Review* 40 (2005): 209.

Alan J. Rom. "'*McDuffy* is Dead; Long Live *McDuffy*!': Fundamental Rights Without Remedies in the Supreme Judicial Court of Massachusetts." *Saint John's Journal of Legal Commentary* 21 (2006): 111.

James M. Rosenthal. "Massachusetts Acts and Resolves Declared Unconstitutional by the Supreme Judicial Court of Massachusetts." *Massachusetts Law Quarterly* 1 (August 1916): 301.

Honorable Randall T. Shepard. "The Renaissance in State Constitutional Law: There Are a Few Dangers, But What's the Alternative?" *Albany Law Review* 61 (1998): 1529.

Henry L. Spencer. *Constitutional Conflict in Provincial Massachusetts A Study of Some Phases of the Opposition Between the Massachusetts Governor and General Court in the Early Eighteenth Century* (Columbus: Fred J. Herr, 1905).

THE AMENDMENTS AND CONVENTIONS

Primary Sources

An Address of the Convention, for Framing a New Constitution of Government, for the State of Massachusetts-Bay, to their Constituents (Boston: White & Adams, 1780).

Amendments to the Constitution of Massachusetts Proposed by the Convention of Delegates, Assembled at Boston, on the Third Wednesday of November, A.D. Eighteen Hundred and Twenty: with Their Address to the People of This Commonwealth (Boston: Russel & Gardner, 1821).

Debates in the Massachusetts Constitutional Convention, 1917–1918 (Boston: Wright & Potter, 1919).

Discussions on the Constitution Proposed to the People of Massachusetts by the Convention of 1853 (Boston: Little, Brown, & Co., 1854).

Journal of Debates and Proceedings in the Convention of Delegates [1820–21] (New York: De Capo Press, 1970).

Journal of the Constitutional Convention of the Commonwealth of Massachusetts, Begun and Held in Boston on the Fourth of May, 1853 (Boston: Wright & Potter, 1853).

Journal of the Constitutional Convention of the Commonwealth of Massachusetts, 1917 (Boston: Wright & Potter, 1919).

Rules and Orders to be Observed: In the Convention of Delegates for the Commonwealth of Massachusetts, Which Met on November 15, 1820 (Boston: B. Russell, 1820).

Commission to Compile Information and Data for the Use of the Constitutional Convention. Bulletins for the Constitutional Conventions, 1917–1918 (Boston: Wright & Potter, 1919).

Harvey *Fowler. Official Report of the Debates and Proceedings in the State Convention Assembled May 4th, 1853, To Revise and Amend the Constitution of the Commonwealth of Massachusetts* (Boston: Wright & Potter, 1853).

William B. Munro. *A Manual for the Constitutional Convention, 1917* (Boston: Wright & Potter, 1917).

Secondary Sources

Jeremy Belknap. "Minutes of the Massachusetts Convention of 1788." *Proceedings of the Massachusetts Historical Society* 3 (1930): 296.

Raymond L. Bridgman. *The Massachusetts Constitutional Convention of 1917: Its Causes, Forces and Factions; Its Conflicts and Consequences; Mention of Every Proposed Amendment* (Boston, 1923).

Michael Brunet. *The Massachusetts Constitutional Convention of 1853* (Thesis (PhD), Clark University, 1949).

George T. Curtis, et al. *Discussions on the Constitution Proposed to the People of Massachusetts by the Convention of 1853* (Boston: Little, Brown, & Co., 1854).

John Dinan. *The American State Constitutional Tradition* (Lawrence: University of Kansas Press, 2006).

______. "Framing a 'People's Government': State-Constitution-Making in the Progressive Era." *Rutgers Law Journal* 30 (1999): 933.

Morris M. Goldings. "Massachusetts Amends: A Decade of State Constitution Revision." *Harvard Journal on Legislation* 5 (1968): 373.

John A. Hague. "The Massachusetts Constitutional Convention, 1917–1919: A Study of Dogmatism in an Age of Transition." *New England Quarterly* 27 (1954): 147.

Augustus P. Loring. "A Short Account of the Massachusetts Constitutional Convention 1917–1919." *New England Quarterly* 6 (1933) 1.

Charles F. Mahoney. "The Case for a Popular Constitutional Convention." *Massachusetts Law Quarterly* 44 (April 1959): 21.

Samuel Eliot Morison. "The Vote of Massachusetts on Summoning a Constitutional Convention, 1776–1916." *Proceedings of the Massachusetts Historical Society* 50 (1917): 241.

Merrill D. Peterson. *Democracy, Liberty and Property: The State Constitutional Conventions of the 1820's* (Indianapolis: Bobbs-Merrill Co., 1966).

Samuel Shapiro. "The Conservative Dilemma: The Massachusetts Constitutional Convention of 1853." *New England Quarterly* 33 (1960): 207.

Henry L. Shattuck. "Martin Lomasney in the Constitutional Convention of 1917–1919." *Proceedings of the Massachusetts Historical Society* 299 (1959): 299.

Sean Wilentz. *The Rise of American Democracy: Jefferson to Lincoln* (New York: Norton, 2005).

■ TABLE OF CASES

■ INDEX

About the Authors

LAWRENCE FRIEDMAN is a professor of law at New England School of Law, in Boston, Massachusetts, where he teaches courses in constitutional law, state constitutional law, and national security law. He has written many articles on these subjects and is the author, with Victor Hansen, of *The Case for Congress: Separation of Powers and the War on Terror* (Ashgate, 2009).

LYNNEA THODY is an associate with Blatman, Bobrowski & Mead, LLC, a Massachusetts law firm specializing in land use and municipal law. She is a former law clerk to the Honorable Karyn Scheier, Chief Justice of the Massachusetts Land Court.

www.ingramcontent.com/pod-product-compliance
Ingram Content Group UK Ltd.
Pitfield, Milton Keynes, MK11 3LW, UK
UKHW021135160926
475595UK00020B/57

9 780199 778683